Farms, Mines, and Main Streets

*Conflicts in Urban and Regional Development,
a series edited by John R. Logan and Todd Swanstrom*

Farms, Mines, and Main Streets

Uneven Development in a Dakota County

Caroline S. Tauxe

Temple University Press
Philadelphia

For my parents

Temple University Press, Philadelphia 19122
Copyright © 1993 by Temple University. All rights reserved
Published 1993
Printed in the United States of America

The paper used in this publication meets the minimum requirements of American National Standard for Information Sciences—Permanence of Paper for Printed Library Materials, ANSI Z39.48-1984

Library of Congress Cataloging-in-Publication Data

Tauxe, Caroline S., 1958–
　　Farms, mines, and main streets : uneven development in a Dakota county / Caroline S. Tauxe.
　　　　p.　cm. — (Conflicts in urban and regional development)
　　Includes bibliographical references and index.
　　ISBN 1-56639-070-2
　　1. Mercer County (N.D.)—Economic conditions.　2. Mercer County (N.D.)—Social conditions.　3. Energy industries—North Dakota—Mercer County.　4. Ethnology—North Dakota—Mercer County.　I. Title.　II. Series.
HC107.N92M477 1993
338.9784'83—dc20　　　　　　　　　　　　　　　　　　　　　　　　92-40264

Contents

Maps	vi
Acknowledgments	ix
Chapter One	Linking the Global and the Local │ 1
Chapter Two	A Century of Transformation │ 25
Chapter Three	Currents in Political Culture │ 60
Chapter Four	Lowering the Energy Boom │ 94
Chapter Five	The Politics of Planning │ 119
Chapter Six	Living with Development │ 149
Chapter Seven	Patterns of Power: Changes in Political Economy │ 182
Chapter Eight	The Price of Progress │ 211
Notes	241
Bibliography	251
Index	267

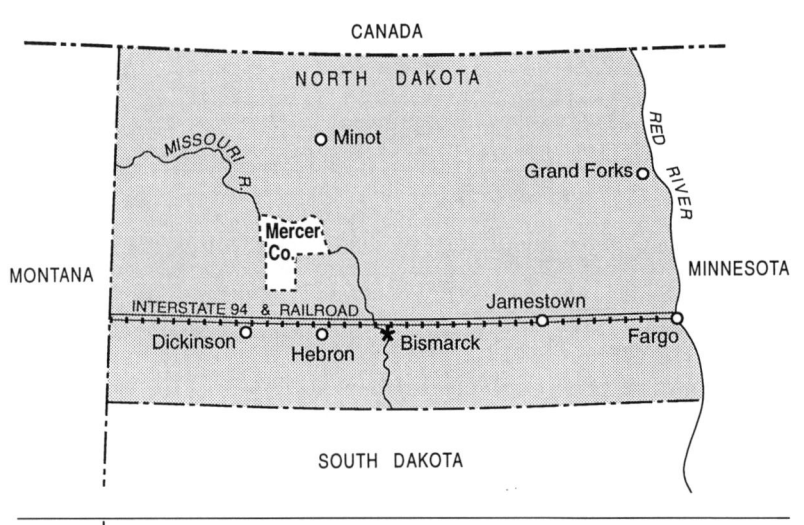

Map 1 | Location of Mercer County

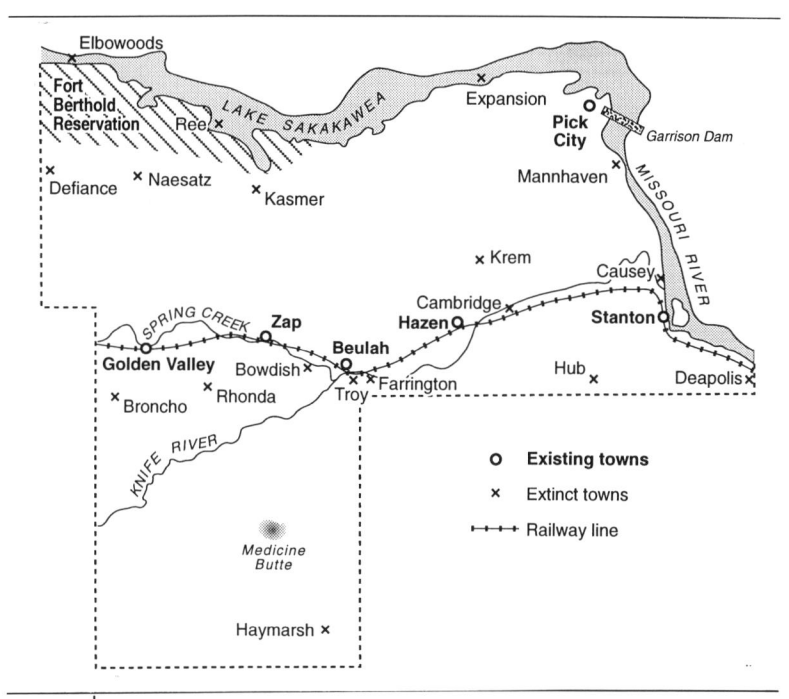

Map 2 | European-American Settlements in Mercer County

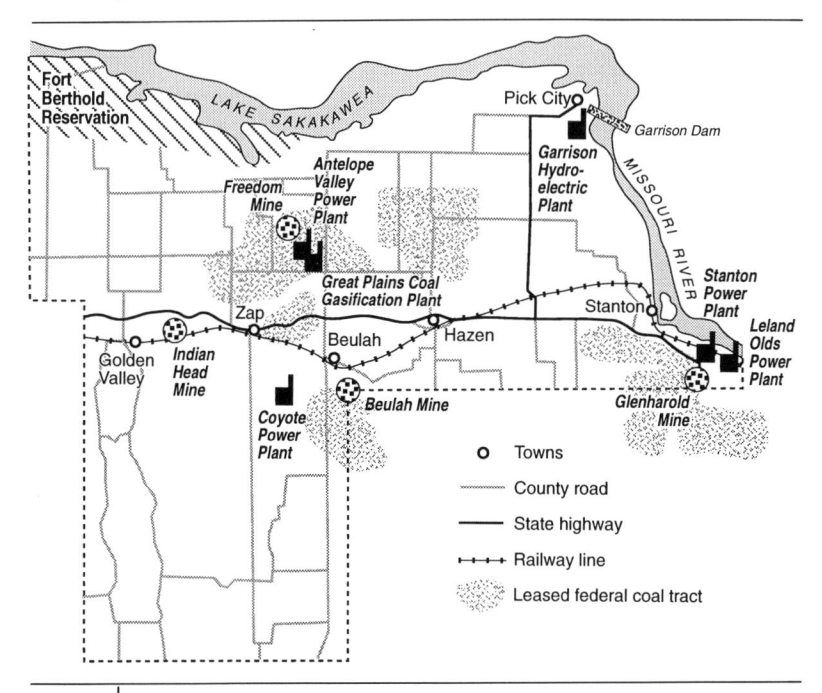

Map 3 | Mercer County Industrial Developments

Acknowledgments

I wish to thank the National Science Foundation for funding the major portion of the dissertation fieldwork upon which this book is based. Grants from the Lowie Foundation and from Hobart and William Smith Colleges also provided financial support.

A number of friends and colleagues have contributed careful readings of earlier drafts and valuable editorial suggestions. I especially wish to thank Jack Potter, Shaunna Scott, Abdi Samatar, Todd Swanstrom, and members of the Geneva Writers Circle in this regard. At various stages in its development, Ted Nace, Pedro Rezende, Ann Markusen, Dick Walker, Aihwa Ong, Christopher Gunn, Michael Ames, and Malcolm Willison helped to bring this book into being. Michael Kirshoff gave me lessons on graphics technology and produced the maps. Miguel Centeno, Tamar Gordon, Anne Levenstein, John Tanquary, and my family have given me unfailing encouragement and support.

Most of all, I am deeply grateful to the people of Mercer County for their friendship, openness, and generosity over the years I have been a curious and sometimes intrusive visitor among them. The subject matter remains controversial and I do not expect my interpretation will meet with universal agreement in Mercer County. I have sought to treat events there with respect for their complexity and to present a thoughtful account.

Those who are looking for themselves and their neighbors in these pages should know that I have made an effort to protect the privacy of those who shared their time and thoughts with me. With this in mind,

I have changed names and, where requested, eliminated other identifying details, giving only relevant positions and official titles.

For this reason, I will also avoid thanking by name those individuals in Mercer County who lived and worked most closely with me. Without their assistance, support, and insight, this work would not have been possible.

Farms, Mines, and Main Streets

Let the sons, then, claim the kingdom they inherit, whatsoever the claim may cost. The day will and must come when through this vast deposit of easily accessible and marketable wealth, the wheels of industry will hum, the chimneys of factories will belch forth and cloud the sky by day and light it by night, and a half million artisans will find employment at good wages, build homes, rear children, clothe and educate them, and add ten thousand times ten thousand to the wealth, prosperity and contentment of this rich state.

—"Coal in Ward County," *North Dakota Magazine*
December 1906

When will it all stop? When we can't breathe the air any more or when the river is too polluted to swim in. There is nothing wrong with energy development but there is such a thing as too much.

—Mercer County resident in 1981

Chapter One

Linking the Global and the Local

As the twentieth century entered its final decade, rural areas of the United States generally were in decline. Small highways and county roads throughout the nation revealed an increasingly dilapidated housing stock, abandoned mines, railroad spurs overgrown with rank weeds, and small towns with boarded-up factories and storefronts from which most of the young and able had departed. The consequences of economic restructuring contributed to a lower quality of life for rural families and communities (Bergland 1988:29; Shapiro 1989). During the 1980s, rural areas lost much of their economic base with the closing of millions of family farms and the movement of manufacturing operations to locations overseas, where desperate poverty and lower worker and environmental protection standards made for greater corporate profits. Some of these jobs were replaced in rural America, but generally at near minimum wage rates that failed to provide families with a decent living or local governments with a sustaining tax base. Corporate farming, with its concentrated ownership of productive resources and proletarianized work force, continued to expand onto lands once worked by independent family-based operations.

Many studies have documented the worsening poverty and loss of control over small communities experienced by rural Americans during these years.[1] These problems are certainly nothing new; as hinterlands have been integrated into the wider economy, rural areas have followed the ups and downs of a developing industrial nation. And yet during the decade of the 1980s, while other sectors of the economy prospered, rural America saw its worst period of devastation since the Great Depression.

This general pattern did not hold everywhere, however. During the 1980s, I spent time in a place called Mercer County, in western North Dakota, that was experiencing an unprecedented industrial boom that allowed it to escape, or at least to postpone, the decline experienced elsewhere. With new businesses, increased population, and modernized infrastructure, Mercer County appeared to be a community developer's dream come true.

As an anthropologist interested in social change and economic development, however, I sought to penetrate this surface appearance to explore underlying conflicts and compromises. Looking closely, it was clear that the costs and benefits of development were unequally distributed in the county. Listening attentively, one could hear conflicting interpretations of the changes underway. Observing the affairs of the residents of Mercer County over a period of years gave me a sense of the trade-offs involved in this kind of development and the limitations of viewing it as a model for other communities to follow. It also showed how much the experience of large-scale, capital-intensive industrialization there has to teach us about the processes of economic development as they occur within the United States and other industrialized areas of the world.

My study of social changes in Mercer County was a longitudinal one, including notes made during an early stay there in 1978, ten months of fieldwork undertaken intermittently between 1980 and 1985, and a return visit in 1991. During this period, the formerly agricultural and smaller-scale mining district that includes the county became a major center for expanding coal-based energy industries. This so-called "energy boom" was a wider regional phenomenon, including rapid development of coal-, oil-, and gas-based industries throughout the northern Great Plains and intermontane West of the United States, in response to the high prices for energy products following the world oil crisis of 1973–1974. My fieldwork took place during and after the most intense period of construction and expansion of several lignite coal strip mines, coal-burning electrical generating stations, and the Great Plains coal gasification plant—the flagship enterprise financed by the now defunct federal Synthetic Fuels Corporation.

The boom associated with construction lasted from 1973 to 1983, but by 1984, falling energy prices and the withdrawal of federal support brought a period of retrenchment and reorganization. By 1991, a new order had emerged, characterized by even more complete dependency on the energy industries. Economic and political pressures on farmers, organized labor, and Main Street merchants had forced on them difficult accommodations to the new developers, yet within the shifting parameters of opportunity, local interest groups continued to contend with each other and with the corporate powers of big capital in efforts to secure both a livelihood and a livable future from their experience with economic development.

Anthropology and the World-System Model

This study of the political, economic, and social transformations in Mercer County during the course of the energy boom and its aftermath focuses on the categories of actors and issues that were most significant from the perspective and experience of local residents—farmers, miners, small town business people, corporate-community relations, and the role of government—while maintaining an analytical perspective based in global political economy. The scope of these concerns may seem ambitious for an ethnographer, trained in the traditional anthropological practice of face-to-face research in relatively small and bounded social groups; but increasing numbers of anthropologists are making use of the global paradigm developed from world-systems theory as a framework for linking the macro level of global and national political economic processes to the micro or local level.

According to the conventions of field research developed in the first half of this century, anthropologists would spend a year or more living in a community observing the habits and practices of its people; inquiring into their lives, beliefs, knowledge, and commentary; and participating as much as possible in their activities. In preparing an ethnography, a written account or interpretation of the group's culture, anthropologists typically sought to convey the local reality holistically and timelessly, as a many-faceted and internally coherent system of belief and practice complete unto itself. This style of analysis had certain advantages. It allowed the ethnographer to showcase the complexities of local tradition in ways that elicited in the reading audience a respect for cultural diversity. It also simplified the task of bounding the subject under investigation, which presents a considerable problem for anyone seeking to conduct and report systematic inquiry into subjects that cannot be contained within the controlled conditions of laboratories, surveys, or experiments.

The biggest drawbacks of this model of "primitive isolates" were the artificial nature of these boundaries, the reification of social cultural systems often not so much a matter of set custom as of continual transformation, and the tendency to distort or ignore contemporary reality in efforts to reconstruct and describe traditional culture as it may have existed in the past. For example, although anthropological studies of tribal societies in the first half of the twentieth century took place mainly in the context of domination by colonial powers, these groups were portrayed as if they were isolated units clinging to traditional ways, self-sufficient and relatively autonomous.

This ethnographic style of representation began to change after World War II, when more anthropologists turned to the study of peasant communities, whose integration into larger civilizations as a subordinate class was more difficult to ignore. By the mid-1970s, anthropologists interested in Marxian models of political economy and social change had completed a theoretical and methodological transformation, convinced that it was no longer possible to make sense of local social, economic, and political dynamics without reference to the global context that helps to shape them.

This realization was shared by other social scientists and historians, among whom a new paradigm was emerging for understanding the relationship between economic development and underdevelopment on a global scale. World-systems theory was developed in reaction to the popular model of the 1950s and 1960s, known as modernization theory. The latter assumed that underdevelopment was a pre-existing condition throughout the world, maintained by lingering precapitalist traditions. Modernizationist theorists such as W. W. Rostow (1960) maintained that development could be induced simply by altering traditional or customary obstacles to progress (such as communal land tenure or ritual redistribution of wealth), encouraging indigenous entrepreneurs, building modern infrastructure, and injecting a strong dose of Western capital and expertise. Political sociologists such as Frank (1975) and Wallerstein (1976) pointed out the failure of this model to explain worsening underdevelopment and poverty in many so-called "emerging" nations that had adopted policies of modernization. They argued that underdevelopment and development were not in fact sequential stages but rather simultaneous processes occurring in different parts of a single integrated political economic system.

The world-system to which they referred was that which had grown with the expansion of capitalism since the sixteenth century. Beginning with commercial trade and progressing though periods of colonial imperialism and the post-colonial economic order, this modern world-system, no longer needing a unifying political structure, is now based on an international division of labor mediated through a system of unequal exchange between dominant "core" (developing) and subordinate "peripheral" (underdeveloping) trading partners. The two economic processes are thus historically linked by asymmetrical power relations: The nations colonized by European powers were underpaid for the food, labor, raw materials, and natural resources they provided, resulting in an enormous transfer of wealth to the colonizers—wealth that financed their industrial development. At the same time, the impoverished economies of the colonies were rearranged to suit their new role in the system, making it difficult to undertake any real development efforts even after the period of political colonial rule had ended.

According to this model, there may exist even within the nations of the developed core similarly structured relationships with their own so-called "internal peripheries," which serve much the same function in providing cheap labor and raw materials to underwrite industrialization and capital accumulation in dominant centers. Appalachia is a good example of a historic internal periphery within the United States; its coal, lumber, and labor fed the industrial furnaces of the developing Northeast, while it became underdeveloped—its people becoming more impoverished and its natural environment laid waste. In similar respects, Mercer County can be seen historically as part of another internal periphery, receiving less than full value for its natural resources, including agricultural land and products and its fossil fuels deposits, while relatively little of the profit they generated was reinvested locally in socially sustaining ways.[2]

Subsequent work within the general world-system paradigm emphasized the processes of dependent and uneven development within peripheral societies, with greater attention to their cultural and historical variability. In shifting the focus away from the determinism of unequal exchange relations to problems of production and exploitation, it sought to interpret events in the periphery not merely in terms of processes originating in the developed centers of the global economy, but also as part of local histories (Roseberry 1989:12). Dependency theory (see Cardoso 1972; dos Santos 1973) explains the processes by which the international division of labor permits industrial development to take place in some areas, but restricts it in others whose economies are understood to be conditioned by the development and expansion of the dominant economies of the core. This means that these dependent economies cannot develop autonomously according to a logic based on the needs of their own people, but only contingently, in the spaces left open by changes in the power centers of the world-system.

As Third World nations pursued development policies emphasizing import substitution industrialization, Green Revolution agriculture, and foreign exchange-earning exports, it became apparent that the benefits (such as they were, given the overall pattern of increasing national debt and poverty) were unevenly distributed. Numerous anthropological studies (see Schneider 1975 and Smith 1980 for summaries) documented a widening gap in income not only between the core and periphery, but also within the Third World nations, where a relatively small number of entrepreneurs and elites reaped the profits of development programs, gaining even greater power and resources with which to further outstrip the increasingly impoverished majorities. Political economists studying such uneven development (e.g., Samir Amin 1976) argue against the possibility of promoting a more equitable distribution of the benefits of economic development through careful planning, since they view such inequality as inherent to a system based on monopoly capital. This is an important question, since the boom growth of energy industries in Mercer County represented, at least from the local perspective, a kind of dependent development vis-à-vis the national centers of corporate and state power, and the benefits were also unequally distributed despite (and arguably by means of) elaborate planning efforts. The local process of development here can be seen in the terms Sunkel used to describe uneven development in the periphery: "Access to the means and benefits of development is selective; rather than spreading them, the process tends to ensure a self-reinforcing accumulation of privilege for special groups as well as the continued existence of a marginal class" (1972:519).

The emergence of world-systems theory offered to anthropologists a powerful vision of the world historical context for many of the change processes they had observed on the local level. Some, such as Eric Wolf (1982:21) and June Nash (1981), have called for a new commitment among anthropologists to writing the ethnography of the modern world-system, by exploring the global historical processes of power that have shaped local social and cultural systems and forged the linkages among them. Others have emphasized the need to represent contested local realities in the contexts of the larger political economy, and to experiment with integrating ethnographic accounts with description of the more impersonal order of political economic processes. This task is not one of writing a universal account of human life in a global village, but rather of placing numerous individual case studies within the context of a world history of uneven development. Among anthropologists, those of the political economy school have been especially inspired by this framework for understanding micro/macro linkages (Ortner 1984; *American Ethnologist* 1978). In attempting to trace the relationship between processes occurring at different levels, some have shifted the analytical focus away from the discrete community to a more regional (e.g., Hart 1982; Schneider and Schneider 1976) and even a global scope (Appadurai 1990; Hannerz 1987). Studies in this growing interdisciplinary body of literature have brought to the fore such problems as the relation of capitalism to other modes of production, the responses of groups on the periphery to the effects of capitalism, the ethnography of transnational corporations and labor organization, the migration of workers, changes in household and gender relations, and forms of resistance to domination.

In creating ethnography informed by the insights of world-systems and subsequent global political economic theory, anthropologists have also criticized the paradigm and brought their unique perspective to bear in compensating for its limitations. The traditional practice of anthropological research emphasizing long-term personal contact, local histories, and native points of view provides an important antidote to the tendency of macro-level scholars to overemphasize the determinism of the powerful forces of the core corporations and states. Ethnographic studies get beyond the assumption that people whose societies have been colonized and underdeveloped are passive victims of the process, and instead can explore modalities of agency and resistance—both symbolic and material—in the context of political economic struggle. Rather than simply documenting the determining power of political economic structures, anthropologists are more interested in exploring how such structures are themselves generated and reproduced, emphasizing the central place of real people doing actual things as agents making society and history. The firsthand experience of anthropologists with peripheralized peoples also leads to a more complex understanding of their relationships with various centers of influence, rather than assuming a capitalism-centered view of a single, unified, and completely integrated world-system.

The following account of the energy boom in Mercer County is linked to this literature in development ethnography in its subject matter, theoretical perspective, and analytical style. Like many anthropologists studying economic development and social change in Third World settings, I found that, although world-systems theory did provide a useful structural framework, the local history of production was at least as important as unequal exchange relations in generating and perpetuating uneven development. By the same token, I also found that the holistic approach of anthropology opened up research to a symbolic and cultural dimension often missing from the work of other social scientists, permitting greater empirical understanding of how power is produced and the processes understood by people on the local level.

If we define culture as a framework of meanings and understandings by which people live, then it both constitutes the conventions of daily social life and is also produced in the constant flow of social action. Cultural orientations are maintained and transformed within local social contexts, and they affect the dispositions, ideologies, and emotions of local actors. The forms of action they undertake, in turn, can influence structural change in ways that are not simply predictable from the nature of monopoly capitalism. Culture is itself constantly adjusted and remade in ways that are intimately bound up with changing social systems. Although social change all over the world is conditioned by the expansion of the capitalist system, the anthropological perspective helps us to keep in mind the dynamic interplay between structural forces and people's cultural and ideological conceptualizations. This perspective also contributes to a more existential understanding of development, in exploring the role of human will and agency in shaping larger social processes.

This study differs from the vast majority of others I have mentioned in one important respect, however. It is set, not in a peripheral society of the Third World, but rather in the heartland of the United States, one of the most developed and powerful economies on earth. This part of the world-system has been relatively understudied by anthropologists and development specialists of the political economy school, and one of the aims of this work is to present this case for comparative purposes.

It is important to bear in mind how uneven development within an advanced capitalist society differs from that found elsewhere. Among the important causes of disparities in the degree and character of capitalist development within and among regions in the periphery are (1) the persistence of pre-existing non-capitalistic economic and social relations; and (2) conditions of low worker productivity, wages, and profits due to historical forces such as the impact of world markets, class struggle, the draining away of locally produced value, or the political consequences of imperialism (Walker 1980:34). Both of these conditions, which may be encountered in terms of political boundaries, cultural differences, and incompatible monetary systems, make for the uneven spread of capitalist development and explain why it is not the same everywhere.

While historical forces such as those listed above do play a part in the following account of social change in Mercer County, a conceptual framework based on concepts of development and underdevelopment alone is not sufficient to explain the kind of economic unevenness and inequality that we see among localities in the United States today. The geographer Richard Walker has argued that unevenness in advanced capitalist economies is due not so much to barriers interfering with investment and profit-making, but rather to the uneven geographic distribution of features that capital finds useful. National corporate capital has the freedom to locate its investments essentially anywhere in the United States it chooses, so location decisions are based largely on the combinations of advantages available in various places: "From the perspective of capital, concrete places contain a specific ensemble of the material of nature, a built environment, labor power, members of other classes, various commodities, etc., as well as the specific constellation of social relations into which these spatially-situated people have entered among themselves and with their environment" (1980:29). The patterning of these conditions (what he refers to as a "spatial mosaic") is itself the result of historical interaction with capitalism, and these factors enter into corporate location decisions because they affect productivity and the speed with which profits can be generated. The result is a spatial differentiation in which places undergo uneven transformations that are really different kinds of development for various purposes, but these localities are not in any sense "underdeveloped" in the process.

Applying an uneven development model to a locality in the United States implies a "vertical slice" analysis in three different senses. First of all, anthropologist Laura Nader (1974, 1980) has argued that analytical models ought to be applied vertically to various strata within a social system, rather than only horizontally within a single class. This not only allows one to avoid incorrectly attributing causality to class position (when in fact the same phenomena might be found at other class levels as well), but also provides a way of tracing the causal or at least conditioning linkages above the local level to more powerful strata in the social hierarchy. Both of these concerns are relevant here, although the ethnographic focus is on just classes present within local Mercer County society.

Furthermore, this study seeks to link the history of Mercer County with national and global events and institutions in terms of articulated political levels. In an argument similar to that of Laura Nader, Eric Wolf has pointed out the need for documenting and analyzing such linkages in a framework emphasizing hierarchies of power and policy: "The period of the present is marked by the extension into all spheres of public life of a set of civil and military bureaucracies, connected through contracts to private concerns. . . . The dominant intellectual issue of the present is the nature of public power and its exercise, wise or unwise, responsible or irresponsible" (Wolf 1974:252). For this reason it is important to look at the formal as well as the informal mechanisms for exercising power, and at the unequal distribution of access to them.

Finally, this study contributes to a kind of "vertical slice" in applying the same concepts to another part of the world-system than commonly has been examined in the past. The analysis of events in Mercer County supports the view that core–periphery dichotomies often have been too starkly drawn. In fact, not only is there a good deal of capital accumulation going on in the periphery but, as this study shows, uneven development also operates at the heart of the core.

In exploring the ways that macro-level power is exercised locally, it is important to avoid reducing "capital" to an icon of exploitation, or the people of Mercer County to mere cardboard "victims." The ethnographic focus in this study remains on the ground; while providing an empirical framework for understanding the vertical connections, it concentrates on how local social structure, culture, and ideology, formed in a crucible of struggle for survival within capitalism, influenced the relationship between the great energy corporations and the local communities, and shaped both the actions of the people of Mercer County and their understanding of events.

Economic Restructuring and Social Change

The white collar layoffs and industrial plant closings of the mid-1980s brought the social problems of economic restructuring in the United States to the attention of the mass media and the public, but it was really not a new phenomenon, nor one confined to urban areas. In its broadest sense of adjusting production to general changes in economic conditions, restructuring is a continual process throughout the capitalist world-system, and one that has always conditioned the lives of people in the United States. This is a central story line in American social history, shaping what C. Wright Mills (1959) called the "main drift" of American social changes, and such adjustments have been an ongoing theme in the classic American community studies in anthropology and sociology.[3] The connection is made explicit by anthropologist Dan Rose, who, in discussing a mined-out area in the eastern United States, remarked on the painful transformations suffered in towns within the continual fluctuations of the wider economy:

> I found in the culture of the region a continuous onslaught of instability and change, reformation, tied directly and indirectly to the world economy. Capitalism . . . transforms the entire planet, but this transformation is painfully felt at the specific town or small city level. In these places, capitalist social forms continually re-create themselves in order to respond to the destabilization of privately as well as publicly induced economic and social transformations. (Rose 1989:42)

Similarly, economic development in Mercer County has not only been an uneven process across interest groups, but also over time; it has never been a progressive evolutionary process, but a series of booms and busts. The ebb and flow of its development has depended on market changes, the short-run interests of investors, and the efforts of local residents to shape their lives within its shifting sands. Each new high tide leaves behind as it recedes a flotsam of transformed economic and social formations, some elements of local society lifted by the crest, others left in the wreckage of dashed hopes and ruined opportunities.

When grain prices were high at the turn of the century, railroad companies, big grain merchants, and the federal government facilitated the settlement of the county with small family farmers willing to absorb the market's risks. When prices fell these farmers had to shift as best they could and came to depend on government assistance for survival. Thousands suffered the disappointment and personal tragedy of bankruptcy and relocation. When energy prices rose dramatically in the 1970s, industrial capital, again aided by the state, reshaped Mercer County according to its new needs. And again, the local residents and the government absorbed the risk. With energy prices falling in the mid-1980s, industrial capital began pulling back, leaving local residents stranded, while the government stepped in to rescue the corporate investment.

Throughout these changing times, those in different positions within local Mercer County society have worked to secure what they have seen as beneficial to themselves, to their families, or to broader constituencies of loyalty and responsibility. And yet their future remains uncertain, still vulnerable to shifts in global markets and other forces beyond their control.

The classic community studies depict industrial fluctuations at an earlier stage in the development of American capitalism. Economic processes have been different in the last quarter of the twentieth century, when rapid capital mobility and monetarist management policies have made the contradiction between capital accumulation and community stability increasingly obvious. The devastating wave of plant closings that swept the country after the oil crisis of the early 1970s left behind abandoned communities, recession, and the highest unemployment rates since the Great Depression. More important for the long run, this was a period of economic restructuring on a global scale, in which manufacturers found it feasible and advantageous to dismantle much of their industrial and manufacturing base in areas with established labor organization, and rearrange their operations so as to transfer those with heavy labor costs to cheaper foreign labor markets.

According to the analysis of political economists, declining rates of profit brought about by maturing international competition produced this era of frenzied capital movement, including the phenomenon economists Barry Bluestone and Bennett Harrison have called "deindustrialization," that is, "the widespread, systematic disinvestment in the nation's productive capacity" (1982:6). They have argued that the pace of industrial investment and disinvestment in the pursuit of quick profits by U.S. companies in the 1970s and 1980s provoked a crisis for American workers and communities, who are used and abandoned by investment managers more interested in moving assets profitably than developing sound companies. In an increasingly competitive international economy, corporate managers looked beyond work force efficiency and streamlining to a strategy of restructuring the geographical distribution of production in order to reduce costs.

Such rearrangements took place within the United States; deindustrialization in the more developed parts of the country was accompanied by industrial growth in other areas with lower average wages and benefits, lower levels of social services, and where union power was less entrenched. The consequences for organized labor were dramatic, as managements could credibly threaten to relocate while pushing for contract "give-backs" in the name of competitiveness. Workers lost bargaining power and living standards in the face of pressure to save their jobs and communities, in competition with even more unempowered and lower-paid workers both in other countries and at home. When workers opt for individual migration in search of better opportunities, this also weakens the community support so important for effective mobilization.

In the context of deindustrialization and runaway shops, potential sites for new or relocating industries competed desperately, offering industrial sites and tax incentives in a manner which June Nash (1989:5) has likened to the magical measures employed by Melanesian cargo cults to attract military supply shipments back to their Pacific Islands after World War II. Such was also the case in Mercer County, where a declining agricultural economy impelled pro-development elements to join the national trend of offering competitive economic enticements in hopes of attracting industries.

The weakness of this position in the face of unrestrained capital mobility is clear. The faster capital can move around, the less attached it is to any one place, the more it can use the threat of leaving as a strategy against labor, and the more local development becomes dependent on outside capital. Such development as can be secured is often ephemeral (the boomtown phenomenon) and the result of location advantages to corporate capital rather than of traditional regional and community development strategies.[4] Given the "spatial mosaic" of features relevant to location decision-makers in advanced capitalism, development is *necessarily* uneven, and there is little that people in any individual locality can do to generate self-sustaining economic development. Increasingly, development occurs as a "top-down" process flowing from decisions made by national corporate capital rather than a "bottom-up" one based on growth generated within a community or region (Walker 1980:32–33).

The instability and uncertainty generated by accelerating economic restructuring presents American communities and their governmental bodies with difficult and sometimes confusing choices. They can suffer the economic decline with its human cost in suffering, despair, and lowered living standards, and its financial costs in terms of declining property values and sales tax revenues that sustain local services. Some, like those in Mercer County, have the option of becoming unequal partners with powerful corporations that have at least a temporary interest in being there. This is a frequent choice—to relinquish some local autonomy and control over the process in exchange for a ride on the tiger of development. A third choice, which may offer more sustainable solutions and greater opportunity to reinvest the results locally in socially sustaining ways, is most difficult. This is to restrain the outflow of locally generated capital and to grow jobs from within rather than to depend on attracting outside businesses to relocate. The difficulties of this path are both structural and ideological, since it entails the invention and institutionalization of new kinds of financial, managerial, and policy practices that no longer favor the traditional business constituency, and with a cooperative design that is unfamiliar to mainstream Americans (Gunn and Gunn 1991).[5]

Anthropologists (Fernández-Kelly and García 1985; Hopper, Susser, and Conover 1985; MacLennan 1985; Nash 1985, 1989; Newman 1985) and regional geographers (Harvey 1985; Logan and Molotch 1988; Massey 1988; Pred 1984; Warf 1988) studying the impact of economic restructuring (and especially deindustrialization) on American communities have stressed the need to avoid viewing these processes as monolithic or evolutionary. Although local responses are conditioned by the global nature of restructuring, what happens in a specific case depends more on the articulation or structuring of local circumstances over time. These scholars have sought to integrate the political economy of regional/global change with local histories of labor. Labor is selected as significant, both because of the powerful ways that changes in production continually shape local society and also because involvement in this process helps to shape the everyday life experience, biography, family formations, and political consciousness of local actors. Viewing these changes over time, it becomes clear that the dynamics of economic restructuring, local social organization, and individual ideology and action are closely interwoven, each continually reproducing and transforming the others.

The locally specific expressions of this process in Mercer County can be discerned in the following account, while the issues to which it speaks are of broad concern to Americans. As part of the critical tradition of American ethnography of the main drift, it develops themes that will be familiar to readers of American community studies—including the ongoing contest between large and small capital and the growing trends of absentee ownership, bureaucratization, social inequality, and economic dependency constraining communities' choices in determining their own future. It concerns the exercise of corporate power in the institutions of the state and the consequences of large industrial interests' operating in rural areas, particularly the activities that make for deteriorating bargaining power for labor, threaten environmental quality, undermine small-scale farming, and place long-term financial burdens on local communities. These trends are characteristic of contemporary United States society; an understanding of their consequences and potentials for ordinary citizens is important if we are to cope with them in responsible and effective ways.

Power and Consent

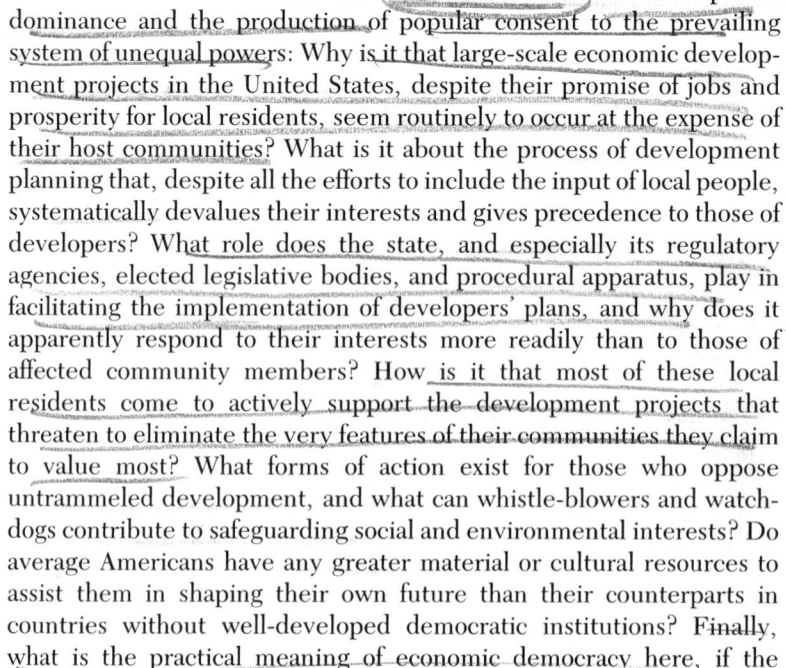

A series of questions emerged over the course of research in Mercer County that have to do with the noncoercive exercise of corporate dominance and the production of popular consent to the prevailing system of unequal powers: Why is it that large-scale economic development projects in the United States, despite their promise of jobs and prosperity for local residents, seem routinely to occur at the expense of their host communities? What is it about the process of development planning that, despite all the efforts to include the input of local people, systematically devalues their interests and gives precedence to those of developers? What role does the state, and especially its regulatory agencies, elected legislative bodies, and procedural apparatus, play in facilitating the implementation of developers' plans, and why does it apparently respond to their interests more readily than to those of affected community members? How is it that most of these local residents come to actively support the development projects that threaten to eliminate the very features of their communities they claim to value most? What forms of action exist for those who oppose untrammeled development, and what can whistle-blowers and watchdogs contribute to safeguarding social and environmental interests? Do average Americans have any greater material or cultural resources to assist them in shaping their own future than their counterparts in countries without well-developed democratic institutions? Finally, what is the practical meaning of economic democracy here, if the economic and regulatory apparatus is structured in favor of developers and the people are culturally predisposed to accept the legitimacy of corporate capitalist logic?

Ultimately, of course, these are questions of hegemony rather than of conspiracy or conscious, intentional action. Dominance is a property of the system of relations that comes into play, resulting not from overt ideological coercion or threats of repression, but from the historical cultural leadership in the United States of those who control its basic economic processes. Antonio Gramsci (1971), writing while imprisoned by the Italian Fascists in the early 1930s, advanced the idea of "hegemony" to characterize the process whereby an economically dominant alliance of classes extends its influence over a society in ways that shape its people's civil institutions, way of life, and patterns of thinking. In formally democratic class societies such as the United States, mass support for the system is maintained through the promotion of a perceived commonality of interests across classes as well as a shared ideological perspective. The power of a dominant alliance of classes is exercised through structural hegemony, in the sense that unequal access to resources becomes built into civil institutions such as wage, commodity, and finance markets, or legal and regulatory procedure, and also through ideological hegemony, which refers to the mass inculcation of system-supporting beliefs and values through socialization by civil institutions such as schools, churches, mass media, and advertising. The result is not a system that simply profits one class or narrow interest group, but rather the perpetuation and expansion of an existing economic and social order, without the need for continuous violent repression. Legal and legitimate sanctions are employed to preserve the status quo when it is seriously threatened, to be sure, but its most significant support is provided by securing the consent of those who are subordinated within the system.

Ethnographic research provides access to empirical data on hegemonic processes, showing how they operate in concrete instances at the interface between the lives of those in Mercer County and the social order of corporations and the state. This meso level between micro and macro is that of civil society, where in this case the values and practices collectively supporting the orderly capitalist development of energy resources are incorporated into such social institutions as political parties, social welfare agencies, farmer and labor organizations, and regulatory bodies, and into employment practices, planning and zoning procedures, finance, and advertising. There is evidence to support the view that the hegemonic structure and ideology of civil institutions ensures that they "naturally" function to favor dominant interests while maintaining the appearance of evenhandedness. It is also clear that local consent to energy development is produced in part through the formation of vertical pro-development alliances that include local interests, and the ideological linking of energy industry growth to American commonsensical notions of "progress."[6]

The assurance of continuing popular consent is necessary for this kind of capital-intensive development to be feasible; since the development is visibly enabled by government agencies, however, this consent must be assured without jeopardizing the legitimacy of the process. Dissent must therefore also be permitted, although in the case of Mercer County, it may be channeled and marginalized through unobtrusive administrative means, and also contained by the widespread acceptance of hegemonic ideology. As heirs to a Western civilization historically shaped by centuries of bourgeois cultural leadership, people in Mercer County (like other Americans) shared a conception of historical change that was basically social evolutionist and progressivist. Corporate publicity invoked elements of this taken-for-granted body of knowledge, in effect a preconstituted discourse, encouraging the county residents to equate industrialization with progress and future prosperity.[7]

Hegemonic control is of course never total, and strains of opposition were present in Mercer County, varying over time in strength and efficacy. A liberal Lockian individualism and free-enterprise ideology linking economic growth with progress and generalized prosperity was for the most part dominant in the local ideological worldview. These beliefs were not simply imposed by monopoly capitalism, but emerged in part from the local history of frontier community building. They existed side by side with other ideological beliefs and values, including those of agrarian populism, democratic labor unionism, and religious and civic morality. It is the encounter with the dominant that spawns the alternatives, themselves not necessarily counter-hegemonic, but rather made up of an intricate and changeable weaving together of resistance and complicity. The contradictions among these juxtaposed strands in Mercer County's political culture generate constant tension, and help explain the complex and shifting attitudes and strategies of the people in relation to energy development locally.

Considering the tension between economic growth and other values, it is not surprising that purely or radically counter-hegemonic opposition to corporate activities was rare in Mercer County. The preponderance of local opinion supported the strategy of pursuing growth, while remaining wary of outside interests. The overall dominance of a growth-oriented ideology despite cognizance of its risks is striking, but perhaps expectable. The United States is, after all, a thoroughly capitalist society where belief in economic growth as inherently good and in the ideals of free enterprise and individualism is already well-developed. The fact that this study is set within mainstream U.S. society makes it different from cultural analyses of capitalist relations in settings of dramatic social change from noncapitalist or preindustrial sociocultural systems.[8] In Mercer County, the nature of counter-hegemonic resources (both material and ideological) is more ambiguous, since they have themselves been historically engendered within the crucible of capitalism.[9]

The role played by the state is central to the American economy and to developments in Mercer County. Although "private enterprise" in the United States is mainly privately owned, the system depends on the operation of state institutions—particularly those responsible for legislative, regulatory, military, and policing functions—to assure the continuance of production and distribution (Heilbroner 1985:104).[10] The government (and indirectly the taxpayer) helps to cushion the shocks of business cycles, assuming risks and subsidizing profits. Public expenditures on education, basic scientific research, social welfare, and physical infrastructure for transportation and communication are accepted means of, among other things, promoting business efficiency and reducing the costs of economic competitiveness to American corporations. Direct and indirect assistance to privately owned firms, in the name of preserving domestic jobs and geo-politically strategic investments, and special tax incentives for business are also commonplace measures. All of these practices are predicated on the people's dependence on employment for survival, and are legitimized by the widespread acceptance of the commonsensical logic that businesses' success will benefit all the people. They are based on the assumption that, in the words of Charles E. Wilson, "What's good for the country is good for General Motors, and what's good for General Motors is good for the country."[11]

The involvement of the state in the development of Mercer County's energy resources was both integral and complex. Federal policies helped shape the energy crisis of the mid-1970s and the subsequent boom in domestic production; Congress created the Synthetic Fuels Corporation, which supported the federal financing of Mercer County's gasification plant. Throughout the energy boom, the national government remained a silent partner, orchestrating the procedural relationships between industrial developers and the local communities. The encounter between the developers' interests and those of local residents took place within a legal and political framework ostensibly serving to mediate conflicting interests, anticipate their problems, define their formal powers, and settle their disputes.

This encounter, however, was not between equal powers. The

corporations had the advantage of efficient bureaucratic organization, control of wealth and information, and greater influence in both the legislative and executive branches of the government. This influence stemmed in part from the commitments of the successive Ford, Carter, and Reagan administrations to support the development of domestic energy resources, because of their strategic importance in international relations. Large corporate developers also had at their disposal advertising and public relations professionals, expert at crafting publicity messages to generate support for policies favorable to them. Particularly on the local level, development agents wishing to minimize popular opposition to their plans had access to the means of manipulating information in the public debate so as to pre-empt discussion on those issues they wished to treat while obviating conflict on those which they excluded from consideration.

An important arena in which aspects of hegemony and conflict can be observed is in the institutionalized practice of planning and regulating the implementation of industrial projects. The practical operation of officially sanctioned development planning procedures allowed the most powerful interests to shape projects, define the parameters for public discussion, and minimize corporate responsibility for the adverse results. This occurred while providing a legally circumscribed space for public and community participation at the local level. The permit-granting process gives local entities veto rights over land use decisions, and potentially great power to slow the pace or limit the extent of industrial expansion, and Mercer County officials and citizens took advantage of these opportunities to limit the damage to their own interests. In the long run, however, local power to actually change the course of development had a very narrow range, and attempts to do so were dampened by the apparent harmony of interest produced through the development ideology of progress and prosperity.

The economic processes at work over the course of the energy boom produced uneven development both as a result of forces external to Mercer County and also as a continuation of ongoing transformations rooted in local history. The benefits and costs were unequally distributed among the towns, and it also affected different sectors of the local economy in disparate ways. Shifts in local-level sectoral power relations were an important consequence of such unequal conflicts. Industrial growth supported the power of coinciding commercial interests while agriculturalists were increasingly excluded from local politics and superseded as a national interest group as well. The massive development of energy industries throughout the nation led to energy-determined rural policies and uneven economic growth at a time of growing crisis in American family farming.[12]

As a class, agriculturalists were the most challenged and transformed by the interaction of the farm crisis and land use struggles of the 1980s. Conflict between energy development and agriculture characterized the implementation of energy projects throughout the western United States. The construction of strip mines, electrical generation and coal conversion plants, and high voltage transmission lines created problems for agriculturalists, leading many of them to conclude that the two land uses are basically incompatible. Conflicts resulted in North Dakota over the issues of protecting prime farmland from industrial use, the enforcement of land reclamation and ambient air quality regulations, and the siting of inconvenient and potentially hazardous transmission lines (Nace 1979:568). Government agencies at all levels struggled to reconcile and prioritize the disparate interests of agriculture and energy developers, at a time when declining prices for agricultural products, federal pressure to facilitate national energy self-sufficiency, and massive pro-development lobbying campaigns all promoted the view that North Dakota's future should not be built on wheat and cattle.

A distinct pattern emerges from this convoluted case history of how and why industrial development occurred in Mercer County. The implementation of policies designed mainly to benefit corporate interests, with the consent and cooperation of a significant portion of local community members, pervades the entire process—a pattern that has been endlessly repeated across the nation. The central issues here are those of power and economic democracy: the relationship between corporate and community interests and among contradictory local interests, and the role of the state. Whether it is a question of boom growth or sudden abandonment by industry, ordinary citizens have little room to maneuver and must cope with accomplished facts; they have small scope for contributing to the major structural decisions that determine the course of their lives. Their legal powers and involvement come into play late in the process, and the participation of the public in proactively planning the future of their own communities is quite limited in practice. Despite these constraints the people of Mercer County remained active throughout the process, working sometimes with and sometimes against the institutions of development, to secure their own place in the new order.

This book does not pretend to come up with answers to dilemmas of economic democracy, but rather explores how large-scale development projects actually occur and why similar patterns seem to be repeated time after time across the country. It is not intended to be merely an elaborate argument against the development for profit of coal or synthetic gas as energy sources through current institutional arrangements. It is a study of power and ideology in late twentieth-century American society that seeks to deconstruct the apparent inevitability of just this kind of development process. The point is not simply to criticize the practice of energy development today, or those who cooperate with it, but to look beyond its perceived benefits at its trade-offs, contradictions, and hidden consequences.

The Setting and the Study | Mercer County covers an area of 1,042 square miles in the relatively dry country west and south of the Missouri River in North Dakota, in the Great Plains at the center of the North American continent. The landscape is open and rolling, endlessly varied in texture and detail, with rugged buttes and meandering streams. The natural vegetation is grassland. The summers are hot, and the winters are very cold. The average yearly precipitation is about 18 inches, much of which falls as snow in winter, and the average growing season between killing frosts lasts only 110 days. Agriculture is further jeopardized by unpredictable rainfall and occasional severe drought. Mercer County was legally constituted in 1882, settled mainly by German-Russian immigrants. Six towns punctuate the county's landscape, each of which serves as a commercial and social center for its surrounding countryside, where coal mines and conversion plants operate amid the farms and ranches (see Map 1).

The distribution and activities of Mercer County people follow a geographical and historical logic. Water is the limiting factor in agriculture on the Great Plains, and the vagaries of yearly rainfall make for unpredictable agricultural incomes. The most productive farmland is in the northern and eastern sections, close to the Missouri River, where the land is wetter, more fertile, and flatter. To the west and south, the terrain is drier and more eroded, and there multi-crop farming gives way to ranching and wheat farming, especially in the sparsely populated southern portion of Mercer County known as the "ten lost townships," where today no towns are located.

Commercial lignite coal mining began in the 1880s. Mining has increased in importance over the last two decades, while agriculture has declined. The Fort Union coal formation underlies the entire county, and is in many places covered by only forty feet of overburden, the soil and rock that is removed in strip mining to reach the coal beds. This enormous geological feature stretches across the entire northern Great Plains. The states of North Dakota, Wyoming, and Montana are estimated to have 230 billion tons of easily recoverable coal, or 24 percent of the nation's reserve. The Garrison Hydroelectric Dam spans the Missouri River in northeastern Mercer County. The reservoir behind the dam is called Lake Sakakawea and is one of the largest bodies of fresh water on the continent.[13] The dam produces electricity, and the lake serves as an inexpensive source of clean water for residential and industrial use. With its undeveloped shoreline and excellent sports fishing, the lake also provides tourist income and a welcome haven from the hot summer sun for local residents.

Such an instrumental view of the land, in terms of its productivity and resources, is important to those who seek to profit from it, but the description is far from complete. Western North Dakota is also a grand and inspiring landscape, where the elemental powers of wind, sky, and land are a constant presence. A city dweller feels exposed under a great overarching sky, creeping over the open surface, immersed in the dramatic and ever-changing spectacle of the weather. It is exhilarating to watch the storms passing miles away, the thunderheads rising up while the sun shines on another part of the land. As one native wrote: "We live in the sky. . . . We watch the sky for signs of rain, signs of drought, signs of our neighbor coming for coffee. We watch the sky for sunsets visible in every direction, for sunrises that promise days of productive work or quiet contemplation while the rain passes" (Jacobs 1975:36–37).

My introduction to Mercer County came while still a college student in 1978, when I held a summer job on an archaeological crew excavating a historical site known as White Buffalo Robe Village, along the Missouri River near one of the new power plants. The energy boom was already underway at that time; in addition to the coal mines, half a dozen large electrical generating plants were operating or under construction there and in neighboring counties. I lived in a mobile home park for two months, where I had an opportunity to observe the life of migrant construction families. Understanding the social consequences of energy development requires longitudinal study, and I later carried out ethnographic fieldwork during five return visits between 1980 and 1985, ranging from one to three months. During these field seasons I stayed in the home of an elderly lady in Beulah, with a young family in Hazen, and also in hotels mainly housing migrant construction workers. When not in North Dakota I kept up with local events by frequent phone calls and correspondence, and by reading two local weekly newspapers, which my knowledge of local background enabled me to interpret critically.

Beulah, Hazen, and the surrounding countryside formed the focus of my research. Located in the center of the county, where the construction boom was most intense, they are also the largest towns in the county and, as rival communities, offered instructive contrasts in terms of their economic and social makeup. I had initially intended to limit my study to one or two towns, since my own urban bias led me to consider them to be key social units in themselves. I soon realized, however, that the community relevant to this study extended beyond the town limits to include adjacent agricultural areas and the county as a whole. The field continued to expand over the course of fieldwork, as I became more familiar with the interconnections among the towns and rural neighborhoods.

In 1978, Mercer County residents lived in small-scale communities composed of people who knew each other well, were familiar with one another's personal and family background, and shared a common body of local knowledge. In 1970 the county's population was only 6,175 people, of whom 3,726 lived in towns ranging from 119 to 1,344 residents. Over the hundred years since the area's Euro-American settlement, intermarriage among those who had remained in the county had added a dense network of kin relations to those arising from lifelong association. The meaning of being "from the area" was inextricably bound up with having kinship connections to local families. Outsiders were a conspicuous rarity and, lacking a position within local social networks, could find it difficult to gain acceptance.

Local residents often cited the close-knit character of community life as an advantage of living in Mercer County, and its loss as the primary disadvantage of social changes brought about by the energy boom. This account, however, is not intended to be a romantic critique of modernization or a lament about the transformation from isolated community to mass society. These communities may have been intimate, but they were hardly pristine holdovers from an earlier rural Golden Age. They have always been integrated into a wider capitalist economy and subject to its laws of motion. Local society has been shaped by its role in the larger economic system, and has long been vulnerable to the booms and busts of the international grain market and the national industrial economy. Many of its settlers were recruited and transported there by the Northern Pacific Railway. Land tenure, settlement, and the location of towns, schools, and roads were subject to the rule of federal bureaucracy and private land development companies. Local communities have always been changing, class stratified, and riven by conflict.

Although social life in Mercer County was conducted on a personal, face-to-face basis, its residents were not necessarily more intellectually narrow, ignorant, or tradition-bound than their urban counterparts. In the 1950s and 1960s, people in Mercer County participated in the popular cultural and ideological life of the nation, seeing the same movies and television programs, reading national magazines and perhaps a city newspaper, and keeping in touch with family members scattered across the country. The changes brought by industrialization were a continuation of historic transformations, rather than the sudden disorganization of hitherto undisturbed communities.

Doing fieldwork in such a setting required modifications of the community study method developed by sociologists and anthropologists working in the United States. All of the people living in Mercer County were my research subjects, in a broad sense, but this number was much too large (it reached 14,359 in 1983) for me to get to know them all. Random sampling to select informants was out of the question, since the people were suspicious of outsiders in general and of inquisitive ones with dubious intentions in particular. Instead, I made friends in various segments of local society who incorporated me into their own social networks. After an initial week of lonely exclusion, I began to meet people. An elderly lady in Beulah befriended me, rented me a room in her home, and introduced me everywhere as her "granddaughter." Morning outings for coffee and late-afternoon bar visits proved to be fruitful opportunities for conversation. I also went to church, played Bingo at the Eagles Club, attended suppers at the Veterans of Foreign Wars, and went to wedding dances, boating trips, and private parties.

In addition, I sought out those in official positions for more formal interviews, and participated as fully as possible in the civic life of the county. I became a familiar figure at planning and zoning, town council, and County Commission meetings, and at those of political organizations. Sitting with my notebook and asking questions during the breaks, I appeared much like the local journalists at my side, and officials often treated me like one.

As an outsider, I was generally greeted with reserve. Others researching the energy boom had conducted rapid surveys and left, and local residents informed me on many occasions that the only way to understand the situation would be to spend a longer time in the area. As my intentions to do just that became clear, people began taking me more seriously; although some remained mistrustful, others were happy to talk with me and even sought me out with information they wished to be included in my account. When I expressed curiosity on some subject, they often introduced me to others with more expertise in the area. A sympathetic article about me and my research appeared in a local newspaper, and soon it seemed everyone was willing to talk with me. Over the course of my fieldwork, I interviewed some 297 people from all segments of local society, many of whom I maintained contact with over all the years that I visited Mercer County. These included 186 men and 111 women, the imbalance being the result of studying civic life, politics, and economics, areas formally dominated by men, and also because of my research among the overwhelmingly male population of migrant construction workers.[14] Many of my questions were also on the minds of local residents as they sought to cope with development, and our conversations together often led to collaborative insights. Following anthropological practice, I have taken steps to protect the privacy of informants by using fictitious names and leaving out specific dates and places of particular interviews quoted in this book. Such conversations are the source of all of the quotes appearing here, except where I have indicated another source.

As I learned more about Mercer County, it became clear that there was no unitary or well-integrated consensus about what was happening, no simple or unchanging "local perspective" on energy development. A principal aim of this work is to give an empirical account of the conditions for the historical constitution and interaction of the many voices in this beautiful and troubled land.

Chapter Two | A Century of Transformation

History is always present in the Mercer County of today. It appears in the form of flint arrowheads and pottery fragments in a plowed field, in ruined country churches and abandoned back road farmsteads, and in the polka bands at wedding dances. It lives on in the hallways of a retirement institution aptly named "The Pioneer Home." The older generations, who saw the sod houses of their homesteading childhoods replaced by mechanized agriculture and industrial plants, never tire of recounting the travels and travails of their families. Well-known tales of life back in the "old country," of settling a semi-arid frontier, and of Dust Bowl horrors provide a sense of historical depth to this newly coalesced society. The people of Mercer County are proud of their history, and the fact of their survival in the face of hardship lends dignity and even glory to the mundane suffering and simple pleasures of earlier days, transforming the memory into a source of meaning for the present.

Theirs is a history of booms and busts, but the wheat and cattle farmers, coal miners, and town builders of Mercer County have not been passive victims of outside economic forces. For the past century, they have worked to shape their own lives and communities, sometimes contending against the commercial forces of the wider economy, and sometimes in cooperation with them. Each new phase has left Mercer County transformed economically and socially; experience and the retelling of memories have helped to shape the content of its people's political consciousness and their forms of organization to meet with the most recent convulsion in this turbulent history, the energy boom of the 1970s and 1980s.

Scarcely a century has passed since European-Americans began to settle here in significant numbers, so much of their history is still within living memory. The following reconstruction of the past is based on numerous conversations with older residents as well as such documentary sources as family histories, town anniversary yearbooks, newspaper back issues, old county directories, and archives at the historical society.

Peopling the Plains | Long before American agricultural settlement, the profitable fur trade made this distant colonial outpost the scene of international rivalry. By the early 1700s, the presence of the English on Hudson Bay and the French at Lake Superior was felt in the Upper Missouri Basin. Trappers and traders introduced European goods and diseases, while military and population pressure in the east stimulated the westward migration of a number of Minnesota and Great Lakes Woodland tribes, including the Hidatsa (Gros Ventre), into the Dakotas.[1] Arikaras (Rees) immigrated from the Mississippi Valley and, together with the Hidatsa people, joined the Mandans already living near present-day Bismarck. A series of epidemics decimated these communities, and after the final U.S. military conquest of the Plains in the 1860s, the area around Fort Berthold, including northern portions of what is now Mercer County, was converted into a reservation for the Three Affiliated Tribes, as they are known today. The descendents of these indigenous people remain important on the northern margins of the County, but their relationship with energy development has been quite different and separate from that of non-Native people, and it is for this reason alone that they are left out of the following account.

The early settlement by people of European descent of what was to become Mercer County took place at the height of the great riverboat era of American commerce (see Haights et al. 1975; Hunter 1969), so it was no accident that the first communities were river towns. During the 1850s, Norwegians and a few Scottish, Irish, and Anglo-American farmers occupied the best river-bottom land and established small towns, including Causey, Mannhaven, and Old Stanton (see Map 2). These served as shipping points for grain crops and landing points for immigrants and also as fueling stops for the steamboats that navigated this far upstream. These towns were later abandoned as river transportation declined in favor of railroads and overuse depleted the once plentiful supply of cottonwood fuel.

Throughout much of the nineteenth century the federal government's budget depended heavily on the profitable disposal of public lands. Encouraging settlement also served to consolidate the young United States at a time of fierce competition with other national powers. By populating the territory with American nationals, and facilitating their westward flow, national expansion was made secure and Manifest Destiny fulfilled.[2]

The Homestead Act of 1862, together with the Pre-emption Law and the Timber Culture Act, provided inexpensive means of acquiring legal title to surveyed lands on the western frontier. Under the Pre-emption Law, settlers owning less than 320 acres elsewhere in the country could buy 160 acres, with proof of six months' prior residence and improvements. The same amount of land—a quarter section—could be gotten for a small filing fee as a homestead, with five subsequent years of residence and cultivation required. Residence was not required by the Timber Culture Act of 1873, but at least ten of the 160 acres had to be planted in trees that survived for at least eight years.[3] However, although homesteads of 160 acres may have been sufficient for farmers in the more humid regions of the Midwest, these were not viable units for commercial agriculture on the drier western plains; from the beginning, farmers sought to expand their landholdings in competition with their neighbors.

In the western states, enormous federal land grants were made to railroad corporations, who surveyed townsites and recruited immigrants from all over Europe to fill them. One such grant of 50 million acres to the Northern Pacific Railway touched off a boom in land speculation that was eventually to fill the northern plains with more small commercial farmers than its semi-arid climate could support. But this rural population explosion initially provided a market for the manufactured goods produced by growing industries in other parts of the United States, and thus a highly productive agricultural sector provided the basis for much of the nation's early economic growth.

Soon after the organization of Dakota Territory by Congress in 1861, settler families had reached the interior of Mercer County, following the creeks that fed into the Knife and Missouri Rivers. The river bottoms had already been occupied for ten years or more, so this new wave of immigrants had to move out onto the open grassland to build their homes. Far north of the projected Northern Pacific railroad route, Mercer County remained for some time sparsely populated and river-oriented, but was nonetheless the setting for numerous speculation booms in the 1880s.

Life on the frontier was difficult and unstable. Pioneers struggled to break the thick layer of sod covering the fertile soil. The mass of matted grass was tough enough to serve as building material, and in the absence of suitable wood, was cut into blocks for constructing reasonably comfortable houses and barns. These sod houses, or "soddies," were sometimes covered with planks on the inside and extra earth on the outside for added insulation and comfort. Settlers sometimes made dugout houses in the sides of hills, to take advantage of the earth wall insulation, which protected the inhabitants from the extreme temperatures of both winter and summer. Log cabins were also built here, but only in the riverside woodlands.[4] Lignite coal outcrops provided an inexpensive source of fuel and small-scale commercial mining for local use took place from the earliest years of settlement.

Isolated frontier farmers had to provide their own food, as well as cultivate commercial grains, using only simple hand plows, hoes, and rakes. Early crops included potatoes, wheat, corn, and vegetables, and settlers supplemented their diet with domestic pigs, chickens, beef and dairy products, as well as wild game. New arrivals needed the help of established farmers to find suitable land and learn the techniques of grassland agriculture. The yearly cycle began with the seeding of land that had been plowed the preceding year, followed by the breaking of new land to enlarge the holding. This was back-breaking work with a hand plow, but from the beginning farmers considered it imperative to maximize the area of cultivation to take advantage of economies of scale. They were already concerned with earning cash income for purchasing machinery and making debt payments. Next came haying to provide feed for livestock, and then harvesting and threshing the commercial grain crop, which required extra workers and neighborly cooperation. Then it was time to plow back the stubble and the new land broken that spring. Women frequently did field work in addition to producing household necessities such as soap, candles, and wheat flour. They also undertook the tasks of carding, spinning, and dying wool, knitting clothes, weaving cloth for blankets, sewing clothing, preparing food, and caring for young children. During the winter months men also produced simple implements like rakes and carts.

During the 1880s a new group of immigrants began to arrive on the scene; these were Germans from the Russian Empire (before 1917), who became the most important local ethnic group by the turn of the century. These people, whose communities are scattered throughout southern and western North Dakota, have an unusual history. In the 1760s, according to numerous published accounts as well as oral tradition, Empress Catherine of Russia, herself a German, wished to colonize the South Russian Tartar steppes in order to consolidate her rule there. Accordingly, her agents went to Germany to attract settlers. Peasants made landless and destitute by the Seven Years' War were offered free land, religious freedom, exemption from military duties, as well as cattle and implements, if they would emigrate and settle in "South Russia," as the region is still referred to in Mercer County.

By 1770, fifty thousand Germans had moved to the lower Volga and to the Odessa-Kiev region of the modern Ukraine, founding more than one hundred agricultural colonies. In the reign of Alexander I, who became Czar in 1801, a new wave of migration brought German refugees from the Napoleonic Wars to settle in formerly Ottoman Bessarabia (modern Moldova) near the Black Sea. The adverse conditions of these areas were good preparation for life on the North American grasslands: The land was semi-arid and the German villages were culturally isolated both from their homeland and from their non-German-speaking neighbors. The colonies consisted of pious and hardworking farming families, with little interest in state-organized secular education.

In Russia they became prosperous citizens, with a social status higher than their poorer peasant and nomadic neighbors'. They were largely left alone by the Russian government until the area underwent a nationalistic Russification program in the 1880s and 1890s. New policies made Russian-language schools and military service mandatory (Voeller 1940). These changes, and the increasing scarcity of land, stimulated emigration, and many left for the New World. Their destinations included the Argentine pampas, southern Brazil, and the Great Plains of North America; and many found themselves unwitting objects of ship captains' immigrant quotas for these various destinations. Their incentives for moving—cheap land for settlement and freedom from cultural oppression—were much the same as in their earlier migration. These groups even resettled in areas bearing some ecological resemblance to the former home of those who had lived on the Russian steppes.

In 1888, when the first German-Russians drove their covered wagons from established settlements in South Dakota into North Dakota in search of good homesteading land, they followed the advice of travelers and farmers met upon the way and finally found themselves in Mercer County, several days' travel north of the nearest railroad shipping points at Hebron and New Salem. These first families were in need of cash and had arrived too late in the year to put in a crop, so they supported themselves by gathering buffalo bones on the prairie, which they sold for six to fourteen dollars a wagon load. This peculiar occupation was common at the time, since the bones of herds previously demolished by bounty hunters could be shipped east to be made into carbon black for sugar refining. During this first year they also broke sod and made houses, using techniques such as those described in this excerpt from a family history:

> In the spring Grandma Dorothea went out to plow or break up the sod with the oxen, and to plant flax. Grandfather Johannes did the building

and went down to the Missouri river to cut thin cottonwood trees, or long river poles, which they used for the roof of their house. They used yellow clay for the roof and to build the walls. With muddy clay they smeared shut the holes so that it wouldn't rain in. (Brenneise 1979:xli)

According to local historians, these first German-Russians had grain to sell the next year, a fact demonstrating that from the beginning, they were engaged in commercial, rather than merely subsistence, agriculture.

New arrivals kept coming by wagon train, so that by the time of North Dakota's statehood in 1889 there were thirty German-Russian families in the county. The migration of many more families directly from Russia was later organized by the Northern Pacific Railway through an agent hired from among the recent immigrants, in order to sell off their federal land grant to individual smallholders to assure themselves of a market for their grain shipment services. Although the country was new to them, these immigrants made successful frontierspeople in the agricultural conditions they found so similar to those in South Russia. These families had brought with them from Europe commercial attitudes towards land and agricultural enterprise as well as the German values of hard work, honesty, and Christian piety. As in their Russian villages, they resisted compulsory secular education and stuck to single-crop wheat farming and a clannish isolationism.

Many of the oldest generation living in the county today were born in Russia and brought up on homestead claims. Some have bitter memories of intergroup conflict: "Back then, German speakers were really looked down on, and they couldn't communicate much with the others . . . and even among themselves they didn't mix with the other religion [Protestant versus Catholic]. The family wouldn't even let you date such a person." Others recall tragic suffering: "There were no doctors in the beginning. . . . I remember quite a few women around died trying to have their babies. And there were a lot of little graves. . . . So many children would get sick."

More often, though, older residents emphasize the positive aspects of their youthful experiences. They readily recount how the countryside was knit together by exchanging work, equipment, and food, and by an emphasis on neighborly cooperation and family solidarity. Traditional wedding dances, held in barns or banquet halls built with volunteer labor, exemplify the interconnectedness of this remembered rural society. After the wedding vows and meal, the neighbors, friends, and relatives were invited to join together for a party that could last up to three days, dancing and drinking. This upbeat version of frontier social life is illustrated in an excerpt from a family history included in a commemorative volume produced for the fiftieth anniversary of the town of Beulah:

> With the birth of their first child . . . Mag had no more time for loneliness, what with the new baby to care for, chores to be done, meals to be cooked, mail to be gotten (this was a 23-mile trip to Nesbit and back), and of course one had entertaining to do. . . . New friends (of many nationalities) were made. Sometimes language was a bit of a barrier,[5] but this was soon overcome, for they all had one thing in common—they were settlers seeking a way to make a good honest living. If a neighbor was sick, you dropped your work and went over and helped; if their barn was destroyed, you had a barn-raising; if there was a death, you comforted.
> (Beulah, North Dakota 1964:126)

Town Building and the Emergence of Inequality

Mutual aid may have been the rule among the farmers of North Dakota; yet each was engaged in a budding commercial enterprise that would eventually lead them to compete with their neighbors. Settlers were intent upon improving their living standard by marketing cash crops of grain, which depended upon the investment of Eastern capital in railroads, banks, grain elevators, and farm equipment. The railroads became busy pipelines for transport back and forth between the nation's rapidly industrializing cities and the expanding agricultural hinterland. The riverboat-based fur trade had made the area into a periphery of St. Louis; now the rails transformed it into a satellite of Minneapolis and St. Paul.

Railroad construction and townsite speculation stimulated an economic boom in the 1870s and early 1880s. The Great Dakota Boom drove up the value of land at a time when farmers and ranchers of the West had to expand their holdings in order to stay in business. Although the state's population increased one thousand percent between 1878 and 1890, 49 percent of the farms were mortgaged by 1890. Overproduction and subsequent falling grain prices during the 1880s contributed to a high rate of farm abandonment and the early demise of many speculation townsites. The limitations of the region's farm economy had become apparent, and the risks were increased by the region's unreliable rainfall. The additional squeeze of elevator, shipping, and marketing costs proved fatal to many such enterprises.

Lines of transportation and the practical exigencies of agricultural production and distribution shaped the definition, location, and founding of many towns. More than fifteen towns appear in local historical accounts of Mercer County between 1883 and 1914, but only six of them survive today. A brief description of the rise and fall of such rural settlements sheds light on the forces shaping rural plains life in an industrializing America. Early settlement consisted mainly of single farmsteads, spread out on the land, rather than clustered in villages. Most of the earliest towns, all of which were subsequently abandoned, began as post offices or general stores. Local entrepreneurs (some with colorful names, such as "Scrap Iron" Bill Bryant, "Four Paw," and "Longhaired Spencer"), operating flour mills, mercantile shops, newspapers, banks, saloons, sawmills, and even a steamboat-building yard, constantly tested the population's ability to support local businesses.

When the county was designated in 1883, it had only two dozen legal voters, yet was already considered a "hotbed of political intrigue," with intense competition for public office, there not being "enough offices to go around" (*The Common* August 10, 1872). In 1885 Stanton won the title as county seat over its rival Causey in a hotly contested fight in which the deciding vote was cast by one "Club-Foot" Wilson, a horse rustler brought in by the Sheriff during the vote. At that time, the county's population was 254, its assets consisted of a shack courthouse, a few log bridges, and a crude road scraper. Its liabilities amounted to several thousand dollars.

Over the years, the county's boundaries have been redefined several times,[6] and the composition of its population centers has been even more fluid. Stanton reached a peak of two hundred residents in 1888, but had been virtually abandoned ten years later. Mercer City, a town platted by the Lutheran Colonization Bureau of Chicago, never had more than one inhabitant, although 25 lots were sold to gullible buyers in Illinois. Mannhaven and Expansion were both founded by locally formed steamboat-building and -operating companies and survived as grain shipping ports and lumberyard centers until the railroads came through another part of the county. Krem was the only sizeable early town built away from the river, and with its flour mill and two general stores became for some time the busiest trading center in the county, although farmers still went to the river to sell their grain. Another victim of shifting transportation structures, Krem was abandoned after 1912 when the new railroad coming through the county passed it by. Kroenthal and Kasmer, founded in 1900 and 1910 respectively, both began as post offices and then experimented with creameries. Kroenthal died abirthing, however, when it was discovered that butter shipped south to market failed to survive the long wagon journey without spoiling. Kasmer fared better, acquired stores and a bank (the German-American). But it ultimately succumbed with the advent of the railroad in the county, as did Ree (also known as Stoeltingen), founded as a branch of the Expansion Lumber and

Mercantile Company and as a grain shipping point on the Fort Berthold Indian Reservation. Bigbend, like Mercer City, was another money-making attempt by outside speculators that failed almost before it began. There, several hundred lots were sold in Wisconsin by Milwaukee speculators, but only one settler actually took possession.

The only town of this period that has survived to this day is Stanton, once a river town, and then a railroad town. Stanton was resurrected in 1907 when people protested that county officials must live and keep records there in the designated county seat, but its future was not assured until the Northern Pacific (later bought out by the Burlington Northern Railway) arrived in 1912. As the railroad route was planned, the Northern Pacific Land Department sold their remaining land to Iowa capitalists, and the Tuttle Land Company undertook the platting and establishment of Hazen, Beulah, Zap, and Golden Valley at approximately ten-mile intervals across the county from east to west, the distance most convenient for a loaded grain wagon to travel in a single day.[7] Grain companies set up storage elevators in each of these towns, and merchants from the older towns moved their businesses (and sometimes even their buildings) to the tracks, leaving behind rural churches and schoolhouses. The thriving inland town of Krem moved en masse to Hazen, that of Kasmer to Zap, while new groups of entrepreneurs tried their hands at trade in the other two towns.

Even at this early stage, not all the railroad towns were equally successful. Hazen thrived while Beulah languished: The former was closer to the agriculturally rich land along the river and benefitted from its trade. When large and accessible coal deposits were discovered in the drier land to the west and south, Beulah and Zap turned to the mining industry for growth. Golden Valley did well for a time because of its proximity to the Fort Berthold Reservation with its Indian commerce. This trade moved elsewhere after the Garrison Dam flooded the reservation's river lands and rearranged the geography of the reservation in the 1950s, and Golden Valley entered into a long decline. In the central part of the county, the neighboring towns of Beulah and Hazen eventually emerged as the largest and most commercially dynamic in the county.

The railroad was crucial in shaping the social geography within these towns, as well. Those towns that were planned along the railroad route are easily identifiable by their characteristic layout. All are what John Hudson (1982:90) has called "T-towns," in which the business district was laid out entirely to one side of the tracks to minimize railway crossings. The tracks run parallel to and one block south of Main Street, with the depot and towering grain elevators somewhere close to a central avenue. Most development has taken place north of the tracks (it is usually less prestigious to live south of them), with businesses strung along Main Street and houses in neatly arranged blocks spreading out from the town center. Any visitor to the Great Plains will immediately recognize this typical town plan, which varies little in its essentials from the smallest village to Bismarck, the state capital. As with everything designed by settlement planners, strict adherence to the cardinal directions and an orderly grid is maintained except where unruly Nature imposes a meandering stream or asymmetrical butte.

The division of land by township and range lines, subdivided by section lines upon which county roads typically run, is testimony to the rational impulse of the federal land disposal bureaucracy. Roads, barns, fences, and even chicken coops are placed parallel to lines of latitude and longitude. This order creates a mental habit of orientation according to the cardinal compass points such that local residents give directions according to them, as in "drive west three miles, then north for half a mile, and the farmstead is on the east side of the road." Similarly, all natives of Mercer County know that the "home quarter" refers to that square fourth of a quarter section of a family's farmland that is set aside for the construction of the house, barn, equipment shed, and other outbuildings. Rural North Dakotans admit to becoming easily disoriented in the little city of Grand Forks, where the street grid is offset from the cardinal norm in order to follow a river bend.

Even though the railway depot towns built after the turn of the century gained importance at the expense of older towns, the focus of life for most farmers and ranchers remained in the countryside. Until the widespread adoption of automobiles in the 1920s, country schools, churches, and general stores thrived amid the many small-holding families. Every rural neighborhood had its sandlot baseball teams, musical groups, and barn dances to provide entertainment, together with basket socials, theatrical productions, and traveling carnivals. It was not until the 1930s, when drought and agricultural competition forced many of these farmers out of business, that the density of farmsteads declined significantly, along with the richness of neighborhood life in the countryside.

Shopping in town was also a social occasion, as this account of Beulah Main Street life in the early 1930s illustrates:

> While the women sat on a bench in front of the Wear-U-Well shoe department and did their weekly visiting, the men were either kibbitzing or playing a game of checkers. . . . If it was lunch time our rural customers would go to the kitchen and get a glass of cider, buy a hunk of sausage and a box of crackers and the family would "dine out." On Saturday nite [sic]

the bench was its busiest, for everyone came to town, the young people would be visiting on Main Street and the women and smaller children would be using the bench and all the chairs the [store owners] owned. By the time everyone went home there would be sunflower seed shells an inch thick on the floor. These were the days when stores would be open until eleven or twelve every nite. (*Beulah, North Dakota* 1964:217)

Small businesses in town depended on the agricultural trade and shared in the farmers' ups and downs. These towns were collections of churches, shops, and banks, their skylines dominated by a grain elevator or two, with little industry of their own. Competition among towns for trade was intense, for their very survival depended on winning out in the struggle for patronage. Towns close to coal mines had an additional source of employment, but were ultimately just as dependent on outside capital as other towns, since coal was also exported for sale outside the region.

Building towns upon such uncertain economic foundations required a cult of civic pride and belief in the region's capacity to sustain growth. In this they resembled the Midwestern towns studied by Lewis Atherton, "where idealism, optimism, materialism, and an abiding faith in progress were strangely mingled . . . progress in terms of growth in numbers and real estate prices" (1954:xiv). The rise in real estate values during successive boom periods was the main engine driving the fantastically rapid transformation of remote and open grasslands into farmsteads and bustling villages complete with all the trappings of civilization. The capital outlay required to finance this development depended on sustaining the appearance of confident progress towards an economically bright future. The emphasis on performing civic duties, as expressed by investment in local real estate and businesses, took its ideological form as boosterism—a form of community allegiance expressly linked to commercial activities. From the earliest years, commercial clubs organized all manner of vigorous promotions and attempts to attract new businesses and services to their communities.[8] While striving to minimize internal competition, such associations undertook civic projects to improve the local business community's competitive advantage in relation to neighboring towns. Organizing harvest festivals, building bridges to facilitate farm trade, and encouraging the railroad commissioner to investigate alleged overgrading of grain in nearby towns are examples of such activities.

A large part of the resources of such associations went into projects with a more indirect effect on the economic struggle among towns, such as support for community bands, town picnics, and athletic events. The effect was to mask the economic nature of the competition and to raise the town spirit through "boosting" the community—making challenging and often symbolic statements to the world at large of the town's superior worthiness through the pride and dignity displayed by its members. Such displays entailed a calculated risk, both financial and in terms of "face," and carrying them off successfully required a united community effort.

Towns that won out most visibly in this competition for trade and social honor centralized the organizing energy of various civic voluntary associations into an inclusive Chamber of Commerce. By focusing these activities and encouraging the proliferation of diversified special interest associations under its umbrella, the Chamber strengthened relationships with farmers living nearby, by sponsoring Farmers Union and 4-H events and encouraging member lending institutions to extend farm credit, and it sought also to unite factions within the community. As the lignite industry grew in the twentieth century, miners became important factions in several of the towns. Their union locals were encouraged to join the Chambers of Commerce and to participate in the civic religion of boosterism.

Despite all efforts, Mercer County grew slowly to its 1900 population of only 1,778 persons. Towns away from the railway lines did not survive the changing economic and transportation systems, but the competition and rivalry among surviving towns remained strong, along with elaborated ideas about the uniqueness of each community's character and special qualities.

Continued immigration had brought together a diverse population in Mercer County by the early decades of the twentieth century. According to the Patrons' Reference Directory of a 1918 Mercer County Atlas (1918), at least 75 percent of the adults had been born overseas. Of these, more than 70 percent were Germans from Russia; there were also a significant number born in Germany, and a few natives of Hungary, Sweden, Norway, Austria, Canada, Bohemia, Ireland, and Brazil.[9] Numbers are not available for women, but only about 25 percent of the adult men in the county had been born in the United States, and fewer than 10 percent of these were North Dakota natives.

The occupational makeup at this time was more homogeneous, reflecting an undifferentiated economy. Almost 99 percent of the working population were engaged in agriculture—as farmers and animal breeders. Most of the rest were employed in businesses, with a very few holding full-time government jobs. In 1918 there were ten banks in the county, principally providing farm credit.

Religion was an important organizing feature on this rootless frontier. After homes, churches were typically the first buildings the settlers constructed. Local frontier communities were socially polarized into Catholic and Protestant (mainly Lutheran and German Baptist) congregations, especially among the Germans from Russia, who had lived in sectarian communities there. Rivalries among families within single congregations over lay positions in the churches were also commonplace. In the memories of the older people in Mercer County today, marriage across religious lines was discouraged, and voting in local elections followed the same pattern.

Church communities were also the rallying point of ethnic identity. The earlier Anglo-American settlers had established Presbyterian, Methodist, Episcopalian, Congregationalist, and Irish Catholic churches. The later immigrants drew together around religious, ethnic, and linguistic solidarity in an alien land where the church was the only major institution over which they could exercise control. The churches sponsored voluntary associations for women, men, youth, and church fairs, festivals, and wedding celebrations provided the major source of entertainment for the settlers.

Ethnic and religious conflicts had class and status dimensions, as well. Mastery of the English language was an important status marker, and many German speakers found themselves subject to the opprobrious taunt, "dumb Rooshians." Their ethnicity was further stigmatized as a result of two world wars and the Russian Revolution, in which the American public came to view both of their countries of origin as enemies. The shift from high to low status that accompanied their migration to America was traumatic for many Germans from Russia. English speakers at first dominated the more prestigious occupations of banker, doctor, lawyer, and teacher, although some recent immigrant entrepreneurs did become relatively successful (i.e., wealthy) and therefore were respected as businessmen, ranchers, or farmers.

The social position and working conditions of coal miners in the early decades of the twentieth century were very poor. Older residents of the towns where mining was important recall the segregation of the miners and their families in poor shacks in the undesirable neighborhoods, one of which was called "Dog Town." Signs at the entrance of some local saloons read "No Miners," allegedly because others considered them dirty and prone to violence. As a group, miners were at the bottom of the status ladder, only slightly above the position of the mules hauling the underground coal cars. The elderly widow of a coal miner recalls with shame and indignation the disrespectful treatment her husband received:

He played the organ so beautifully; he played in the church. I overheard other people saying that they didn't expect that from a dirty coal miner. . . . When he went to get his driver's licence, all neat and clean of course, the clerk asked his occupation. "Coal miner." The clerk looked him up and down and said, "You don't look like it!" . . . He and I used to joke about it to the children, "Poor kids: a dumb Rooshian for a mother and a dirty miner for a father!"

Despite such social discrimination, some old miners recall with nostalgia the warm camaraderie of the underground work crew, and avoid discussion of their low status. A retired miner recounted: "In the underground mines there was a good feeling; the workers were more close, working together every day. If something happened, people always jumped right in to get the job done. That's what I liked. It was fun having all your friends there."

Commercial mining by a major coal company to serve a state-wide market began here in 1917. The Beulah Mine, owned by the Knife River Coal Corporation, employed 220 men in 1930, working underground seams at depths of 30 and 170 feet. In this mine, labor-intensive pick and shovel work produced about 230,000 tons per year. Subsequent equipment modernization brought employment down to an average of 206 in 1931, 165 in 1935, and 108 in 1942, when these few workers produced 362,000 tons of lignite. Earlier mines on farmers' property had been worked seasonally by farmers after harvest, but the larger ones were year-round operations. But sluggish demand made for unstable and often part-time employment; some miners were also part-time farmers, while others had no other source of income. The mines at Zap—Lucky Strike, Zap, and Indian Head mines—produced a community of miners to rival that of Beulah. Zap Collieries, and later the North American Coal Corporation, employed numbers comparable to those of the Beulah Mine.

Landless farm laborers and tenant farmers also had low status, and many miners were drawn from their ranks. As was common in the United States, social honor and prestige were largely determined by income and property ownership, seen as concrete evidence of shrewdness and hard work. On the local level, land owners gained superior status over propertyless laborers, and residence in town (generally associated with nonfarm business activity) was more prestigious than a rural address. Those at the top of the class structure, who owned the railroads, grain elevators, and large underground mines, were generally absent from the County and conducted their business through hired subordinates.

Farming and Mining: The Roots of Dependency and Resistance

Since the late nineteenth century, rural residents of western North Dakota have been mainly commercial producers of wheat and miners of coal, both primary product commodities subject to unstable prices, in a region with concentrated control of credit, transportation, and marketing. The agrarian populist efforts to gain greater local autonomy and the labor struggles of organizing mine workers helped to shape local political culture, including both the ideological and organizational forms with which people in Mercer County encountered big capital during the energy boom.

During the late 1800s, the Northern Pacific and Great Northern Railways, together with an association of Minneapolis wheat buyers, controlled the rural grain elevators, and freight shipping, and the terminal elevators at the shipping terminus in Minnesota. The cartel gave rebates to wheat buyers in the group, ruled against trackside loading (so that farmers could not ship directly but had to go through the big company elevators), and regulated the size and location of elevators along their rights of way so as to drive independent buyers out of business. They were also accused of low-grading the quality of wheat when buying, and raising it when selling; paying below-market prices, using false weights, and docking purchase payments excessively for chaff and other impurities.[10] Farmers also felt they were the victims of tight-money banking and unfair credit policies.

Farmers organized early against the grain shippers and merchants.[11] Outspoken protest in North Dakota began in 1881, and by 1884 local groups had begun to organize mutual protective associations for cooperative selling and for buying coal and twine. Local groups combined in 1889 to form the Dakota Farmers Alliance, whose goals were a free grain market and legal reforms to be achieved through electing farmers and their supporters to public office. At that time there were 744 local alliances, with 28,000 members, and the statewide organization joined with both the National Farmers Alliance (known as the Northern Alliance) and the National Farmers Alliance and Industrial Union (the Southern Alliance), which laid the organizational foundation for the rising Populist Party.

European immigrants in Mercer County had some experience with radical organization. In Russia, the German farmers had operated cooperative granaries and associations for fire insurance, livestock herding, and tree planting. The Norwegian settlers were heir to a long history of agrarian labor activity. The Norwegian Labor Party, founded in 1849, was the result of years of united struggle on the part of agricultural and industrial laborers to organize unions, strikes, cooperative purchasing, and sick funds, and to win the right to vote. Still, organizing the scattered Dakota farmsteads was not easy. The predominantly German-Russian population of the western counties had a perennial distrust of "outsiders" of any sort (including Populist organizers), and knew their income to be dependent upon the good graces of the buyers and shippers of grain. It was also difficult to dislodge the political machine of Alexander McKenzie, the boss of the railroad interests, who had established a strong patronage structure throughout the state.

In spite of these obstacles, some reforms were enacted during North Dakota's brief Populist years,[12] and a strong tradition of anti–big-business politics was established. Already, the dual character of North Dakota politics had become clear: Businessmen and the entrenched political machine of the Minnesota capitalists supported Republican policies, and the agricultural community was torn between a traditional loyalty to the Republican Party and resentment against the railroad barons, grain magnates, and bankers.

The decade and a half after the turn of the century was a time of progressive reform in American politics and of shifting power relationships among North Dakota interest groups. In 1910, Progressives won control of the state legislature and enacted numerous reforms, yet their identity remained essentially liberal and middle class (Hofstadter 1955), and it was left to the farmers to organize more radical projects on their own. On the farms and in the small towns of rural North Dakota there was widespread sympathy for radical measures. As one historian relates:

> In the struggle, the people of the state, feeling keenly their entire dependence upon the railroads, could hardly be expected to admire the giant corporations, so obviously rich and powerful, which, moving in secret ways, influenced public officials and exploited townsmen and farmers alike, reducing their incomes by freight rates designed to earn a return on fictitious capitalization. (Robinson 1966:241)

Organizing efforts continued among farmers throughout the Progressive years. They were successful in establishing a network of rural elevator cooperatives (managed by what came to be known as the Farmers Union Cooperative) and, in 1908, passed legislation for their long-held dream of a farmer-controlled cooperative elevator at the Minnesota terminus.

With the rise of the socialist Nonpartisan Political League in 1915, the earlier populist themes were forcefully rearticulated (Saloutos

1946). In their weekly newspaper the situation of farmers dependent on "Big Biz" or "the Interests" was described as "colonial" (*Nonpartisan Leader*, February 10, 1916). The League's founder, Arthur C. Townley, campaigned throughout the North Dakota countryside. His colorful style is exemplified by this line attributed to him: "If you put a lawyer, a banker, and an industrialist in a barrel and roll it downhill, there'll always be a son-of-a-bitch on top."

Although it harbored members with extremely radical views, the party as a whole favored a moderate program of reforms, including rural credit banks, state hail insurance, and state-owned flour mills and terminal elevators. This platform was only slightly more radical than that of the progressive movement, and was generally appealing to farmers, even to the staunchly conservative German-Russians of Mercer County. Yet even so, the stigma of the title "socialist" was simply too great for the party to attract a majority following. Eventually, Townley resolved to move the organization and its platform of state ownership into the Republican Party itself. This reorganized Nonpartisan League was an immediate success with farmers all over the state. Its immensely effective grassroots organizing involved farm-to-farm visits and well-planned sales talks to arouse the resentment of farmers against big business interests.

In control of the state legislature by 1917, the League began to realize its platform: The state constitution was amended to permit the state to engage in business, the Bank of North Dakota was chartered, and the state Mill and Elevator Association established. Legislative conflicts, internal disputes, mismanagement, the opposition's charges of disloyalty during World War I (which were partly responsible for a boycott of the League's bonds by Eastern capital), as well as the relative prosperity of farmers during the war years resulted in the failure of most of these socialistic measures. By taking over the burden of risk from farmers, the state enterprises exposed themselves to the wild fluctuations of a grain market that remained essentially beyond their control. The state bank survived, and a single state mill and elevator were eventually constructed, but the Nonpartisan League as a centrally controlled political organization had collapsed by 1922.[13]

The fate of this experiment in state enterprise illustrates some of the ideological peculiarities of North Dakota politics. Since these continue to influence political activity in Mercer County today, they deserve explication. Although the interests of farmers were in conflict with those of freight, milling, and banking firms, both groups tended to operate within the same party, confining much of their struggle to the level of primary elections. The historic strength of the Republicans in North Dakota is due to a powerful party loyalty and does not in itself indicate a consistently conservative climate. Both the Populist and Socialist movements failed as third (or even second) parties, and power could only be gained by working under the Republican rubric.

Observers have often noted the apparently dual nature of the area's political orientation—alternately conservative and socialist. This political ambiguity can be explained by the ambiguous class position of petty commodity farmers, who are one part businessman and one part small family operator. Although they think of themselves as entrepreneurs, they have no control over the circulation of money, commodities, and capital (MacLennan and Walker 1980:39–40). This dual economic personality made it difficult for Mercer County family farmers to maintain a consistent ideological outlook; they tended to praise the "free-enterprise system" when times were good, and reverse their position when times were bad, demanding increased state economic intervention. Another problem is that analysts' classification of issues as either conservative or progressive does not necessarily correspond to the views of Dakota farmers, who were concerned with their own very specific sets of interests. What may appear on one level to be ideological discrepancies makes more sense within a particular culturally constructed logic of self-interest and locally specific form of production.

Independently of the fortunes of political parties, the cooperative movement among farmers gained strength throughout the 1920s and 1930s. It attracted farmers of all political persuasions, because it specifically addressed their dependent and peripheral relation to the market. Farmers were much more interested in addressing this issue than that of overproduction, which was at least as serious a cause of their economic problems.

Although the rest of the nation enjoyed economic growth and prosperity after the First World War, farming experienced a persistent depression. Mortgage debts were owed on seven-eighths of North Dakota farms worked by their owners in 1921; between then and 1930 farm tenancy rose from one-fourth to one-third of the state's farmers. Overextension of credit by the numerous small rural banks led to a general bank collapse in the early 1920s. With decreased European and U.S. Government demand for wheat and with the deflationary tight-money policies of the Federal Reserve Board, cash flow into the state was sharply cut at a time when farmers were having to withdraw savings to make ends meet. Ninety-nine banks failed in the state in 1923, and during the next ten years total failures reached 573 out of the original 898 banks in business in 1920 (Robinson 1966:377). An exodus of discouraged farmers began during the 1920s, which has continued on and off ever since.

A Century of Transformation | 43

The cooperative movement was strengthened by adversity. Farmer-owned cooperative elevators constituted one-third of all elevators in the state by 1921, and in 1922 legislation was passed exempting agricultural cooperatives from anti-trust laws. Many such attempts to eliminate the middlemen failed under pressure from the grain establishment, but one great cooperative venture achieved widespread success (Tucker 1947). In 1927 a merger of regional farmers' organizations established the North Dakota Farmers Union Grain Terminal Association (also called the Farmers Educational and Cooperative Union). It organized with thirteen thousand members and an extensive line of services, and kept growing. Mike Jacobs offers an explanation for its success that emphasizes the farmers' particular views and interests. According to him, farmers saw cooperatives "as a middle road between corporate capitalism, which robbed them, and state capitalism, which they felt they could not trust" (1975:74). In other words, the cooperative organization enabled them to act independently of state financing and control, while avoiding some of the middlemen. When the energy boom began, every town in Mercer County had a Farmers Union elevator and service station selling gasoline and other essential agricultural materials at reasonable prices that private companies had to match to stay in business.

North Dakota's agriculturally based economy was severely weakened by the farm depression of the 1920s, and when the 1930s brought the Great Depression and the Dust Bowl crisis, the area suffered even more than most parts of the country. Older residents of Mercer County recount that throughout the early 1930s farmers would plant and "nothing would come up but Russian Thistles [tumbleweed]." Drifting dirt and dust covered up fences, and finding forage for the animals was a serious problem. One tale is told of a local farmer who shipped his lambs to market in St. Paul, only to receive a telegram from the railroad saying that profits from the sale had not even paid the freight costs, and that he owed them money. His reply? "Don't have any money, but can send more sheep!" In some years, farmers scarcely brought in enough of a crop to produce seed for the next planting. The crops suffered not only from persistent drought, but also from the ravages of billions of grasshoppers and an exploding population of jackrabbits. There was no work for farm laborers. When the drought abated in the late 1930s, depressed prices still brought producers little return for their investment. A retired farmer recalls his family's financial troubles:

> In 1929 in the fall wheat was $1.17 a bushel when they started the harvest. The price of oats was so low it didn't pay the freight cost. Same with sheep, selling them to the government. Wheat storage in town cost a half a cent a

bushel per month. Next spring wheat was selling for 78 cents a bushel, and by the fall of 1930 it was 45 cents a bushel. It kept going down, to 21 or 22 cents a bushel. Pigs on the hoof were 3 cents a pound. We dressed them there on the farm and sold them to the miners in Zap for 5 cents a pound, thinking that at least the miners would have some money. But they ate and didn't pay.

Gasoline was 17 cents a gallon. A week's supply was five gallons, a week's supply of kerosene was two gallons. I went and worked underground [in a coal mine] for six years. They paid us 44 cents a ton of coal mined by hand. That was about 50 cents an hour or four dollars a day. You didn't dare complain, though, because there were nine guys waiting for the job.

During the Dust Bowl years, over 121,000 people left North Dakota, most heading west to Washington, Oregon, and California. This was a tragic disruption for tightly knit local communities. Many Mercer County families who lost their farms through forced sales and foreclosures either emigrated or moved to town to find relief work. Tax delinquency soared, suicides became more frequent, and a police officer was killed while confiscating equipment forfeited in a farm foreclosure. In 1936 over half the county's population was on relief assistance of some kind. This in itself was hard on these proud people, who felt that accepting charity was shameful.

The poorest families suffered most during the Depression. Ellen, a resident of Hazen, recalls with sadness her difficult childhood on a nearby farm. Her mother died in childbirth at the age of twenty-nine, leaving four children, of which seven-year-old Ellen was the eldest:

> We had to work all the time. The only time I ever got to play was on Sunday afternoon, and then I didn't know *how* to play, just didn't remember how anymore. We were so poor in the thirties, in the drought, when the harvest just gave enough to pay the interest on the mortgage. Sunday dinner was the big meal of the week, and that was just those little tiny potatoes with cream on them. . . . Our clothes weren't warm enough for winter. We always had frostbite on different parts of us. We didn't even have any shoes, can you believe it? Just socks and newspaper in overshoes, but we still walked to school in the snow. The teacher didn't know how bad off we were. . . . You didn't waste anything; had to haul water to the two-room shack, only so much coal, kerosene and such. Everybody just went to bed early to not use up so much. . . . All the children got a pad of notepaper for Christmas. It costed a nickel, and it had to last all year in school.

As a result of forced sales and farm foreclosures, landholdings became more concentrated in two ways. Millions of acres in North

Dakota devolved to corporate and public institutions, but the far-reaching Anticorporation Farming Law of 1932, requiring all corporations holding farmland in North Dakota to sell it within ten years of acquisition, successfully prevented the penetration of agro-industrial enterprises into this family farming state. Lands forfeited by bankrupt farmers were also bought up by their more fortunate neighbors to enlarge their own precious holdings. The process by which surviving farmers expanded by absorbing their failed neighbors' land was fraught with ambivalence, because of the close cooperative ties and competitive undercurrents among neighboring farmers. The state-owned Bank of North Dakota held most of the mortgages in Mercer County, and after a bankruptcy occurred, even those people most interested in acquiring the property would let it stay with the bank for a year or two before making a move to buy it. As one local farmer explained to me: "It usually stayed vacant or rented for a year, because no one really had the heart to go in and grab their neighbor's land.... You're so friendly with your neighbors, you know." Similar pressures exist today, and since one person's gain is so frequently another's loss, the subject of land aquisition is treated with extreme delicacy.

Despite the thinning of its ranks, the family farm has survived as an institution largely because of its flexibility and capacity for "self-exploitation."[14] Agricultural families have been able to meet seasonal labor demands with minimal recourse to hired labor, and to reproduce themselves nearly independently (Friedmann 1978, 1980). This institutional survival has cost individual families dearly, however. Many lost their livelihood, and even the lucky few who prospered have suffered family dispersal. Household production required the lifelong commitment of some family members, but it could only support a fraction of each generation, and forced the rest to leave.

The traumatic years of drought and depression left an indelible impression on the minds of generations still living in Mercer County. The desperate poverty and fruitless effort of those times are a frequent subject of conversation among older people and provide a fund of experience upon which they draw for argumentation. Their stories of the Great Depression often contain a moral or political lesson, as in the following narrative included in a collection of local family histories:

> On this farm they weathered the dust storms of the '30s, the disappointments of low prices for the farm products, and the endless, back-breaking work of farming your homestead without the help of modern machinery of today. The worries were many: whether or not you'd have enough money to feed and clothe your family through the long North Dakota winters; then with the coming of spring, whether you'd have

enough money to buy seed; and after seeding came the longest wait and worry of all, would it rain, and if you had a good stand, you'd wonder if you could get it off before you "hailed out" (as crop and hail insurance was unheard of in those days). They were a frugal and strong-willed couple; so they withstood all these hardships that plagued them during the greater share of their farming days, and they made a success out of their farming operations. (*Beulah, North Dakota* 1964:161)

In such stories, hard times are portrayed as having natural causes rather than social ones, and as temporary setbacks in the family's progress toward prosperity. They imply that the courageous response is to wait it out until times get better. Those of determined spirit will overcome all obstacles, pulling themselves up by their own bootstraps. The struggles of pioneers and their descendents are rendered quietly heroic, because of their association with American individualist values of independence, hard work, and self-help. Their glory is contrasted with the shame of those who failed to overcome hardship on their own and were reduced to accepting charity. Emigration, on the other hand, is considered to be an appropriate response to economic failure in such accounts.

Some survivors express more sympathetic interpretations. A retired farmer described conditions this way:

Everybody in the area was in the same boat. People didn't make enough to pay the taxes on the land, and they were only thirty-two dollars per quarter of land. They went into the hills to dig coal for their home use. My mother stayed on the farm with one boy. There was a girl from Zap living with them and working. Her folks couldn't afford to feed her so they farmed her out. Didn't even ask them to pay wages, just said, "buy her a winter coat." Everybody was on [government] assistance.

If there had been none there would have been a revolution. . . . Hunger recognizes no boundaries. But I still find people [who] tell me "I feel terrible I'm going on Welfare." People think they're a failure if they need it. I always tell them they are only getting back now what they got a right to from the government, after paying taxes all their lives. There should be nothing shameful in it at all.

Many of those who survived the 1930s without having to accept relief seem to have emerged more conservative than ever, claiming that since they were able to make it by the sweat of their brow, all recipients of welfare and other such programs must be worthless freeloaders. Others, praising the justice of federal programs that helped them overcome this crisis, maintain a more liberal outlook. In any case, although the cooperative movement has remained strong and the Democratic Party has made inroads into Republican dominance in North Dakota politics, none of the Populist reforms resulted in fundamental changes in the structure of the American agricultural economy. The Farmers Union cooperative has come to behave much like any other business, and some members complain that its urge to invest in growth has made its service to farmers suffer. The problems that reached a dramatic crisis during the Depression have continued to plague family farmers since then.

World War II brought prosperity to Mercer County, with good rainfall and higher prices for beef and grain. In the state as a whole, average personal income shot up 145 percent between 1940 and 1945. Tenancy fell, as the ten-year deadline established by the Anticorporation Farming Law fell due, and families were able to buy back farmland from corporations at low prices. When the state bank and the Federal Land Bank sold back their holdings, however, they retained half of the mineral rights, and so gained extensive control over lignite reserves throughout the western portion of the state. This action was later to impair the efforts of Mercer County farmers in the 1970s and 1980s, in their attempts to prevent their own lands from being strip-mined. Although farm foreclosures and out-migration did continue at a slower pace, people remember the 1940s as a time of growth and of paying off accumulated debts. Roads were improved, bridges built, and the formation of a statewide organization of rural electrical cooperatives under the auspices of the federal Rural Electrification Association brought electric power to all but the remotest farmsteads.

These improvements in the quality of life for Mercer County residents did not change the structures of political conflict in the state. During the 1940s a revitalized Nonpartisan League again took over the state's government, under the leadership of Governor William ("Wild Bill") Langer. Throughout the 1940s there were numerous legislative faceoffs between the Farmers Union and the Greater North Dakota Association (GNDA), a business organization of out-of-state railroad, banking, and manufacturing interests founded in 1925. The GNDA, with its numerous member organizations, undertook the long-range goal of diversifying the state's economy by promoting industrialization, irrigation projects, tourism, highway improvements, and diversification of farm products. The newly formed Republican Organizing Committee orchestrated the resurgence of conservative power in the prosperous period following the war. In 1956 the Nonpartisan League finally left the Republican Party to join the Democrats, forming a strong second party for the first time in the history of the state. Bill Langer was then a U.S. Senator and especially popular among the German-Russians of Mercer and surrounding counties. When he refused to follow this move to the Democratic Party, so did most of the Leaguers of this area, which thus remained a Republican stronghold.

Republican Mercer County, with its burgeoning business community, participated in this conservative trend, yet after the peak in farm prosperity in 1947, the structural squeeze between falling prices of farm products and ever-increasing costs of production came into play again for the county's agriculturalists. Overproduction and the increasing mechanization of agriculture continued to eliminate marginally profitable operations. By the mid-1950s, net farm income in North Dakota had fallen to the disastrously low average of $2,683 per year, and emigration rates were so high that by 1960, 48.9 percent of all those still living who had been born in the state then lived elsewhere. In Mercer County and other rural areas, these trends were reflected in the small towns dependent on the farm trade. As a result, merchants became especially interested in the possibilities of expanded industrial development as a means of freeing themselves from the unstable farm economy.

Lignite coal mining has represented a significant industrial activity in North Dakota since its settlement by Europeans and Americans. Many western settlers dug coal on their own property for home use, and several cooperative community mines operated in the area that includes modern Mercer County. The ready availability of lignite was used as a selling point to promote settlement and investment west of the Missouri. The Northern Pacific Railway opened mines along its right of way and sold coal to settlers. The state's Department of Agriculture also advertised this mineral wealth in efforts to boost the western communities (cf. *North Dakota Magazine* 1906, vol.1[4]:13).

In 1908 there were sixty-five operating mines in the state, producing 320,742 tons of coal a year. By 1911 the number had risen to one hundred mines yielding 486,842 tons, which by 1920 had reached one million tons. Mercer County was a center of mining activity from the beginning. Most of its early mines were underground operations, although strip mining was practiced at the Red Flag Mine at Zap as early as 1909. In the early decades of the twentieth century, there were large mines northeast of Hazen (at the Truax-Traer Mine, which ran a company town near Krem), at several sites near Zap (by various companies, including Zap Collieries and later the North American Coal Corporation), and north of Beulah (by the Knife River Coal Mining Corporation). The latter was one of the largest producing underground mines in the United States, and continued to operate underground until 1954 when it became a strip mine. The overburden (layers of soil and rock covering the coal deposits) here is mostly clay and shale, not strong enough to safely support extensive underground excavation;

cave-ins and surface subsidence continue to be a major problem as the town of Beulah expands onto undermined land.

Mercer County miners were a diverse group; some were recent immigrants from other mining regions, some were landless "extra" sons from local farming families, and others were active in both farming and mining simultaneously. They faced a number of problems, including low job security, seasonal underemployment, unsafe working conditions, and low wages which the labor shortage of World War II did little to alleviate.[15]

At one mine east of Zap, the company maintained a camp, with a company store, for miners and their families to live. It was known as "Little Moscow," because most of its residents were poor German-Russians. Former residents describe conditions there as miserable: poor housing, no running water or electricity, and too far away from town. The fifty or so families living in the camp had to live on credit at the company store during the summer season when workers received no wages because the mine could not sell coal until fall. The camp was shut down when the unions came in,[16] but no one seems to have been sorry to leave it. A retired miner describes how labor was treated in the early days at the Zap mine:

> Young people today can't really believe how hard it used to be to hold down a job. Foremen and supervisors could tell you to do anything and you had to do it. Even things not on the job; whatever, like, "Don't drive your car on Saturday," or "Clean up your yard at home." They treated labor just like slaves, just like they owned you. . . . They used to start up the stripping machines for the season right on July Fourth, just to spite the workers—nine times out of ten they did—so they didn't get the holiday. And there was no Thanksgiving or Christmas off either.

Low status and residential segregation were not unusual for industrial workers in the rural United States earlier in the twentieth century, conditions that some rural sociologists at the time argued could only change through labor's real empowerment: "In the little town . . . the classes who are not in possession of the social machinery remain voiceless, their masses inchoate, their conditions unprogressive" (Douglass 1919). The union movement in Mercer County began even before the Great Depression. Some of the smaller mines had their own "in–house" unions, and the United Mine Workers of America, a much stronger and more militant national association, was organizing other mines. The "Dirty Thirties," with their soaring unemployment, checked this nascent labor movement. One retired miner recalls that "at that time, there were forty guys for every job, people from all over trying to get mining jobs." Anti-union feeling ran high in the area, and miners themselves were split over the issue of union organizing: "People were afraid to say anything against the company's treatment for fear of losing their jobs."

The wartime labor shortage and new contracts for selling coal to power plants in the mid-1940s improved the bargaining power of the mine workers in the county. With more jobs and more hours of work, the men could afford to make demands. As one miner explained: "Finally, the men got more disgusted—wanting more money and stuff—and had more leverage. When a big market opens up like that and more men get employed, the unions try to go out and organize." So the impetus for union formation came both from within the local mines and from the efforts of national mine workers' unions.

During the late 1940s, local miners began to organize in earnest. This was accomplished through the cooperation of internal cliques of miners with the traveling union representatives and organizers from both the United Mine Workers and the Progressive Mine Workers. The first major successful strike in many years took place at a Zap mine in 1951, with about half the work force organized. As in later such actions, the female members of mining families played a major role. These women had strategic importance not only because of their ability to mobilize large groups of supporters through their own networks, but also because of the free-for-all character of the encounters between union sympathizers and police. Violence directed toward women was considered cowardly and immoral, so forcing the issue with sensationalist tactics helped make the police out to be shameless villains.[17]

In this landmark strike, women sat on the railroad tracks to prevent the coal trains from leaving, and when the police came to drag them away, one of the women bit an officer's leg. A group of women held a policeman while painting him yellow from head to toe, while another group held one captive and threatened to stuff him into a wool sack, until he "cried like a baby." The violence was not all one-sided; in a later strike at the same mine, police threw a cherry bomb into a group of women to scatter them with the smoke, and the explosion injured a striker. In addition, police monopolized the legitimate use of firearms and the sanction of arrest. While such violent clashes stopped short of any killing, its threat was always there: Miners were well aware of incidents in regional labor history,[18] such as the massacre at Ludlow, Colorado, during a United Mine Workers strike in 1914, which remained part of oral tradition among unionized miners in Mercer County even during the period of my research, more than sixty years later. A retired Mercer County miner told me the following version:

The miners lived in company housing. When they struck, the company run 'em out of the housing, and they set up a kind of a tent colony, living in these tents. Then they [the mining company] sent John D. Rockefeller's boys, the Colorado State Militia, out there to get 'em. Now, the men had dug basements under the tents, to protect from the gunfire and all, but then they come and set fire to the tents! They shot four or five miners. Thirteen women and children died.

One of the most dramatic effects of the new power gained by Mercer County coal miners through their unionization was a transformation in their social status in the towns. According to older miners, during the prolonged strike that accompanied the United Mine Workers' organizing of one of the large mines, many mining families had run out of credit with the storekeepers in town. Anti-union feeling ran high among local merchants and miners received rude treatment from all sides. When the union stepped in and paid all these debts, others suddenly gained more respect for the striking miners.

When their prestige on the job changed, it also changed in the community. Since the 1950s, coal miners in Mercer County have lost much of the social stigma that had marked them as inferior, and have become respected members of the local society. This change corresponded to the period in which the underground operations were closed and miners became heavy-equipment operators in the new strip mines. In addition to the respect they won through successful union struggle, this shift away from dirtier and more laborious work to activities more closely resembling those of farmers and construction workers changed the local public perception of miners' status.

In spite of vigorous union activities, countywide class consciousness among miners was offset by other forces that divided them among competing mines, mining companies, and unions, as well as intertown rivalries. Workers at the two largest mines in the 1950s and 1960s did not get along well with one another. Based in neighboring Zap and Beulah, they were affected by the booster-style chauvinism pushed by competing business communities. In addition, the mines were owned by different companies, which attempted to promote high morale and productivity through their own sort of "booster" activities aimed at creating company loyalty and pride.

Mine ownership in the state has become progressively more concentrated since the early days of cooperative and seasonal neighborhood coal pits. In 1935, there were 357 mines in operation, and almost as many different owners. By 1975, over 99 percent of the lignite produced in the state was mined by four large companies, only one of them actually headquartered in the state (Jacobs 1975:59). This fact has not been lost on the people of Mercer County, where sentiment against outside control runs deep. A miner told me of the role this factor played in local public opinion during a strike at the Indian Head Mine at Zap in 1975.

> At first everybody was against the strikers, but by the end they were supporters. . . . [A farmer activist] came up to me at the end and said he didn't used to realize what that little mine was, that it was a big corporation that would eventually take over more. He said he used to think it was just a little mine settin' over there not bothering anybody. . . . It really woke 'em up when they realized it was their own kids that were being treated so badly and that Murray [head of North American Coal Mining Corporation's Western Division] was from Ohio [i.e., an outsider].

Other forms of industrial raw material were available for exploitation and, together with coal, formed the basis of the energy boom of the 1970s and early 1980s. Exploration for oil had begun early in the century, and it was discovered in 1951 in the western part of the state, not far west of Mercer County itself. Newcomers flooded the oil region, seeking drilling leases and mineral rights. By 1961, 2,806 wells had been drilled, and 110 million barrels produced, along with some $28 million worth of natural gas. The state's remoteness, its lack of refineries, and the worldwide surplus production of crude oil all held back the development of the industry. Major petroleum corporations began constructing refineries and processing plants in the state by the 1970s, and although much of the oil still had to be exported to refineries in other states, North Dakota had taken an important step towards broadening its role as an energy supplier.

Promoters touted this movement away from the agricultural economy toward a strategy of industrial development as a way of escaping from dependence on an unstable farm produce market, and as a vehicle for modernizing the local towns. Glowing images of economic independence and prosperity outshone any realization that this kind of industrialization would produce even greater dependence on another notoriously undependable market—that of energy commodities. Without effective long-range planning or adequate environmental protection laws in place, and subject to a flood of corporate propaganda, the state's government embarked on a new wave of development, this time with the land itself at stake. The script was different, but the roles were the same: Rural North Dakotans continued to bear the risk in responding to the needs of the national economy.

Town and Country on the Eve of the Energy Boom

This history of economic peripheralization within American industrial society has left its mark on community life in Mercer County. During the first half of the twentieth century, the social geography here was characterized by the presence of three distinct features, known in the classic rural sociological literature as "community," "village," and "neighborhood" (e.g., Brunner et al. 1927, Sanderson 1932; Smith 1940; and Taylor 1933). "Communities" were areas surrounding and including a small retail center, or "village," which was the focus of common identity and all town-based activities for all the agriculturalists in its orbit. "Neighborhoods" were clusters of rural farmsteads, not including a town, whose residents frequently socialized together. These were often formed around the rural schools and churches.

Unlike the rural market towns typical of peasant societies (Skinner 1964:63), the small "central places" of Mercer County never served primarily for the horizontal exchange of locally produced goods. From the beginning they were the spatial nexus of highly verticalized exchanges; farmers brought their produce to town only to ship it by rail to distant wholesale buyers, and local merchants sold manufactured goods produced outside the area. Local residents did exchange local products, but primarily in the form of reciprocal gift exchange within dispersed personal networks rather than central marketplaces.

By 1970, increased mobility brought about by automobiles and paved roads, together with the depopulation of the countryside, had brought about the demise of most rural neighborhoods. The number of villages had decreased, and rural residents were no longer limited to shopping in the closest town. Most, however, continued to identify with a particular one—under which their telephone number and mailing address were listed, where their children went to school, and the source of their fire and police service. As the rural neighborhoods declined, the towns gained importance. They became centers for more consolidated public services and social activities. The gradual expansion of industrial activities and concentration of agricultural land shifted residents off the land and into the towns. Although the total population of the county declined 9.2 percent between 1960 and 1970 (from about 6,800 to 6,200 according to the U.S. Census), all but two of the towns experienced modest growth (see Table 2, p. 151).

Although town and country were conceptually opposed in local culture, they were economically interdependent and socially integrated. Legal boundaries separated town and countryside but the social fabric was spread continuously over the whole land, with various areas of denser and looser weave. The various parts of the county were interconnected by ties of kinship, friendship, business relations, and lifelong acquaintance. The values and lifeways of the farm were the foundation of social life even for town dwellers. Agriculture had been the economic basis for settled life in the northern Great Plains since prehistoric times, and until the 1970s it was recognized as "everybody's bread and butter" in Mercer County. Most of the older town residents had grown up on farms, and this experience provided important common ground. Basic farm knowledge was widespread, even among those who had never actually lived outside of town. Nearly all local residents counted farmers and ranchers among their extended kin.

The towns were centers of social activity. School, church, shopping, banking, and recreation brought rural residents to town almost every day. Government offices and agencies were located in the towns, and nearly all voluntary associations met there. In the past, wedding dances had frequently been held in rural barns, but by 1970 the practice was declining in favor of festivities in town community halls. Entertainment facilities were clustered in the towns, and even the smallest of them had at least a small restaurant or cafe and two bars. Eating out, going to sports events, and social drinking were important recreational pursuits. Bars functioned as social clubs in the evenings, each with a distinctive set of steady clientele: most towns had a particular bar where farmers and ranchers living nearby would gather, while some had other bars frequented by mine workers. The small local cafes and restaurants were important daytime gathering spots, especially for women and retired men.

There remained a structural tension between rural residents and townspeople, however. Wealth produced on the land flowed into the towns, as farmers sold products at low wholesale prices to local elevator and livestock companies, and bought supplies from merchants in town at retail prices. From the farmer's perspective, townspeople did not work as hard as they did, yet enjoyed a higher material standard of living. Rural people resented the commercialism and urbane pretensions of merchants and town elites. Townspeople, on the other hand, tended to regard farmers as ignorant and slightly paranoid in their suspicions about banks and storekeepers' taking advantage of them. Town-dwelling miners and service workers viewed farmers seeking extra income as a threat to their own jobs, arguing that the farmers had no right to take work away from others, since farm people could live on their own produce during hard times. In any case, by the 1950s, a new generation was growing up in the towns whose basic orientation was urban; these young people no longer identified with farmers or the rural lifestyle.

There were six towns in Mercer County when the energy boom began, built in three successive waves of past development. Stanton, located at the confluence of the Knife and Missouri Rivers, was a busy riverboat landing point in the late nineteenth century. Hazen, Beulah, Zap, and Golden Valley were railroad towns built along the Northern Pacific tracks, and Pick City began as a government work force encampment when the Garrison Dam was constructed in the late 1940s and early 1950s. Each town had its own character, due to unique combinations of economic base, occupational makeup, location, and size, and each was situated differently to take advantage of opportunities offered by the energy boom.

Most of the local towns were situated in slight depressions in the open landscape, with surrounding hills and windbreaks of trees to shield them from tornadoes, blizzards, and high winds. Mature shade trees lined the older residential blocks of small wooden houses, many of them brightly painted, with neat little lawns in front and vegetable gardens in back. The more prestigious houses were located near the center of town, as were the numerous churches. Children played in the streets and yards and with their bicycles had easy access to the entire town, nearby rivers, and countryside. Stores and offices were located in sturdy structures along a wide Main Street, parallel to the railway tracks (except in Stanton, which predated the railway), where businesses requiring more room, such as lumberyards and farm implement dealerships, leased space on the right-of-way. Grain elevators, which served initially as nuclei for other commercial developments, towered over the other buildings.

Stanton, the oldest town, was located on the richest farmland, and was the only one to have a significant population of Scandinavian descent. As the county seat, this sleepy little town experienced a revival during the 1960s, when a large surface mine opened nearby, and two rural electrical cooperatives constructed coal-burning electrical generation plants southeast of town. The number of Stanton's businesses doubled from 1962 to 1972 to a total of about twenty. The town remained small despite this growth, with a 1970 population of only 517.

At the extreme western end of the county was Golden Valley, nestled among gentle buttes and grey-green rangeland. This was the smallest and most countrified of the towns, although during the 1920s it was the largest of the railroad towns in the county, and then had three banks. It was a German-Russian settlement; the preeminence of cowboy hats over farmer's caps among shoppers and loungers still indicated its orientation toward the ranch lands to the west and south. Golden Valley had no significant industry, and was one of only two

Mercer County towns to lose population during the 1960s. In the mid-1970s, it was on the verge of extinction, with little more than a hardware store, a gas station, and a bar or two still open on its dusty, unpaved Main Street.

Pick City was also a small settlement. Located near Garrison Dam and the Lake Sakakawea recreational area, it was a seasonal resort town. Few Mercer Countians were wealthy enough to own year-round vacation homes at the Lake, so Pick City never developed an organized business association or stable year-round population, and its residents had little sense of community.

Because of their location, Zap, Beulah, and Hazen became the center of energy boom development in the late 1970s and 1980s. All three were German-Russian settlements and were centrally located in the county. Zap and Beulah both had a long history of lignite mining, during which differences in mine management shaped the different character of the towns. As a local business woman explained, "Zap was a miners' shanty town, and Beulah was the alternative for the better-off miners and related people who wanted to avoid the dirt-poor and seasonal mines." By the 1970s, Beulah was many times larger than Zap and interunion rivalry persisted among the two towns' coal miners.

Zap's particular claim to fame is as the site of a bizarre event that occurred one weekend in the spring of 1969. Because of its attractive name, students from North Dakota State University who were organizing a sort of prairie Woodstock chose Zap as the site, neglecting to notify anyone there of their plans. With the Zap-In advertised nationally, some three- to five-thousand "hippie-type" young people from all over the country descended on Zap for a rock concert. Their wild antics, thought to be inspired by drugs and drunkenness, amazed and horrified a good part of the local population, only ending when the National Guard and Highway Patrol entered the town at dawn on the second day. The "Zip to Zap," as it was also called, has since become a landmark event in town history and a source of revenue from Zap-In reunions and memorabilia.

In the smaller towns before the energy boom, there were generally no street signs, and most of the store fronts were "unimproved," with faded lettering and the once-popular brick-patterned tar paper nailed on, rather than the more modern aluminum siding sported by some stores in the more prosperous towns. There were fewer national corporate franchise stores than in the larger towns, and they were of an earlier vintage. With the exception of Hardware Hank and SuperValu grocery stores, the only franchises in the four smaller towns were automobile dealerships, service stations, and bulk oil dealers. People living in these smaller towns valued their homey atmosphere. As one man explained, "You can't come uptown [to Main Street] without seeing people you know—old friends and relatives—and stopping to talk." Here there was less status differentiation than in the big towns, a stronger feeling of community and a sense that all there were "common working people."

Beulah and Hazen were by far the largest of the area's towns. They both had well-developed chambers of commerce. In 1962, each town had approximately seventy businesses and professional offices, and these numbers increased by more than ten percent in both towns over the following decade. Although Stanton claimed the lion's share of local government offices, some were located in Hazen and Beulah. Both had several grain elevator companies, while the smaller towns had only a Farmers Union elevator. The Main Streets of both these towns were relatively bustling, paved, and more than four blocks long. But although Hazen and Beulah were larger than the other towns, they were still of a size where all the residents knew one another, as well as each other's family backgrounds and connections.

These two larger towns differed little in appearance, but Beulah's industrial history was evident on closer inspection; a 35-megawatt coal-burning electrical generating plant built in 1923 graced one end of Main Street, producing energy for local consumption. The old mining sites on the outskirts of town were marked by numerous large, thinly overgrown piles of earth. These "spoil piles" were the residue of surface mining in the period before the law required the restoration of the original landscape. The land for miles north of Beulah was riddled with abandoned mine tunnels and chambers close beneath the surface. These had been subject to cave-ins, leaving the surface honeycombed with sinkholes.

The rivalry between Hazen and Beulah was as old as the towns themselves and by far the most intense in the county. Local people remarked that "Hazen and Beulah go at it like cats and dogs," and numerous explanations and interpretations for the competition were current. Although both communities participated in the rivalry, it was more conscious and deliberate among residents of Beulah than those of Hazen, who tended to interpret it more narrowly in terms of business competition. In the words of people from all over the county, "Beulah always wanted to be a *city*!"

Social life in these small towns was intense and personal. Active gossip networks more far-flung than neighboring groups provided important channels of communication countywide. News traveled fast in these towns, and people of both sexes kept up with the latest gossip. Groups of women met regularly in their kaffeeklatsch,[19] and telephoned each other frequently. Men gathered in their own coffee-drinking groups at the restaurants early in the morning to exchange and discuss the news. Little that happened in the towns went unnoticed or unremarked upon. Gossip was important for communicating news and information of all kinds. The buzzing grapevine made it possible for individuals to know from day to day (even from hour to hour) what was going on and to form "public opinions" in response to events.

Voluntary associations have always been numerous and active in the rural United States (Kolb 1959; de Tocqueville 1835), and Mercer County had a wide variety. These included golf clubs, art associations, athletic leagues, card-playing groups, insurance associations, Boy Scouts, Girl Scouts, singles' clubs, senior citizens' groups, youth groups, homemakers' clubs, commercial clubs, farmers' associations, stockmen's associations, trade union locals, volunteer fire departments, veterans' associations, secret societies, and many more. Such groups organized an endless series of events, ranging from church breakfasts to rodeo tournaments. Thanks to them there was always some entertainment to enjoy.

Churches were the most important voluntary associations. Most local families attended church on Sunday mornings. Churchgoers told me they enjoyed attending because it made them feel spiritually uplifted, and because they liked the ritual and music, and the opportunity to see their friends and acquaintances. My own impression was that going to church also provided them an opportunity to display their best clothes and fine manners, and to take their place in society as moral and upstanding citizens. All except the young children behaved with studious decorum there, and sermons stressed such themes as the value of discipline, the joyful servitude of the faithful, and submission to the will of the Lord. The Roman Catholic Church and various Lutheran and German Baptist sects of Mercer County all belonged to regional and nationwide organizations that are to a greater or lesser degree strictly hierarchical and authoritarian, and congregations had little autonomy in terms of dogma and policy. Social differentiation was reflected in the variety of churches of each major denomination in each town, and the wealth and prestige of a church's membership were reflected in the accoutrements of the building.

Perhaps the most significant and characteristic feature of social life on the eve of the energy boom was its intimacy. Despite the structured conflicts generated by the nature of their integration into the dominant national economy, residents of Mercer County in the early 1970s still lived in face-to-face communities, the result of generations of intermarriage and lifelong association. The towns ranged in population from 119 to 1,344 in 1970, and residents were generally familiar with one another and shared a common field of local historical, geographic, and social knowledge. These were relatively safe enclaves, with little of the crime, traffic, or encounters with strangers that add stress to urban living. A shared cultural legacy emphasized self-sufficiency, a strong work ethic, and a pervasive distrust of government and of outsiders in general.

This sense of belonging and rootedness was explicitly valued. In later years, people spoke nostalgically to me about how pleasant it had been to walk down the street, visit the stores, or go to church, and know everybody they met. The negative side was also remembered in complaints about the lack of privacy and the impossibility of avoiding people even when they wanted to. Before the accelerated changes brought by the energy boom, outsiders who trickled in were gradually assimilated and business was done on a credit basis, while disputes and negotiations took place within a public arena in which little could be kept secret. The web of personal relationships enforced some accountability of local officials to their constituents; with relatively little external authority present, local people exercized great control over day-to-day community affairs. This style of community life was already beset by internal conflicts, however, and was soon to be threatened by the rising tide of industrial growth.

Chapter Three | Currents in Political Culture

The people of Mercer County have a history of building their lives and communities under the unstable conditions of fluctuations in the wider economy. In the course of this experience, with its shifting patterns of conflict and alliance, they have also developed a complex political culture with several distinct ideological currents. This complexity was impressed upon me from the beginning of my conversations with residents of Mercer County about energy development there.

Although they freely explained to me their opinions about and involvement in what was taking place, it was difficult at first to discern much ideological coherence in their statements. Not only was the "local voice" far from unitary, but its varieties did not break down neatly into discrete, corresponding interest groups. Argumentation by members of the local occupational groups with a stake in energy development included multiple rhetorical strategies. Indeed, individuals themselves shifted political rhetorics according to the situation, invoking one or another alternative ideological frames to suit their purpose of the moment. What I heard was not a coherently integrated, neatly configured system of thinking, but arrays of ideas invoking patterns of meaning that included not only complementary, but also inconsistent, and even contradictory aspects.

This patterning was not random, however, nor simply following an internal symbolic logic, but in many respects it mirrored the complex and dynamic material relationships among the people—relationships imbued with tension between cooperation and individualistic competition. The main ideological currents of agrarian populism, labor unionism, and the boosterism of small town entrepreneurs all contain a mix of elements, some opposed to and others in harmony with the ideology and practices of corporate capitalism. This coexistence of alternative forms also reflects the ambivalent position of these groups in relation to big capital over the course of local history.

The currents of political thought and the configuration of alliances and antagonisms among Mercer County farmers, miners, and merchants in the early 1980s shaped their initial response to energy development in their county. This chapter is concerned not so much with actual statements of political ideology as with the generation of their variety, complementarities, inconsistencies, and contradictions. It explores the connections between social and economic conditions, the experiences of work, and political participation (both in the sense of political activity and political thought) for the principal groups whose history and makeup is described in the preceding chapter. The purpose is to evoke the complexities of political culture in Mercer County as its people encountered the energy boom. Political life there in the early 1980s was openly conflictual, as occupationally defined interest groups contended over the reallocation of resources which accompanied industrial development. Although each group was internally differentiated, farmers, coal miners, and small town business people each tended to see and interpret the world from the perspective of their own position within the economic and social system. Each group has a distinctive political subculture—that is, a set of interests, experiences, relationships, resources, and ideological frameworks that together constitute contingencies for them as political actors.

The term "ideology" is used here in a nonpejorative sense, for any more or less systematically articulated set of ideas that express and justify the perceived interests of some group. This usage departs from anthropological tradition, in which "ideology" is used broadly to refer not only to systems of political ideas but also to more holistically conceived ideational frameworks that can include economic, social, religious, and cosmological dimensions (Hobsbawm 1977). Marshall Sahlins (1976), Louis Dumont (1986:4–12), and other cultural economists have argued convincingly that these more general cultural worldviews play an important part in shaping the perception of self and group interest. Therefore the term "ideology" in the account here is not restricted to its critical sense as essentially linked to maintaining domination, although it is integral to power relations. The traces of dominant American ideology can certainly be discerned in Mercer County, for example, in the emphasis on individualism, but this account is more concerned with Mercer County people's expressed political conceptual frameworks, such as agrarian populism, labor unionism, and Main Street boosterism, that are more limited in scope and grow out of local historical experience in ways that are accessible to ethnographic inquiry. The received meanings and values they provide, contested and reformulated in each generation, help people in Mercer County to organize and interpret their own experience and the behavior of others. Thus, ideology is not simply a distorted mask obscuring some "truer" reality, but a constitutive element of reality.

The ideas and values with which the people of Mercer County formulate their condition are not "false consciousness" in the sense of an incorrect understanding of class interest, opposed to an empowering structural critique. In fact, they provide flexible and sophisticated vehicles for interpreting events and mobilizing action. The people are not rigidly confined in their thinking by single unifying dogmas. Rather, they have various alternative ideological frameworks at their disposal, which they may use to understand and articulate their interests. Foucault's (1980) analytical framework is useful for understanding this relationship between structure, meaning, and agency. Rather than focusing on ideology, a term he considers imprecise and compromised by its diverse usage, he sees actors in a field of relations, strategies, and discourses that they may use selectively as instruments to produce power. Thus, ideological discourse does not merely serve as a tool of domination, but has a more free-floating character, available also for others to use in support of their own perceived interests.

The political culture of Mercer County cannot be reduced to an assortment of ideological forms, however. It is also about the lived experiences of hardship, struggle, defeat and triumph, and the systematic inequalities that shape people's relationships. Understanding these dimensions of political culture for the three principal groups interested in the energy boom clarifies the cross-currents that are generated in their political life, and the character of their participation in its power struggles. In order to convey the dynamic nature of their relationships, it is helpful to invoke a social-historical context that is relevant from each group's perspective, despite the potential confusion of shifting time frames and tenses. The discussion here is limited to farmers, miners, and merchants because, although nonindustrial wage workers represented about half of Mercer County's working population by 1980, this group lacked a consolidated political identity as an occupational group and offered no organized response to energy development. As a class, they were politically invisible during the energy boom, but in order to avoid too distorted a picture of local society, I will include them in the discussion of civic life at the end of the chapter. The public ideology of small town living, with its moralistic emphasis on egalitarianism and neighborliness, constitutes in its own right another strand of relatively coherent values and meanings that those in Mercer County carried with them into the energy boom.

Family Farmers | When most Americans think of Great Plains agriculture, they picture waving fields of wheat and hay, and this image was more or less accurate for Mercer County in the early 1980s. At that time, about half of the farm operators also raised some livestock, chiefly beef, and were thus "mixed" operators. Only a few made their living exclusively from livestock, and these lived in the drier rangelands in the south of the county. Since these true ranchers were mostly outside of the industrial area and its conflicts, the focus here is on the farmers, including mixed operators, in the rest of the county.

Social and Economic Conditions | Understanding the participation of farmers in the energy boom begins with an examination of their position in local society and the economic contingencies they encountered as a group. Since the beginning of the twentieth century, they have gone from a position of dominance in local Mercer County society, both in terms of numbers and influence, to being an embattled minority. According to the 1918 Mercer County Atlas, almost 99 percent of the county's households were then engaged in agriculture, and there was little social differentiation by class or status. Dick (1954) has described this Great Plains frontier society as being relatively fluid in terms of individual mobility. With the drought and depression of the 1930s, however, rural society throughout the region was becoming much more hierarchically differentiated, with limited opportunities for individual upward mobility.[3] An anthropologist studying rural South Dakota in the 1940s summarized this process:

> There is an increasing tendency for towns to be composed of a smaller entrepreneur class and a larger submerged group composed of ex-farmers, unemployed farm and town workers, and stranded itinerants. While doctors, schoolteachers, craftsmen, and retired farmers still live in towns, they are proportionately fewer in number and less significant in community life. The impact of these changes has led to the development of communities sharply divided into distinct strata. (Useem et al. 1942:331)

Those farm families who weathered the Depression were able to recoup their economic position by buying back lost land, but it took longer to regain respectable social standing, and as a class they remained subordinate to town dwellers in status ranking. This was a painful lesson for country children to learn when they were old enough to go to school in town. In the 1980s, adults who had been raised on farms recalled the humiliation of being taunted and bullied during their school days. One man recounted to me his introduction to the awareness of his social inferiority on the first day of school, when he was knocked down and called a "goddam dirt farmer." A woman, retired from farming in 1980, explained, "I'm ashamed to admit it now, but when I went to college I didn't tell anybody that I was from a farm." In later years, the status of successful farm families rose with their economic fortune. The same woman spoke of these changes: "Now the farmers have really come into their own. The farmers think, 'I'm just as good as anybody.'"

Already by 1970, agriculturalists made up only 30 percent of the working population of Mercer County (U.S. Census 1970). The historic trend towards concentrated ownership of farmland presented in Chapter 2 had continued in North Dakota during the 1970s. The number of farms in the state decreased in just five years by 6 percent, from 46,381 in 1969 to 43,366 in 1974, and average farm size increased 4 percent, from 930 acres to 970 acres; the average value of the land and buildings per farm increased from $87,000 to $190,000 (U.S. Census, 1969 and 1974).

Although the average size and number of agricultural operations in Mercer County increased over time, and the number of farmers decreased, the number of landowners did not drop proportionately. This is because there is not a simple correspondence between ownership and operation. Indeed, almost half of North Dakota's landowners lived out-of-state at that time; they were not remote corporate investors, however, but rather relatives of farmers who had inherited parts of family operations but no longer lived in the area themselves. A 1974 study of North Dakota farm operators found that 41 percent owned all the land they farmed; another 46 percent were part owners and part renters; and 13 percent rented all the land they farmed (U.S. Census 1974). In 1980, most farmers owned at least some land, but more than half also rented acreage to assemble enough land for a viable operation. Agricultural land is leased out by retired farmers, by those who have more land than they wish to operate in a given year, and by landowners who live outside the area. The configuration of rental arrangements changes from year to year as owners and operators adjust to changing market strategies and personal circumstances.

It is possible to survive on a farm with very little income, if land and machinery are paid for. During the 1980s there were farm couples living on as little as $2,500 a year, raising their own food and seldom coming into town. This was becoming rare, however, and since the Great Depression, farm operations have become increasingly commoditized. Agricultural households now rely heavily on supermarket purchases, although they still keep kitchen gardens and some domestic livestock. They no longer produce their own cloth, soap, or simple farm implements, and capital investment in land and machinery has risen steadily. To supplement agricultural income, more and more farmers seek to deploy family members in off-farm wage work. Especially among younger families, whose debts tend to be greater, farm wives work as store clerks, waitresses, and schoolteachers, while their husbands seek work as mechanics, carpenters, and coal miners between the planting and harvest seasons. The importance of off-farm work increased dramatically for American farmers after World War II, from 29.3 percent of farm family income in 1949 to 51.6 percent in 1969 (Shaw 1979:651). These figures indicate that off-farm work has become a long-term structural feature of family farm operation, without which many could not continue in business. This semi-proletarianization further fragments the class outlook of farmers (MacLennan and Walker 1980:34), whose class character was already divided between business entrepreneur and small family producer.

Farms in Mercer County are family operations. Although a few farmers are bachelors or have survived their spouses, most operations have a married couple at their core, usually with several children. Although husband and wife cooperate in farm work, he normally has primary responsibility for managing the commercial business, while she is responsible for household maintenance. As is common on American farms (Fink 1987), the wife is conceived of as "helping" her husband on "his" farm, even if it is jointly owned and the work is shared. Hired hands, more distant relatives, or foster children are sometimes a part of the household, but a limited acreage can only support a limited number of individuals, no matter how productive they may be.

The typical farm operation in Mercer County can only support a single nuclear family at a time. Grown daughters marry out of the farm and extra sons must leave, while a daughter-in-law marries in to bear the next generation. Normally, the father assigns a part of the enterprise to be carried out by the son, and pays either a wage or the profits from that part of the operation. As with the Canadian farmers studied by John Bennett (1969:231–232), the terms of father-to-son succession are drawn up in a formal business contract including terms for debt transfer and a payment by the son for the farm to provide retirement income to his parents.

Despite the emotional closeness of family members, the potential for both intergenerational and sibling rivalries is great. Grown sons who are eager to take up farming on their own must wait for their parents to retire before gaining access to the family land. The individualistic ideal of being one's own boss makes them chafe at the bit under their father's management. The older generation holds the power to bequeath the land as it sees fit and can even sell the land outside the family over their childrens' objection. There is no normative rule other than that of male preference to determine which of the offspring will take over the farm. Bitter disputes can occur where more than one of them wish to do so. There is strong cultural pressure for the farm to stay in the family as a symbol of family continuity, but sometimes none of the children want to take it over, especially if it is unprofitable. This situation also lends itself to dispute within the family. As offspring reach adulthood they may come to question their parents' authority and business decisions. Asserting their independence, young adults begin the family cycle anew.[4]

Together with these pronounced structural rivalries, there exists a strongly father-dominated pattern of authority and a clear division of labor by gender. The father is the household head with extensive authority over his wife, children, land, and livestock. He is normally responsible for planning and carrying out the family's commercial agricultural operations, while the mother takes care of housework, child raising, and cultivating the kitchen garden. Girls and boys are taught to perform activities considered appropriate to their gender, such as field and mechanical work for men and food preparation and housekeeping for women. Household members of all ages contribute to its maintenance and perpetuation according to their abilities, and hired labor is kept to a minimum.

The case of the Holzman farm is typical. After losing their farm in the 1930s, Robert and Louise were able to buy back 640 acres from the bank. They rented another half section, bought six milk cows from his parents, and made an adequate living for the growing family of three daughters and a son. They raised and preserved their own vegetables and kept chickens, turkeys, ducks, and pigs for household use. Over the years, they bought more and more efficient farming machinery, and when opportunities arose, they bought more land adjacent to the farm. At the time of Robert's death in 1974 they owned 2,200 acres.

All three of the family's daughters had married local boys and gone to live near their husbands' jobs in Dickinson, a small city about a hundred miles away. Eric, the only son, had married and lived with his wife and child in a trailer home next to the old farmhouse. After Robert's death, Louise gave each of her children a quarter of land, and also sold Eric the quarter where his trailer was parked. She kept 900 acres for herself, but Eric rents all of the original acreage from its current owners and farms it as a unit. Louise lives alone in the big old farmhouse and has no plans to retire to town. Their family's history exemplifies the fall and rise of successful farm families from the 1930s to the 1980s in Mercer County.

Working and Worrying | Like other Americans, the people of Mercer County spend most of their waking hours at work, and identify with their jobs and with others who share the same occupation. For all of the groups here, the organization and experience of work influences their values, interests, and political orientations. The conflicts and alliances both within and among occupational groups are shaped by the conditions of their work lives and the ways its problems are understood and expressed.

For farmers in the early 1980s, the amount of agricultural work varied with the seasons, but the level of worry about financial survival was always high. The organization of work and worry pits individual farm operators (and their families) against one another in a system which they see as a zero-sum game—you can get ahead only at the expense of other families, and your loss may be another family's gain. In hard times, this system generates suspicion and isolation, making it difficult for farmers to cooperate, even when they recognize a common threat.

Farm work is generally isolated and lonely. Family members spend the day engaged in separate tasks in different parts of the operation. Even when two persons are working on the same field, conversation is impossible above the din of machinery. The work itself can be monotonous, "driving in circles all day," as one operator described it. He spoke of the overwhelming immensity of the harvesting task: "Sometimes it seems like you'll never get through it, just looks like a big ocean out there. The only thing to do is to go out there and work on it to get through." Farmsteads are widely separated, so most daily contact is with other household members. These farm operators are used to doing things on their own as their own boss with few personal contacts with outsiders.

Farming is a costly business, requiring investments of hundreds of thousands of dollars in land, machinery, livestock, seed, feed, fertilizer, pesticides, and fuel. Young farmers may inherit a going concern, but machinery is soon worn out or obsolete, and the inheritance itself can be a financial burden, because of high estate taxes and debts. It is more difficult for younger farmers to get production loans, since they have not yet established personal relationships with bankers in town; older producers with established credit relationships but no more collateral than a new farmer find this less of a problem. Although some established farmers, whose land and equipment are paid for, are relatively well-to-do, most carry heavy debt burdens from past expansions and live under the constant threat of financial failure. This insecurity induces stress and deepens the competitive undercurrent of interfarmer relations, while at the same time producing some sense of shared hardship and solidarity.

Darrel is a typical example of a young farmer trying to make a go of it. He hopes to inherit land from his father some day, but until then he prefers to farm on his own rather than work under his father's direction. As an independent farm operator, Darrel is raising crops and cattle on about three thousand acres, some of which are rented from his father and the rest leased from other landowners. He is proud of his operation, but fearful about its future. It is not easy to finance such a venture, as he explains:

> I don't have much capital so I can't get a good deal on my credit. I have to borrow at high rates, so I can't break even. . . . I have to pretend my dad's machinery is mine just to get to borrow on my equity. Three weeks ago the bank almost foreclosed on me—that was very traumatic, I can tell you! . . . I have to pay taxes, but I sure don't have any money now. Nothing to show for a year's work but more debt. . . . Last year I was $90,000 in debt and this year I'm down to $130,000 in debt.

The Mercer County farmers still operating today are survivors of several generations of difficult economic conditions which have forced most of their neighbors out of business. This and their own experience have created an obsession about land. When land becomes available, farmers will attempt to buy it even when it is priced above whatever profitability it will add to the operation. Farmers identify closely with their land. To them, land ownership is their means of subsistence and a security against whatever misfortunes might disrupt the rest of the world. Selling one's land is considered only a last resort. This sense of almost inalienable identity can become a burden when times are bad: "Having a farm is even worse than being married. You can get divorced, but you're stuck with a farm." The result is that many farmers feel compelled to take advantage of any opportunity for expansion—by purchase or lease—in an effort both to achieve a more profitable scale and to enhance their sense of material security.

Productive land is a resource of limited availability and farmers jealously guard their own property while casting a roving eye on that of their neighbors. It is understood, but not openly talked about, that if one farm operation fails, good land might become available to other producers. For this reason, land sales, inheritance, the progress of crops and livestock, and the productive potential of particular land parcels are fascinating but touchy subjects. While driving along a country road, a farmer's gaze habitually shifts left and right, keeping track of how production is progressing in the neighborhood. The conspicuous success of one operation is a source of envy and nervousness to its neighbors, since any extra income may be invested in expanding that farmer's land holdings, perhaps at the expense of financially vulnerable neighbors. Tardiness in mending a fence break that allows cattle to feed and trample on another's wheat field can be interpreted as an open act of aggression.

Any chance meeting of farm operators is an opportunity for intense gossip about the fortunes of other farmers. Such subjects are treated delicately in face-to-face encounters with those whose operations are being discussed. Farm gossip about an operation in the presence of its operator or of someone likely to inform him of it is frequently punctuated by such qualifiers as "of course, people shouldn't look at each other's operations," to which all present heartily voice agreement. A direct and serious offer to buy a piece of farmland is a hostile and threatening act, and likely to provoke an angry response.

Young farming men often gather at their favorite local bar in the evening, to drink beer and exchange news. Most are married, but their wives only occasionally accompany them on these outings. Because of their large debts, this age group is the most financially vulnerable, and they are acutely aware of how their neighbors' operations are doing, although discussion of the subject is oblique. In spite of their friendly camaraderie, each knows that the failure of one might make land available for another. Although the discussion is potentially inflammatory, conversations turn again and again to the fortunes of particular crops and livestock, which pieces of land one or another covets, and so on. Young farmers' obsession with land, and the tension it produces, are the magnetic lines of force through which they navigate in conversation. There is a repetitious thrust and parry where one will make an inquiry about another's operation, and follow quickly with praise of their abilities—"You're a smooth operator"—or a disclaimer such as "I have enough problems of my own without going around looking at other people's."

The joking behavior associated with the subject of land loss and acquisition indicates that it is a focus of great anxiety. Farmers relieve psychological stress by satirizing themselves and their economic lot, as in the following story, attributed to A. C. Townley, a Nonpartisan League organizer of the 1910s: "A doctor, a banker, and a farmer were each asked what they would do if they were given a million dollars. The doctor answered that he'd get a big new house for his wife, and the banker said that he'd invest the money and watch it grow. The farmer thought for a minute and then replied that he guessed he'd just go on farming for a couple of years until it ran out!" Another joke runs, "Did you hear about the farmer arrested for child abuse? He gave his farm to his kids!"

Taking over each other's land, either by purchase or by staking it in mock bets, is the most frequent topic of jokes on such evenings. Drinking beer together also helps to air the touchy subject in a relatively unthreatening way. This way, young farmers feel freer to make known which land they most desire to obtain, and why. It is important to make such wishes public knowledge in case the land should become available, yet it must be done with delicacy and tempered with joking and beer-hall camaraderie.

When admitting to coveting specific pieces of land, some familial connection to it is often cited, as if to validate the would-be claim. If one's great-grandmother once homesteaded a given quarter section, for instance, this fact can be offered as an explanation of why one wishes to obtain the parcel. Likewise, if the parcel borders on one's own land, it is reasonable to claim one wants it for reasons of efficiency. Such arguments also help render the statement less aggressive and threatening.

Men and women who are members of farming families also discuss their other concerns at social gatherings. The weather is a continual source of worry, since drought, hailstorms, or an untimely wet spell at harvest time can destroy a season's effort and investment. New techniques, machinery, and crops are also discussed constantly, as operators struggle to keep up with the rapid pace of technological innovation in agriculture. The other perennial topic of conversation among operators is prices. Producers have to buy and sell in complex and unstable agricultural markets, and a great deal of information and advice is passed by word of mouth.

The pervasive uncertainty about staying in business, paying off debts, the covetousness of neighbors, and unpredictable weather contributes to the farmers' view of the world as dangerous and uncertain, in which one's neighbors, underneath their civility and camaraderie, may really be plotting to take over one's farm. Their isolated style of life and labor, and the economic pressures they withstand, contribute to a psychological profile early noted by rural sociologists,[5] including individualism, conservatism, introversion, shyness, suspiciousness, mysticism, and frugality. The social and cultural horizons of Mercer County farmers today have broadened, yet these traits are still characteristic of many. Farmers are habitually frugal and self-sufficient; they are accustomed to independent action, resent outside authority, and avoid contact with strangers. Among the older generation especially, farmers keep back-up supplies of grain, hay, and "good-laying" hens, even when the practice lacks economic rationality. The farmers' deeply held suspicion of big business—which motivated their participation in the Populist movement—also characterized their response to the growth of energy industries in Mercer County.

Political Participation | The political power of farmers rests in their numbers and in their position as the acknowledged economic base for the rest of the local economy. Because voting is organized according to place of legal residence, country dwellers do not participate to any great extent in the formal political arenas of the towns. As the largest occupational category in the county, however, farmers wield considerable influence in the election of countywide officials, as well as state and federal representatives and senators. The County Commission is a governing body of three elected officers charged with decisions regarding the legal operation of the county and all its political subdivisions, including school, fire, water, and police districts; the maintenance of county roads; and the management of social services. They make decisions about land use outside of the towns, and are responsive to the agricultural community, which constitutes a large constituency. Most County Commission meetings are open to the public, and hearings are held about matters for major decisions, to give residents an opportunity to express their views. This is the main public political forum regularly available to the farmers.

The focus of Republican Party power was in the towns, while the Democrats found theirs in the agricultural base established by the Populist and Nonpartisan League movements. Among local Democrats it is a truism, in the words of one town-dweller, that, "The Democrats have always been for the farmer and the small businessman, but the Republicans are for big business." This basic partisan division has blurred since World War II, however, as farmers have become more like other businessmen. This shift is described by a local farmer who had been active in the Farmers Union for many years, referring to Mercer County farmers of a generation or two ago:

> They were always greatly interested in politics, and they drew up lines more than you do today. Now you can belong to anything and nobody pays any attention whether you're a Republican or a Democrat. . . . [Then] they thought you should just be for the ones that supported the *farmers*. They were very emphatic about *that*! . . . and of course they always thought the Democrats supported the farmers. Now they jump back and forth, they don't go according to party lines like they used to.

Mercer County's farmers are firmly committed to the Jeffersonian agrarian ideal of independent landowners prospering in the free-enterprise system by working hard and living frugally.[6] This vision of a free and independent yeomanry is partly the product of an immigrant experience of escaping state control and building communities on a remote and socially relatively unstratified frontier. Farmers' political strategies are also informed by the rich history of grassroots organizing, and make use of the populist ideology of class conflict between small farmers and big business. The collectivizing rhetoric of the populist movement is belied by the goals of the Jeffersonian vision, however, which are really more reactionary than socialistic—looking back nostalgically to a Golden Age of free enterprise that is largely imaginary. Farmers want a chance to make a decent living as individual, independent, and competitive entrepreneurs, in a market free of the influence of monopoly capital, and equally free of government interference. They see dependence upon federal programs as a regrettable but necessary outcome of these "artificial" distortions of the economy. Similarly, they see cooperative organizing not as an end in itself, but as the only way for small farmers to survive hard times, and as a strategy for circumventing and challenging the power of big capital.

The history of economic hardship and of grassroots organizing to counter what they saw as the immoral dominance of big business was a potentially counter-hegemonic tradition, but its oppositional character was countered by the farmers' more basic commitment to individualism and isolation. Although they joined the cooperative movement in the 1930s and 1940s, the Farmers Union had long ceased to represent anything more than a wholesale supplier to most Mercer County farmers. Other ongoing organizations in which farmers are active, such as 4-H youth clubs, neighborhood weed control boards, and rural electrical cooperative associations, are sponsored and organized by government agencies.

Farmers' rhetoric shifts along with individual fortunes. In good times, they tend to praise themselves for their success, and condemn others for not being able to pull themselves up by their own bootstraps. When times are bad, blame is placed on the big corporations, the exploitive practices of buyers, and a government that fails to appreciate the economic contribution of small farmers. Individuals may be held responsible for their own misfortunes, but when many are affected by an obvious big business adversary, threatened farmers are capable of banding together. At such moments, their grassroots protest rearticulates the old populist themes.

It is a local truism that farmers are hard to organize and find it difficult to cooperate, even when this is an economic necessity for them. This is said to be because they are so independent and value their individual freedom so highly, and because as business people, they are also in competition with one another. These obstacles are real, and are manifested in a local tradition of antipathy toward extra-familial authority and an atomized pattern of decision making where each farm is planned as a separate undertaking.[7] And yet the notion that farmers do not cooperate well is belied by those who remain active in the Farmers' Union organization. It can also be contradicted by the cooperatively organized ad hoc associations formed by rural neighbors in response to collectively felt difficulties, such as those involving upkeep of farm-to-market roads and bridges, water drainage problems, or nearby mining activities.

Coal Miners | The coal miners of Mercer County and their families comprise another group with clearly formulated and consciously shared common interests and political views. In 1970 they made up 20 percent of the working population in the county. Although they represented a minority of the wage workers,[8] their key position as energy industry workers, their well-known history of union struggle, and their high level of organization lent them power and significance disproportionate to their numbers. As individuals and as a group, they are also embedded in complex webs of sympathies, loyalties, and conflicts that at times generate turbulent political cross-currents.

Social and Economic Conditions | Like the family farmers, coal miners and their families had experienced an improvement in their financial well-being and their social status since the hard times of the 1930s. Their transformation from dirty, badly paid, and poorly protected underground diggers into unionized heavy-equipment operators brought them up in the estimation of others. By 1980 they no longer occupied the bottom of the status ladder (held instead by other laborers such as farmhands and mechanics and by the unemployed poor) and could at least claim to be town people rather than "hicks" or "hayseeds." But their position was still decidedly below that of the small-business and professional class.

The mining men (and they were almost universally men) of the early 1980s were locally born and raised, and not ethnically distinct from others in Mercer County. Local commercial-scale mining had been going on for half a century, and there were some three-generation mining families. The companies did not rely heavily upon hereditary recruitment, however, perhaps because the labor union ideology is most highly developed in these families and the corporations at times sought to avoid hiring labor activists. Hiring from other families also reflected the companies' desire to spread their ties over a large number of local families. By giving many families a stake in the industry, the coal companies added support to their position in local political conflicts. A rationale for hiring workers specifically from farming families was that the cost of reproducing their labor force and training them in heavy-equipment operation had already been borne by the agricultural sector of the economy. As local mines expanded, men were also beginning to be recruited from the declining Iron Range of the neighboring state of Minnesota, over the protests of local mining families who resented this loss of employment for locals.

Miners are pulled in many directions. Most live in towns, and yet they work in the countryside. Many have farm backgrounds, and yet their work damages farmland. As industrial laborers, their relationship to corporate ownership and management is potentially antagonistic within the work setting, and yet their jobs depend on the industry's continued operations in the county, which they must support against other local interests. This web of conflicting loyalties is deepened by the extensive kinship networks that entangle miners with others in local society.

At least half of the county's miners have been raised on farms. Some are extra sons who did not take over their parents' farm operation, but others remain active farmers during planting and harvest seasons. For some, mining is a part-time activity and a source of supplementary off-farm income, but for most it is their only job and the center of their economic life. The commitment to trade unionism is strongest among those who depend entirely on mining for their survival. Part-time farmers tend to be less ideologically committed to labor unionism, and many of the other miners resent those with two sources of income, since it is felt they are occupying jobs that others need more desperately.

As town dwellers, mine workers are also involved in the activities and rivalries spearheaded by the business class. Their union locals belong to the chambers of commerce, and town loyalties divide miners by place of residence, weakening their countywide solidarity. As homeowners and taxpayers whose children are educated in local school districts, mining families have an interest in local town politics, but unlike the businessmen generally do not enter into civic leadership roles. Miners' wives participate in neighborhood socializing and exchange networks that, because of residential segregation as well as social distance, include mostly other households of the same class.

Mining families differ from farming or business families, in that they are not involved in household enterprises. Husband and wife spend their days in different workplaces, engaged in separate activities. Instead of working alongside other family members in the fields, men labor in someone else's enterprise and for someone else's profit. In place of dedication to the family-owned and -operated farm or business, mining men develop strong feelings of camaraderie with their fellow workers. Wives and family members are peripheral to this laboring brotherhood, maintaining their own networks of friends and workmates as housewives, mothers, and sometimes as wage workers in other businesses. Historically, women have played a crucial role in union activity, however, particularly on the picket line when strikes are called. Many are no less versed in union ideology than are their husbands and fathers, and defend the interests of the mine workers as a class with determination and loyalty.

Men at Work | Visiting a modern strip mine, one cannot fail to be impressed by the scale and complexity of the coordinated activities carried out there by men and machines. The mining process entails several operations. Once the land agents have smoothed the legal path for the big machines, the upper layer of fertile soil is removed by bulldozers and huge dragline shovels. They dump the topsoil nearby, and then remove the rest of the overburden to be stored in a separate pile. These storage piles form miniature mountain ranges visible for many miles across the prairie. Road workers then construct ramps down into the exposed coal bed, where dragline shovels scoop the coal into gigantic dump trucks that haul it to the crushers. Crushed, and then sorted by size, the coal is distributed to various buyers, principally to power plants that burn it to produce electricity. A power plant is often located at the mine mouth to minimize transportation costs and loss of energy-producing capacity due to the lignite's volatile chemical properties; there, a conveyer belt runs the crushed coal directly to the burners. On areas that have been mined out, reclamation laws require returning the overburden and topsoil, using road graders to create the desired contours, and reseeding the land with a mix of grasses suitable for pasture.

The electrically powered draglines are the greatest of the earth-moving machines employed in the mines. The larger of these have a 75-cubic-yard bucket and a 310-foot boom. In the operating cab, almost invisible at several stories off the ground, sits a man skillfully shifting levers and pedals in a monotonous rhythm to work the great cables that pull and tip the scoop, taking heavy bites out of the ground and swinging the boom around to dump the load. The sequence is repeated every few seconds, while two engineers tend the inner works of the giant machine. It pays to work these behemoths around the clock, and at night they are easily located in the darkened landscape, their lights strung along the booms like reeling Christmas trees.

The working lives of coal miners foster a distinct consciousness of themselves and their place in society. Today's miners are specialized industrial workers who cooperate in large groups to accomplish complex tasks. They operate enormous, powerful machinery that changes the very structure of the land. Task assignments are handed down to the workers, and the work itself can be lonely. Instead of the shoulder-to-shoulder teamwork that characterized work in the old underground mines, heavy-equipment operators in a modern surface mine labor alone in their machines, isolated from their fellow mine workers except for radio contact. Socializing during the lunch break, at the locker room, and in town is important in building camaraderie and maintaining solidarity. Particular bars in Zap and Stanton, in one case owned by a retired mine worker, serve as evening gathering spots for local miners to relax over a beer and discuss developments at the worksite, talk union business, and keep up with the local gossip.

Unlike most others in Mercer County in the early 1980s, miners earned their living by working within large bureaucratic organizations. Both the coal corporations and the mine workers' unions were stratified organizations that encouraged class identification. The antagonistic interests of labor and management were emphasized in this industrial setting; the miners' power struggle was directly with other people, as opposed to the farmers' conflict with abstractly perceived market forces and faraway banking, milling, and railway firms. Experience in these large organizations also encouraged broader social horizons and more personal involvement in national concerns than typical of other local people. Unionized miners are encouraged to be aware of industrial activities across the world, and to identify with fellow laboring people everywhere.

In the early 1970s there were three large coal mines in Mercer County. The Pennsylvania-based North American Coal Corporation operated the Indian Head Mine near Zap, which employed some 60 miners; Knife River Coal Corporation, a wholly owned subsidiary of Montana-Dakota Utilities, operated the Beulah Mine with about 160 miners; and the Glenharold Mine near Stanton, employing some 170 miners, was owned by the Consolidation Coal Corporation, a subsidiary of Continental Oil, itself owned by DuPont. Then Consolidation sold out its coal interests in Mercer County to the Basin Electric Power Cooperative. Basin was one of the largest of the rural electrical cooperatives, and resembled a private corporation in its organization and behavior.

Historically, two unions have vied for the support of the Mercer County miners. Before the energy boom, workers at the Indian Head and Glenharold Mines were solid United Mine Workers members, while the representation of miners at the Beulah Mine was in dispute. As an underground mine, it had been organized by the UMW, while the associated tipple and power plant were represented by the smaller Progressive Mine Workers (PMW).[9] When the underground operation was closed, all the miners were laid off and only those willing to go with the PMW were rehired. Rivalries with the other mines were fostered by Knife River management in an effort to discourage UMW affiliation. By 1974, the UMW had organized the Beulah Mine, but the labor relations board threw out the election results at the request of the company, ruling that since two mines in Montana also belonged to the same company, they ought to have the same union representation and combined elections. The company also introduced an in-house union, the Midwestern Miners (MM), resulting in a four-way factional split among UMW, PMW, MM, and nonunion supporters at the Beulah mine.

Retired miners telling tales of their experiences working in the mines over the years are an important part of the oral tradition shared among miners. These are told impromptu—as first-, second-, or third-hand accounts—at evening beer gatherings in a workingman's bar, at early morning coffee in a cafe, and almost non-stop in union hall conversations. The stories are often thrilling, full of danger, courage, tragedy, and humor, and they nearly always have a moral. The moral need not be explicit, but reflects the teller's attitude about the relationship between labor and management. Because of the persuasive intention of such storytelling, coal miners who knew I was "writing a book" were eager to tell me accounts supporting their own views. Reuben and Roy, two retired miners, hold opposing positions on the role of labor unions, and these are reflected in their stories of mine work.

Reuben's life as a coal miner is typical of many in his generation. He was born in 1907 in a South Russian village, and he homesteaded with his family near Krem, a now-extinct town in eastern Mercer County. He first worked as a teenager in 1922 at the Krem Mine, a small, seasonal shaft mine about sixty feet deep serving local farmers. According to Reuben, it was run on something like a cooperative basis: "If they wanted their coal cheap and in a hurry, the farmers had to help out with the mining there, in addition to the regular miners. That's what I was doing there, for no pay. It was hard work, all by hand . . . and I thought labor was treated very badly at the Krem Mine. I worked in that mine off and on every fall." Later, Reuben worked with his brother for two years in the Kessler Mine, six miles northwest of Beulah. This was an underground mine, but the lignite was so close to the surface that trucks simply drove into the hillside entrance and drove out again with their loads.

After that, Reuben worked for the Knife River Coal Company at the Beulah Mine for thirty-six years until his retirement. He started out at the tipple, loading coal for transport, and in 1936 was transferred underground. The equipment there was more modern than at the other mines where Reuben had worked—they used machines instead of shovels for moving the coal—but much of the work was still by hand. He worked for a while as a car spotter, assisting the mule skinners who drove the mules hauling the coal carts in and out. Then he was selected by the cutting machine operator to be his helper in cutting the coal so it would fall correctly when blasted, setting the fuses on the dynamite shots, and igniting them. In 1952 Knife River shut down the underground mine, keeping open only its more mechanized and profitable surface operation. Many miners were laid off or relocated, but Reuben stayed on, working first as a caterpillar operator, then as a truck driver hauling coal, and finally as the operator of the Beulah Belle, a large dragline with a twelve-yard bucket, until he retired in 1972. The switch to surface mining came easily to Reuben because of his youthful experience with heavy machinery on the farm.

Reuben is loyal to his former employer: He praises the company's good treatment of its workers, and complains about "meddlesome" labor unions. But other miners of his generation, such as Roy, do not share these opinions. Roy comes from a mining family. His father worked at the Zap Mine, as did Roy and his brother, his sons, and his brother's sons. As a young man he lived in the company-owned mining camp outside of Zap, where conditions were miserable. During the 1930s when work at the mine was sporadic, the family nearly starved. They had only a little corn to eat and were reduced to consuming jack rabbits caught by the dog. Neighboring ranchers observed their distress but did nothing, according to Roy, "because they didn't want to have the miners there at all, because it meant land away from them."

In 1941 Roy lost most of one hand operating an unsafe coal-loading machine on the job. The workers had complained previously about the defective design, asking the company to install a guard over the exposed gears which mangled Roy's hand, but had been told that the company would fix it only when it broke down or caused an injury. At that time there were no medical benefits in the miners' contract, and he received only eleven dollars a week for 195 weeks in worker's compensation. When the union came along in 1950, Roy was an avid supporter. While Reuben's fondest memories are of the camaraderie of underground work, Roy's are of the excitement and sense of empowerment on the picket line. He and his wife, who also "manned" the picket lines in 1950, praise the United Mine Workers union for regularizing seniority and safety matters and for the contract benefits it brought them.

Political Participation | The participation of mine workers in county politics before the energy boom was shaped by their geographic concentration. They were most powerful in the town of Zap, where most of the Indian Head workers lived. There were also many miners in Beulah and Stanton, but there they were outnumbered by the nonmining voting population. The activities of the coal mines were their main concern, and this focus limited their involvement with county issues such as road maintenence or the vitality of the local retail economy. Union locals joined chambers of commerce more in an effort to secure legitimacy and respect than out of any identification with small-business interests. Although many mine workers were politically active, this activity was concentrated in the absorbing realm of labor–management conflict, and articulated through labor organizations.

Mercer County coal miners' attitudes towards the unions were complex and apparently contradictory. More radical unionists characterized the relationship between labor and capital in terms of class conflict, in which the interests of ownership and management are seen as fundamentally antagonistic to those of workers. According to this view, it is the nature and role of capital to try to extract the greatest amount of profit, and it will use every possible form of manipulation to do so. Workers must therefore be organized for their own protection, to form an opposing force in order to reserve a fair portion of the value they produce for themselves. When the situation is understood to be structured in this manner, the attempts of both sides to further their interests can be seen as a kind of wrestling match. In this grappling game, both sides constantly exert themselves to maintain their hold and seek new openings to enhance their position.

This view is expressed in the following model of social structure offered by a retired coal miner who had participated in the violent strikes of the 1940s and 1950s, described in Chapter 2.

> I see it [society] is like a stack of barrels. There are, say, four on the bottom, then you can only put three on top of them, then two and finally one on the very top.... The ones on the bottom are the common working people, and the other layers they're supporting are the higher classes. You can see how there are fewer and fewer people in the higher classes....
> Now, what happens when you take out a barrel from the bottom rank?

What happens when someone on the bottom wants to move up? The whole structure comes crashing down! And the ones up there on the top will do anything to stay up there.

Mercer County coal miners, however, were less concerned with abstract formulations of labor–management relations than with managing their concrete problems and personal gripes with management at work.[10] Particularly despised bosses and owners were singled out for hostile remarks and ridicule—statements attributed to them and details of their personal lives were repeated and mocked in the in-group discussions that maintained and reinforced mine-worker solidarity. The personalism of such conceptions of class conflict is explained by Piven and Cloward:

> People experience deprivation and oppression in a concrete setting, not as the end product of larger abstract processes, and it is the concrete experience that molds their discontent into specific grievances against specific targets. Workers experience the factory, the speeding rhythm of the assemblyline, the foreman, the spies and the guards, the owners and the paycheck. They do not experience monopoly capitalism. (1979:20)

The character of their commitment to labor unionism is not uniformly oppositional, however, but also reflects the values of community harmony and of free enterprise. All but a few hard-core anti-unionists believe that the union's historical role has been socially beneficial. It has helped them to achieve higher wages, better benefits, and safer working conditions, thereby supporting the economies of the small towns where workers shop and pay taxes.

On the other hand, while most miners would claim that unions are necessary to protect the workers from corporate greed, they do not go so far as to believe that unions should challenge the operating principles of capitalism. On the contrary, all but the most radical anti-unionists argue that unions exercising proper self-constraint on their demands make an important contribution to the success of free enterprise. This is because, miners claim, union laborers are hard-working, better-trained, and more safety-conscious than nonunion workers. They make good profits for the company, and deserve not only good wages but considerate and respectful treatment in return.

Unionized miners see the ideal labor–management relationship as one in which the union represents the workers' legitimate interests and works with a management that is humane and not blinded to the workers' needs by "dollar signs in their eyes." They are appreciative of any show of personal attention by management, and argue that mutual respect is key to profitable mine operation. Miners claim that wisely managed companies will, after a serious labor dispute, "work hard to get morale back up, because unhappy workers don't work very hard!"

This way of thinking might be called the "harmony of interest" model. According to this view, both owners and workers gain through cooperating in the production process. Their interests are not identical, but they harmonize well as capital and labor join forces to make a living and build the nation. This ideal conception of labor–management relations reflects the dominance of liberal values, with its emphasis on working within the system, as well as the reciprocal and cooperative values of community ideology.[11]

Both the class conflict and the harmony of interest models are used by laborers in Mercer County, in much the same way that farmers shift from populist to free-enterprise rhetoric depending on their fortunes. Their ambivalence can be compared to that of the tin miners studied by June Nash, who recognize both their oppression by the mining companies and their dependence on them (Nash 1979). The class conflict outlook is dominant during times of crisis and repressive management policies. It has historically proved to be the miners' most powerful weapon during the post–World War II expansion of the national economy. Through labor union struggle during this relatively permissive period, they achieved a middle class standard of living and the status of respectable workingmen. It has given them bargaining power and respect on the job as well, and a stronger sense of themselves as a class with distinct interests opposed to those of ownership and management.

On the other hand, a harmony-of-interest rhetoric is employed by both miners and management especially when times are better, to keep their working relationship on an even keel and to improve morale. It provides miners with an idiom for relating to management without evoking conflict, one that can be used to discuss issues such as the responsibility of management to show respect for workers, without appearing unreasonable or antagonistic.

Unionized miners believe that it is only their presence in strength that forces nonunion companies to offer competitive wages: They see the labor movement as the cause and primary guarantee of decent wages and working conditions throughout the economy. But new recruits from farm families, as well as from other parts of the country where high unemployment has already undermined unionism, do not always share this conception. Some older miners who lived through the era of struggle complain that young miners take for granted all their elders fought for, and do not appreciate what the union does for them. North Dakota has long had "right-to-work" legislation, which permits companies to hire nonunion labor even in unionized operations, and prohibits their coercion by fellow workers to join unions (although union miners assert that such workers end up joining the union anyway "the first time the company screws them over.") Each mine has its anti-union faction, and paternalistic management policies encourage workers to become complacent about labor relations.

The attitude of other townspeople toward the miners, their labor unions, and their occasional strikes is ambivalent. Some older businessmen who also remember the pre-union days claim that union power means more steady income entering the community, and entering their own cash registers as well. But the owners of small businesses are employers themselves, and identify more readily with mine owners, rather than with workers. As petty capitalists, they feel threatened by the radicalism of class-conflict rhetoric.

Among the nonmining population, there is a strong undercurrent of anti-unionism, even in towns whose major source of income is from mining.[12] The gist of this anti-unionism is that miners already make more money than most other wage earners, and so even in seeking simply to maintain the wage and benefit levels won in the past, they are demanding more than their fair share. In this "limited good" conception of wages, other wage workers complain that unionized miners make more money than they themselves do, implying that if miners made less there would be more available to workers in other sectors of the economy. Such a view is expressed in this letter to the editor of a local newspaper, in which a farmer's wife blames the labor unions for problems in the farm economy: "Because of their higher and higher wages, our operating cost [sic] have gone up and up, and asking for higher prices for our products would only give labor another chance to strike, and we would end up with less than we have now. . . . Labor is cutting for themselves a bigger and bigger piece of the pie" (*Beulah Beacon* March 1, 1979).

Some business people also argue that it is best not to antagonize the coal companies because of the risk they could shut down their local operations in favor of areas with a more docile labor force.[13] Although local business people may sympathize with individual miners, and may even close up shop in support of a strike in Stanton or Zap, where the miners are a political force to be reckoned with, their use of the proverb "You can't buck big business" is both a condolence and a warning.

Small-Business Entrepreneurs | Although they represent only about 5 percent of the county's population, those owning local businesses—collectively known as "Main Street"—consider themselves to be the most important townspeople. To them, their businesses represent the core of the community, its reason for existing, and they see themselves as having the greatest investment in its survival and growth. The nature of their involvement in the local social structure and economy gives them a characteristic outlook and a common set of interests that are distinct from those of both farmers and miners.

Social and Economic Conditions | The owners of small town businesses, together with well-paid professionals such as lawyers and doctors, made up the politically powerful and socially prestigious local elite, sometimes referred to by others as "society people" or "uppity-ups." As has been typical in rural American towns (Ferrell et al. 1973; West 1945), these entrepreneurs were only a small proportion of the working population (less than 5 percent in 1970), yet they enjoyed disproportionately greater control over town and county affairs. This power is exercised through personal networks, as one would-be entrepreneur explained: "In this town, it's not what you know, but who you know that counts. They all know each other and work together to run things. And the in-crowd can get themselves elected to any position they want."

Local entrepreneurs have played a vital role in the economic development of Mercer County towns. In the earlier decades of this century, a budding entrepreneur inspired by the vision of succeeding in a free marketplace with its healthy competition required only some starting capital, gumption, and a lot of luck. The story of Frank Kramer illustrates this style of entrepreneurship. Frank was born at the turn of the century in Neu Glueckstahl in South Russia. At the age of seven his family emigrated to the United States with him, and he grew up on a Mercer County farm. Lacking formal education because there was no school nearby, Frank started his career as a cowboy, and then worked for a year in an underground lignite mine. He married, and moved to Beulah in 1923.

After an unsuccessful attempt to start a dray (hauling) line, Frank and his wife opened a creamery there in 1924, buying, processing, transporting, and selling dairy products. After some time, he added work shoes and work clothes to his stock of goods, and eventually was running a complete grocery and dry goods store. He taught himself to read by observing the lettering on packages and sacks. In 1932, Kramer leased a Beulah service station, and built his own soon afterward, also acquiring a Plymouth and Dodge franchise. In 1935 he leased out the grocery and dry goods business and built a garage. Two years later he bought a Ford garage and switched his sales franchise to Ford. In 1939, Frank built what is now known in Beulah as "the old post office." Automobile sales declined in the war years, so to his garage he added hardware stock, which soon became a thriving business on its own. After selling the garage and hardware store in the 1950s, Frank Kramer bought ranch land and a feed lot with part of his profits and capped his entrepreneurial career by buying a bank in Beulah together with his son-in-law and another partner. For many years this was the only bank in town. Having no sons of his own, Frank worked there with his son-in-law, who succeeded him as bank president when he retired, while his eldest daughter became the vice president.

Business success translated into civic leadership for Kramer. He became the first mayor of Beulah when it attained official city status, served on the nursing home board of directors, and sponsored a city ordinance to ban outhouses in town, to save the water department from bankruptcy. His career spanned the change to a money-dominated local economy: "Sometimes I would take cattle as a down payment on a vehicle; I have always enjoyed bartering" (*Beulah Beacon* June 5, 1980). The same newspaper article also quotes him as saying, "What business did I enjoy the most? All of them . . . as long as it made money. Show me a business that can make money and I'll go into it!"

The owners of small family businesses face many of the same economic pressures as operators of small farms. As on the family farms, the work of unpaid household members is essential for survival. Although some of the larger, more successful businesses and professional offices employ wage workers, the economic situation of the typical cafe owner or shopkeeper was marginal in the early 1970s. One such petty entrepreneur explained that, "You can't be hiring people to work for you if you expect to make money. You have to do all the work yourself."

Small businesses, like farms, are often passed down within a family. As with farms, there is a preference for male offspring to take over a family business, and sons are sometimes groomed for the role from an early age. Many young people from the business class are encouraged to go to college; young women who do so usually leave permanently, but young men destined to take over a family business return as adults and take up their life where it left off when they went off to college. With their more cosmopolitan experience and their city wives, this group is important in bringing urban culture to Mercer County; they are its first "yuppies."

The relationship between the small town merchants and people of the surrounding countryside has some contradictory features. Until recently, agriculture was the primary source of wealth in Mercer County. Businesses existed by serving the needs of farmers, angling for their hard-earned dollars, and competing with one another for their trade. And yet there was a tendency in the towns to downplay this dependence and to despise country people. This enduring structural antagonism within rural America has been best described by Charles Galpin, a founding father of rural sociology, in a passage that was as true in 1970 as when it was written:

> The banker, storekeeper, and blacksmith know the farmer as the goose that lays the golden egg. The problem is one of pleasing [him] and getting his trade without building him and his mind, capacities and wishes into the community fabric. The farmer's money is good and necessary and must be obtained, and his goodwill retained; but how to accomplish this object is a problem. Thoroughgoing incorporation of the farmer into the stream of village activities is frustrated by the fundamental conception of the self-sufficiency of the village. (Galpin 1915:x)

Agriculturalists felt unwelcome in the towns their labor had helped to build, and the urbanization that accompanied the energy boom accentuated this alienation. It was the practice of storekeepers to extend credit to local residents, and as long as the agricultural community constituted a large proportion of their clientele, the chronic troubles of the farm economy hit small town businesses hard. Merchants were anxious to be liberated from their dependence upon the agricultural market, and welcomed the prospect of industrial development.

The Work of Commerce | Work for the business owners is quite different from that of either farmers or miners. Family members may work together, as on the farm, but at much closer quarters, and in constant contact with customers and the bustle of Main Street traffic. They need to be attentive to the needs of clientele, maintain reliable wholesale supply sources, weather the ups and downs of the local economy, and keep an eye on the competition.

The entrepreneurial career of Anna Hanson, a native of Zap, illustrates something of this experience: She began her business experience after an illness forced her to leave school in the eighth grade; reluctant to return to school after her peers had moved ahead of her, she began working in various businesses around town. Anna asserts that this experience "was an education in itself"; she learned not only the technical aspects of running a business, but also the skills of customer relations: "You have to get good at dealing with the public. You have to be tough sometimes and sometimes smile, even when your insides are burning up." After her marriage, she and her husband ran a cafe in Zap, with their daughters' help. All family members old enough to work served alternately as waitress, cook, cashier, and cleanup crew. Anna's husband died when the children were still young, but she continued to run the cafe, situated next door to their trailer home, until her older children were grown up and moved away. After "flipping hash over there for 18 years," Anna sold the cafe and has built up a thrift shop, souvenir, and hairdressing business in her home.

Possessed of a truly entrepreneurial spirit, Anna is always on the lookout for an opportunity to do business. When college students overran the town for the Zap-In rock festival in 1969, she was on hand to sell them hot dogs and firewood, and she later took advantage of the boom-time housing shortage in the early 1980s to fix up her basement into rooms to rent at the elevated prices of the time.

For the small-business families of Mercer County, survival has been almost as chancy as for the farmers. As independent firms, they depend for their livelihood on maintaining the goodwill of the largest number of potential customers. This is the significance of Anna's remark about smiling "even when you are burning up inside." The need for good customer relations contributes to the pressure on business people to be "good neighbors" and demonstrate their dedication to their town through contributions to community benefit drives and projects. As C. Wright Mills pointed out, "running a business often involves a calculating posture towards other people" (1951:31). The social relationships between business people and other community members are colored by the necessity for the merchants to exploit these relationships directly for economic gain. Their closest friends and relatives are also their customers, employees, and suppliers. Personal relations are used for selling, for example, when a dress shop owner calls up a close friend to say she has "something just perfect for you." "It helps to know your clientele so well," I was told.

One can be too close to the clientele, however, as in the case of one greenhouse owner whose relatives requested so many free seedlings that she was forced to go out of business. Employer–employee relations are sometimes so overlaid with personal relations that the employee feels obligated to accept lower wages and extra work demands they would not tolerate in a purely economic, contractual relationship.

Groups of small-business owners have also countered their economic vulnerability by organizing in each town to reduce competition within their ranks and to present a unified front in competition with the business groups of other towns. The early formation of these commercial clubs and chambers of commerce in the larger towns, as well as the serious character of intertown rivalry, are discussed in the preceding chapter. The civic boosting activities they organize are an important part of the work required of business entrepreneurs, both to enhance customers' loyalty to their own town and to keep good relations with the other local merchants. The mood at the Chamber of Commerce meetings is good natured and informal, as members spend a lunch hour talking about their collective problems, formulating plans, and pressuring each other to carry them out. Privately, business people complain about the great demands made on their time by the "volunteering" required of them to produce the endless series of boosting events sponsored by their chambers of commerce.

The yearly calender of such events is marked in the larger towns by a late-summer open air market and street fair, known in Hazen and Beulah as Crazy Days and Krazy Daze, respectively. At this time, the downtown business strip is roped off for pedestrian traffic, and merchants are encouraged to dress up in goofy costumes and display their wares in outdoor bins and stalls. The atmosphere is festive, with carnival decorations and interesting contests, such as turkey-sweeping races, blindfolded wheelbarrow slaloms, and a hilarious event in which contestants build colorful contraptions composed of toilets mounted on wheeled platforms and propel themselves, seated thereon, down the block with bathroom plungers. In the evening, a band provides music for dancing, while others relax in a German-style beer garden.[14] The yearly county fair also includes parades and other events requiring the participation of local business groups. Such events are enjoyed by all, but require many hours of volunteer planning and effort.

Political Participation | The positive orientation toward growth that characterizes the business community's perspective is a vital part of business ideology nationwide, and is the central element of the small town ethos of boosterism.[15] Chambers of commerce function like business unions, and sponsor a number of voluntary associations to further the careers of local business people and promote the morale and loyalty of community members to their own town. Jaycees, or Junior Chambers of Commerce, are part of a hierarchically organized nationwide association for young business people, and in Mercer County have served as a stepping stone for political as well as economic power. Commercially oriented clubs such as the Elks, Lions, and Knights of Columbus promote town business unity and growth and intertown rivalry through sponsoring projects and activities to which local merchants are invited to contribute. Boosters' clubs were formed early in the larger towns of Beulah and Hazen as promotional committees for businessmen only, working under the umbrella of chambers of commerce that also included miners' union locals and other nonbusiness townspeople's associations.

Essential to the booster ideology is the assertion that growth is good and benefits everybody. Progress is equated with economic growth and capital accumulation, the negative consequences of which are regarded as inevitable, if at times regrettable. Small merchants identify with big business rather than with the farming members of their own class of petty entrepreneurs. Booster ideology conceals the structural roots of the threat to small businesses and family farmers alike. Whereas the majority of local farmers have some consciousness that theirs is a struggle between small and large capital on a national scale, and therefore mistrust outside developers, the business community looked to the entrance of giant corporate entities into the local economy as a panacea for all the problems of economic decline. Many business people expected to profit personally from rapid growth, and evaluated the potential costs and benefits to the wider community in financial rather than social terms.

Governing the county and its towns is ostensibly everybody's business, but only a small proportion of the population actually participates in day-to-day decisions. Business leaders play a dominant role in politics, particularly in the larger towns. This is the case partly because the generally low level of interest in formal goverment activity among the rest of the town population results in a small field of competitors, and also because merchants recognize their stake in overseeing decisions that affect their group interests and their personal commercial success.

Each town has an elected council, the chair of which serves as mayor. Nearly all council members in the larger towns are business owners or professionals. The man who was mayor of Beulah throughout most of the 1960s and early 1970s was a wealthy Republican gravel pit owner. After selling his gravel mines, he bought land that had coal on it, which he sold to a mining company at a handsome profit. Other important figures in the leadership of this town included a banker and a mine superintendent. In Hazen, the local banking family was politically powerful, along with several other business leaders. The link between business and political power extends vertically from Mercer County towns to district and state business and party organizations. A number of local power figures in Hazen and Beulah have also been important in the state Jaycees organization and have held offices in the Republican Party organization.

Traditionally in the region, there has been a heavy reliance on personal relations in the establishment of political followings and the mobilization of support. Because of the small scale of the political arena of such towns, or even of entire rural counties, it was possible for individuals to attain high levels of personal power and exert tremendous influence on the course of events within their sphere. Indeed, there is a preference in local political culture for individual, rather than collective, leadership.

Small town leaders depend on kinship, friendship, and patron–client relations. Early morning coffee-drinking groups of men in cafes and restaurants around town are an essential element of informal power organization. Each group tends to revolve around a central leader and constitutes not merely a gossip or loafing group, but a political clique. Quarrels within one group can result in members shifting to other coffee-drinking factions, and political realignments occur continually. Loyalty to particular leaders is demonstrated by being present most mornings, and although the setting is informal, important political business is transacted there.

Managing Tensions in Community Living

It is useful to disentangle the distinctive experiences of farmers, miners, and merchants from the jumble of social reality, in order to view them more clearly. Exploring the economic constraints and ideological constructs characteristic of these positions provides insight into the relations of competition and cooperation both within and among them. In real life, however, these groups are not so distinct and separate; they are made up of individuals who may belong to more than one of them, and who have important relationships with people in other positions in local society. These groups are not "corporate" at all, in the anthropological sense of having well-defined rules of membership, recruitment, rights, and duties. Their boundaries are fuzzy and fluid; their memberships mingle and overlap with one another and with the rest of local society in forming whole communities. Some miners also farm, while others run small businesses in town after retirement; members of farming families also work in town for wages. About half of the County's population did not fit into any of these three groups.

The communities of Mercer County in the early 1980s were still very closely knit and intimate, but they were also socially stratified and had internal conflicts. These conflicts were all the more potentially disruptive to community life because of their personal character. Reasonably harmonious daily living in spite of them was achieved through an informal code of nonconfrontation, egalitarianism, and neighborliness. The emphasis on social harmony in civic life helped to paper over conflicts that threatened the status quo upon which everyday lives depended.

Before the energy boom, Mercer County society was divided into five locally distinguished occupational categories, which were ranked in status according to income and prestige. These were: an underclass of rural and town unemployed; nonindustrial wage workers of the towns and farms; farm and ranch operators (including a combinations of owners and renters); coal miners; and the merchants and professionals whose ranks included the social and political elite. However, while I have refered to these as "classes" in the colloquial sense of the word as referring to categories of social status, these occupational groupings actually corresponded only roughly to economic classes defined in terms of their differential access to strategic resources Nonetheless, these occupational categories were the most relevant divisions of society to people in Mercer County, who grouped themselves in ways that cross-cut economic class lines. For example, agriculturalists viewed tenant farmers and even some farm laborers as future farm owners rather than as members of a distinct class. "Sidewalk farmers" who lived by agriculture but had a town residence had an intermediate status rank, slightly above other farmers generally, but still a rung down from other town residents. Small town merchants saw themselves as socially superior to, and with different interests from, their rural farm-owning counterparts, despite their common petty bourgeois character. The few salaried professionals regarded their fellow wage-workers of "blue collar" status as socially inferior, and service workers in general failed to identify with the labor unionism of their fellow wageworkers in the mines.

Class prejudice, such as that reported in rural communities by West (1945) and Useem (1942), was also strong in Mercer County before the energy boom. Its expression was mitigated by extensive cross-cutting ties of kinship and close acquaintance, as well as by a moralistic and democratic civic ideology suppressing high status display. Conspicuous consumption was rare among the wealthy of the older generation, but the elite displayed their position in other ways. They staked their high status claims by joining the most elite churches in town, by becoming a member of the Eagle's Club and the Golf Club, and by participating in the private social life of the upper class.

Wealth and occupational prestige were the primary determinants of social status, yet education remained important as a symbol of elite sophistication. A college degree, preferably from the more prestigious University of North Dakota, rather than North Dakota State University or a community college, was important for "society" women as well as for men. Members of the social elite were prominent in sponsoring intellectual and artistic events, and they dominated their local public library, the historical society, and musical, theatrical, and visual arts associations. By the early 1980s, ethnicity had become less significant as a status marker, since recent generations of German-Russian-Americans no longer differed from others in their command of the English language.

In this context of social stratification and structured conflict, day-to-day relations among community members were mediated by a subdued and nonconfrontational style of public interactions. People of all sorts met and mingled in town doing daily errands, drinking and eating out, at sports and civic events, and in church. Despite underlying tensions, Mercer County residents, especially the older ones, maintained a dignified emotional reserve and self-control in public. People did not wish to call attention to themselves and they avoided making scenes that would provide grist for the gossip mill. Even when tempers were high, antagonists would keep their voices low and avoid conspicuous displays of anger. Violence among adults in public was extremely rare (I witnessed only one occurrence in all my time in Mercer County). Conflicts were present, but their overt expression was suppressed.

Such discipline in public behavior was strikingly evident at church, where adults remained orderly and silent except when the service called for their participation in unison. At one church the extreme decorum resembled a military exercise; instead of breaking into chatty groups when the service was finished, congregants remained seated and still until they were dismissed row by row with a curt nod from the ushers.[16] Religous sermons reflected the contradictory currents in community life. Pastors, ministers, and priests interwove contrasting themes like "loving thy neighbor" yet competing with others for entrance into heaven.

The studied friendly reserve appropriate to public life, however, could be abandoned in some settings. Emotional demonstrativeness was encouraged within same-sex groupings. There was a high level of gender solidarity throughout the life cycle, and both men and women seemed more relaxed and confiding in unmixed company. Athletic competitions were also opportunities for emotional outpouring, especially games between the most structurally significant rival groups, such as a football match between the Beulah and Hazen high schools. The younger generation also let off steam with wilder parties in secluded spots like streams and woods on the edge of town. Away from the discipline of society—both literally beyond the view of parental and police authority and symbolically in the "wilderness," teenagers might get drunk, smoke marijuana, play with fire crackers, and discover sex.

More restrained social drinking offered adults an opportunity for frank expressiveness. Beer was available on all sorts of nonreligious informal occasions, and people liked to unwind under its influence. Alcohol's function as a social lubricant was apparent at wedding dances, for example, where guests would sit and drink quietly for the first hour or two and only then become more sociable and communicative. One young woman recalled the expression "Let's get drunk and *be* somebody!" from her high school days, and explained that people feel inhibited about expressing themselves openly in public, and believe this is easier when drinking socially. Submerged conflicts could erupt under the influence of liquor, but even bar fights were rare. Instead, people adopted a joking style of expressing conflicts that they felt like airing.

The relationship between the values of intimate community living and the communitarian civic ideology of egalitarianism is complex and fluid. Despite the strength of social divisions and competitive relations, the values of democratic and harmonious community life remained an explicit ideal. These "small town" values, deriving from the interdependence of pioneer neighbors, provide a moral and rhetorical basis for community ideology. The latter consists of a more elaborated and articulated set of ideas drawing on these values, which serves to soften the impact of inequality without challenging its structural basis. Before the energy boom, there remained enough genuine community, in the classic sense of networks of social relations characterized by intimacy, mutuality, shared experience, and affective ties,[17] that small town values and communitarian ideology were mutually reinforced in public interaction.

In Mercer County people were deliberately informal and friendly in public, greeting one another with a "Hello," a wave, and a humorous comment. They considered handshaking slightly pretentious and laughable on less than solemn occasions, because it implied a level of formality inappropriate to life in a small community. Local elites downplayed social and economic differences in public, to avoid being considered unfriendly and snobbish. Public figures cultivated a hearty, democratic style, and even official business was conducted on a first-name basis.

Similarly, the ideal of neighborliness across all social ranks was stressed in public life. Being neighborly implies having a helpful attitude and behaving with reciprocity toward others. Housewives cooperated in child care and other work, and maintained networks for borrowing and exchanging garden produce and other home products. Neighbors felt some responsibility to care for each other in trouble and infirmity, which might entail checking on them daily, bringing food over frequently, taking them to the doctor, and loaning them money. This kind of intense neighboring was mostly practiced by older people living alone, for whom it worked as a social safety net if their families had either moved away or failed to care for their daily needs. The practice of neighboring is far from egalitarian, however; these mutual exchange relationships existed almost exclusively among people of similar social standing. It may be that "Everyone knows everyone else" in these small towns, but this does not mean they will share their stock of homemade pickles with just anybody.

The ideal relationship of individuals to other community members involved an extension of idealized family sentiment, and the values of family cooperation and caring served as a rhetorical model for moral behavior among them. People explaining community morality to me (often on occasions when it had been breached) invoked the rules of social reciprocity: "Good neighbors" deal in good faith, do not take unfair advantage, and lend a helping hand when needed. People should not be greedy, and all should contribute actively to the community. In return, it is implied, they receive a variety of services and life-enhancing opportunities. Local government and chambers of commerce were often characterized as institutions devoted to organizing this exchange.

The civic ideology emphasizing communitarian values and neighborly morality helps prevent internal conflicts from erupting openly, and was especially useful to the business class. It served to soften the economic character of their transactions with customers, and it promoted town solidarity, which could be expressed in customer loyalty in a context of intertown competition for retail trade. Publicly extolling the virtues of small town living also diverted attention from the potentially negative consequences of business class boosterism, which sought "progress" in the form of growth, modernization, and urbanization, all of which pose a threat to the small town lifestyle.

The expression of this moralistic and democratic ideology was not limited to the business class, however. It resonated with local people's values, and with some of their lived experiences. It also represented the way they wished their communities to be, and the face they liked to present to outsiders. Philip Olson has pointed out that the contradiction lies in "publicly upholding the virtues of rural life and at the same time adopting the technology and culture of the larger society" (1964:348). Becoming dependent on increasingly complex agricultural and mining technology or, more recently, that of synthetic fuels development, implied more absentee decisions affecting the everyday life of rural people. Civic ideology, however, resisted seeing this process as one of outside control or exploitation, focusing instead on the friendliness and neighborliness of the corporate or government agents, ideas more compatible with the comfortable image local residents had of their communities.

Chapter Four

Lowering the Energy Boom

The sudden increase in large-scale strip mining, coal-based electricity generation, and coal gasification that began in Mercer County in the 1970s followed in the wake of the higher world energy prices resulting from the so-called "oil crisis." It was facilitated by federal government policies encouraging national energy self-sufficiency, and a red-carpet welcome to industry on the part of pro-business elements in North Dakota state politics.

Although it linked up with local interests and ambitions, the impetus for the energy boom came from the top down, and understanding the articulation of these events and conditions requires a "vertical slice" approach. In recommending that anthropologists lift their gaze from the local community to study power relations more broadly in the United States in the context of its bureaucratic organizations, Laura Nader (1980:284) encourages anthropologists to "get at the mechanisms whereby faraway corporations and large-scale industries are directing the everyday aspects of our lives."

Yet for many Americans, such vertically integrated power structures, operating semi-autonomously and partly beyond democratic control, remain abstract, obscure, and largely invisible. As anthropologist Dan Rose describes the shaping yet unseen part played by major corporations in the United States: "It was they who helped make this so-called life on the ground that ethnographers study a possibility. A hierarchy of institutional forms [rises] out of sight to the ordinary citizen of the country" (1989:42). People in Mercer County were offered hints and glimpses of the process by which the energy boom was "lowered," but piecing together even what was not shielded by secrecy required an investment of time and energy that few could afford. This, as much as anything that happened subsequently, indicates the obstacles to economic democracy and local empowerment faced by advocates of community-based development.

The coordination of corporate and government action in the design of energy policy is complex, and speaks to the general relationship between capital and the state, and of both to the wider American political system of which they form a part. C. Wright Mills (1956) and numerous subsequent sociologists have provided extensive documentation of the close ties among those occupying the most powerful command posts of American society—leaders of the largest corporations, the military institutions, and the highest political officials.[1] Their alliance, some argue, goes beyond the obvious commonality of strategic interests, to the more thorough integration of personnel, life experiences, and world view that is characteristic of a ruling class.[2] Researchers on this "power elite" differ in the extent to which they view the consolidation of power at the highest levels as beyond the reach of the democratic forms of civil society, yet all of them agree that it is there, at the highest levels of decision-making power, that people who are usually unknown to the public formulate policies that shape our everyday lives in ways we are scarcely aware of.

This chapter traces some of the connections and policies that resulted in Mercer County's energy boom, following the layers of power from the top down. It begins with the corporate impetus for Western energy resource development, and goes on to the intricate dance of government policy, legislation, and regulation at federal, state, county, and municipal levels. National concern over future energy security, and big developers' interest in big profits, were given priority over local and short-term concerns by political and planning institutions throughout the process, in ways that ensured that the most powerful interests were secured in the long run. And yet the people of North Dakota and of Mercer County were neither passive nor powerless recipients of the development plans. Pressure from elected representatives, organized interest groups, and vigilant individuals achieved a sort of class compromise with significant protections responding to local concerns: environmental legislation requiring the reclamation of mined-out land, and special taxes on the coal industries to compensate negatively affected communities. The struggles described in this case study—between local and national levels, big and small capital, corporations and communities, and among corporate, state, and social interests—reflect the state of these relationships in late-twentieth-century America.

In this case, the American state, that is, the more or less integrated organizations (both coercive and administrative) that control the national territory,[3] is shown to be not a simple handmaiden of corporate or dominant class interests but rather as operating within class-divided socioeconomic relations in which corporate power is hegemonic. We see here that despite an overall pattern of cooperation, the interests of the state are not identical to those of capital; the state must compete with capital in appropriating resources from the economy and society through taxation, and must continually balance its function of facilitating the accumulation of corporate capital with the necessity of retaining the basis of its own legitimacy—its reputation as responsive to democratic influence. These two major functions of the state, accumulation and legitimation, are often at odds. As James O'Connor puts it, "the state must try to maintain or create the conditions in which profitable capital accumulation is possible . . . [and] it must also try to maintain or create the conditions for social harmony"(1973:6).

In formal democracies such as the United States, the state's task of facilitating corporate profit making, while not appearing to do so at the expense of other classes, is complicated by the fact that it operates within an overall political system that includes some institutionalized representation of public and community interests in policy making and implementation. The power of local residents is at least potentially great, since local control over land use gives towns and counties formal powers to place conditions on construction and operation permits, and even to refuse them. If the voters of Mercer County had opposed the energy development projects in overwhelming numbers, they might have been prevented. From the point of view of pro-development decision makers in both corporate and government spheres, the orderly exploitation of Mercer County's resources required a careful campaign designed to contain political opposition and to convince the local population that they too would benefit from the development.

The Corporate Decision

The nature and timing of investments in North Dakota lignite can best be explained in terms of profitability. The owners of the large and accessible coal deposits in Mercer County had long wished to capitalize on them; the technology for coal gasification had been available since World War II;[4] and for decades there had been political support for diversifying the state's economy away from dependence on agriculture. Nevertheless, it took the dramatic increase in the market price of oil (and consequently of other energy commodities such as coal, natural gas, and uranium) in the wake of the 1971 and 1972 negotiations with the Organization of Petroleum Exporting Countries, and the political impetus of the subsequent Arab embargo on oil sales to the United

States, to attract the financial and political backing needed to develop this resource at the level of profits which energy investors had come to expect.

Although the major oil corporations (with the exception of Tenneco) did not join the electric utilities and gas pipeline companies directly in undertaking the developments in Mercer County, they were indirectly involved in several ways. The market for lignite coal, natural gas, and other energy commodities had been dominated since the early 1960s by a small number of giant transnational oil corporations. This group, known as the "Seven Sisters," included five American companies (Exxon, Mobil, Gulf, Texaco, and Standard Oil of California), one British company (British Petroleum), and one British-Dutch company (Royal Dutch Shell). Together, they controlled some of the world's richest oil fields and most lucrative refining and distribution opportunities. Because of the strategic geo-political importance of oil, they enjoyed the full backing of their respective home governments in matters of both foreign and domestic policy that affected their business (see Tanzer 1974, ch. 4). Most of the less profitable domestic energy development at this time (including that in North Dakota) was undertaken by smaller oil-drilling and coal-mining corporations and by public utilities rather than these transnational giants. Although the Big Seven's influence on this domestic development would therefore seem remote, Mercer County's energy boom was profoundly affected by the energy pricing and policies designed to benefit big oil.

Beginning in the early 1960s, the major American oil companies began quietly buying up rights to alternative fuel sources in the United States, such as coal, oil shale, and uranium, in anticipation of rising market prices for all energy commodities. Since the oil companies' control is exercised through intricate corporate networks and administrative structures, and much of the information is not made public, it is difficult to determine the extent to which big oil had succeeded in monopolizing the non-oil domestic reserves, yet there are indications that they were extremely successful (see Ridgeway 1973). U.S. Senator Conrad Aiken testified at the Senate Subcommittee on Antitrust and Monopoly in 1970 that oil corporations "have now virtually gained possession of the larger mines of this country" (quoted in Tanzer 1974:33). Although many of the details of ownership and control of the nation's coal reserves are obscured by the maze of subsidiary ownerships, interlocking directorates, joint ventures, and hidden stock holdings, the big oil companies' coal reserves give some indication of their concentration. Seven large corporations control coal reserves in North Dakota, and some of those operate lignite mines in Mercer County. Although the Knife River Coal Corporation also mines in the county, it is only a regionally based company, with smaller total reserve holdings (Table 1).

A significant portion of the nation's energy, financial, and industrial capital was interested in exploiting Mercer County coal. Figure 1 shows some of the primary and secondary interlocked directorships of the Continental Oil Company (Conoco), a DuPont subsidiary, whose own subsidiary, Consolidation Coal, operated a large mine in Mercer and Oliver counties. The investment of oil companies and financial institutions in the coal industry is vertically integrated, and includes extensive investment in domestic gas and electric utilities (Jacobs

Table 1 | Corporations' Coal Reserves in the United States, 1974 (1.5 billion tons or more)

Company	Coal-Mining Subsidiary	Reserves in Billion Tons
Burlington Northern*		11.4
Continental Oil*	Consolidation Coal**	10.8
Union Pacific	Rocky Mountain Energy	10.0
Kennecott Copper	Peabody Coal	8.9
Exxon	Monterey Coal & Carter Oil	7.0
North American Coal*	North American Coal (including Falkirk, Coteau Properties, Quarto Mining, Oneida Mining, NACCO Mining, Florence Mining)**	5.0
American Metal Climax*	Amax Coal & Meadowlark Farms	4.9
Occidental Petroleum	Island Creek Coal	4.4
United States Steel		3.0
Eastern Gas and Fuel	Eastern Association Coal	2.6
Gulf Oil	Pittsburgh & Midway Coal Mining	2.6
Pacific Power and Light		2.5
Atlantic Richfield*	Arcoal	2.2
Bethlehem Steel	Bethlehem Mines	1.8
Texaco*		1.65
American Electric Power	Central Appalachian Coal	1.5
Kerr McGee*	Kerr McGee Coal	1.5
Pittston	Clinchfield Coal Division	1.5

Source: Compiled by and used by permission of Mike Jacobs (1975), from *Keystone Coal Industry Manual*.
*Total includes North Dakota reserves.
**Corporation does lignite mining in Mercer County.

Not shown are interlocking directorships by which many of these companies in turn share directors with other energy companies and with corporations doing business with Conoco.

Companies with which Conoco shares directors:

Abitibi Paper	General Electric	St. Joseph Minerals
Coca-Cola	Institute for the Future	Time
Colgate Palmolive	National Cash Register	United Airlines
Corp. for Public Broadcasting	Owens Corning Fiberglass	

Conoco Subsidiaries	**Companies with which they share directors**
Bankers Trust of New York	American Express, Commonwealth Fund, Consolidation Coal, Mobil Oil, Mutual of New York, Prudential Insurance, Rockefeller Foundation
Consolidation Coal Company	American Electric Power, Northern Natural Gas, Union Carbide
Continental Illinois National	Aetna, Commonwealth Edison, Consolidation Coal, General Dynamics, Northwest Bancorporation, Standard Oil of Indiana, Texaco, Universal Oil Products
Equitable Life Assurance	American Electric Power, Burlington Northern, Chase Manhattan, Commonwealth Edison, Consolidated Edison, Mellon National Bank, Rio Algom, Rockefeller Foundation, U.S. Steel
Mathias Coal	Detroit National Bank
Morgan Guaranty Trust	Aetna, Atlantic Richfield, Burlington Northern, Chubb, Cities Service, Duke Power, Exxon, INA, John Hancock, Niagara Mohawk Power, Panhandle Eastern, Penn Mutual, Standard Oil of New Jersey, U.S. Steel, Union Carbide

Source: Used by permission of Mike Jacobs (1975).

Figure 1 | Continental Oil Company (Conoco), Its Subsidiaries and Their Shared Directorships, 1975

1975:91). Even if this control did not include all the lignite reserves of Mercer County (and the answer lies hidden in the corporate organizational maze), the fact remains that, once holding substantial rights to American non-oil energy reserves, the big energy and financial corporations had a powerful incentive to drive up the market energy sources' prices before exploiting them.

The development of coal mines and conversion facilities had to take place in a coordinated fashion, because of the chemical peculiarities of North Dakota lignite. Once exposed to the air, the mineral begins to volatilize, losing thermal heating potential, and so cannot be transported long distances to market. A trainload from Mercer County would lose thirty percent of its heating value by the time it reached Minnesota. This fact further encouraged conglomerates and cooperation among the mining, electric, and gas industries.

In addition to its rising market price, the profitability of exploiting western coal was enhanced by several factors on the production side. These included the availability of nonunion labor, the area's clean air, its supplies of cheap water, the ease of establishing a low-cost transportation network, the low-cost of obtaining the coal, and the willingness of state legislators to facilitate industrial growth through tax benefits and other financial incentives. Let us examine each of these elements in the case of North Dakota.

Labor conditions in the West were more favorable to capital than in the eastern coal fields. Union solidarity in North Dakota was undercut by the state's right-to-work laws, which permitted companies to hire nonunion workers in any facility, even a unionized one, and restricted the on-site activities of organizers. Despite a history of localized labor/management confrontation, most of western North Dakota was simply too unindustrialized to support a strong labor movement. The industries were willing to offer union-scale wages (if not benefits) in exchange for a complacent work force, and could legally exclude unionists from new installations. Perhaps even more important, labor costs would be further reduced in the western strip mines by more heavily mechanized production techniques. As few as twenty workers are required to run a million-ton-a-year surface mine in North Dakota, as compared to four hundred miners in a comparable underground operation (Environmental Policy Center 1974). Strippable reserves were severely limited in the East, and abundant in the West.

The sparse population and low level of industrialization in North Dakota prior to the 1970s also meant that the people there breathed some of the cleanest air in the nation. The air of the crowded and heavily industrialized Northeast, on the other hand, was already severely polluted, making it difficult for industries to obtain permits to release still more impurities into the atmosphere. There had never been a serious challenge to the quality of North Dakota's air, and the environmental protection movement in the state was relatively undeveloped. The coal-based industries hoped to take advantage of these conditions.

The proposed developments required a great deal of water, most of it for cooling the coal conversion plants. Water is a scarce resource on the Plains, and western North Dakota is no exception, receiving an average of only 15.4 inches of precipitation annually. For decades, economic planners had looked to the Missouri River as an abundant water source to meet the area's needs. The Garrison Dam and its reservoir, Lake Sakakawea, were originally constructed by the Army Corps of Engineers as a part of an enormous diversion and irrigation plan designed to improve the agricultural economy of the region and to provide water for home and industrial use.[5] The energy industries expected no difficulty in obtaining access to the water of the reservoir, which was being underused while the Garrison Diversion Project remained stymied in political dispute. Since Lake Sakakawea forms the northern border of lignite-rich Mercer County, and the Missouri River its eastern boundary, the low cost of transporting water supplies was an important factor in the decision to locate so many proposed plants here.

Transporting the output also appeared to require a minimal investment. The railway system was originally designed to move wheat from the vast hinterland to a distant metropolitan market, and would serve equally well for moving lignite more locally, where the conversion facility was not located at the mine mouth itself. The Burlington Northern Railway (of which the Northern Pacific has been a part since the mid-twentieth century) was itself a major owner of western coal reserves, and eager to oblige the industry. Little resistance was anticipated to the construction of the gas and water pipelines and high power transmission lines, which would also be necessary for production and export of the electricity and synthetic gas, because of the area's low population density and its residents' inexperience with such installations.

The lignite of the western plains could be obtained at a lower cost than eastern coal for a variety of reasons. Because of their investments in western coal, the loan policies of many large financial firms discouraged its development elsewhere (Environmental Policy Center 1974). The concentration of Mercer County coal ownership and mineral rights also simplified the tract-leasing process. In 1975, 40 percent of Mercer County's coal was owned by only six government agencies and one private corporation (Jacobs 1975:138).[6] The federal Department of Interior had reserved mineral rights on homestead lands after 1909, when this area was still being settled; the railroad was permitted to retain such rights when selling off its land grants; the Bureau of Indian Affairs held the coal on the Fort Berthold Reservation in trust for the Three Affiliated Tribes; the state of North Dakota also reserved mineral rights on much of their school land grants sold after 1935; and the Federal Land Bank and the North Dakota State Bank had both accumulated coal ownership when bankrupt farmers defaulted on loans during the Depression. Even where surface owners remained in possession of the minerals below their fields and pastures, in many cases the rights to exploit them had already been sold off to brokers and speculators during the hard times of the 1930s or the oil boom of the 1950s.

The energy corporations exploiting domestic coal could legitimately portray themselves as responding to the Presidential call for national energy independence, and they anticipated government cooperation in leasing western federal coal rights at bargain prices. These expectations were frustrated for some time by a moratorium on federal coal leases imposed by Secretary of the Interior Rogers Morton. The ban was supposed to remain in effect until a coherent coal development policy and comprehensive land reclamation legislation could be worked out. Although environmentalist organizations insisted that these conditions were never adequately met, the moratorium was summarily lifted in 1976 by President Ford's incoming Interior Secretary, Thomas Kleppe, under intense pressure from the energy lobby. At that time, four and a half million acres in North Dakota alone were opened for exploration (Berg 1977:74). Extensive federal coal acreage was subsequently leased at low cost in Mercer County, permitting the expansion and more efficient operation of mining operations there. As the scope of lignite development plans became clear, North Dakota's Governor Arthur Link voiced the concerns of environmental and community development interests: "Is the massive shift from eastern to western coal really necessary or economically responsible on a national basis? Will the production create boom towns and unemployment as in historic coal regions?" (*Bismarck Tribune* August 22, 1974).

Clearing the Way | The final attraction for developing western coal was financial and regulatory incentives. Federal and state policies and decisions structured events in Mercer County, circumscribing the limits of local power and action. The energy lobby is powerful in Washington, D.C., because of the strategic importance of oil to the nation and because it represents some of the nation's largest corporations, banks, and investment firms, all with extensive interests in western coal. Not surprisingly, federal energy policy has been responsive to the energy lobby, which has also been successful in influencing public opinion. For example, during the oil supply shortages of 1973 and 1974,[7] the oil industry campaigned to frighten the American people and public officials with images of a weakened United States, helplessly dependent upon the whims of fickle foreign suppliers. According to Sherrill (1972), efforts to exaggerate the perception of the energy crisis began as early as 1968, in order to pressure the Federal Power Commission to allow increases in natural gas prices. The price increases of 1971 and 1972 were publicly blamed on OPEC alone, and the oil embargo of 1973 offered the opportunity for additional pressure on the U.S. government to improve the profitability of the domestic oil production in which big oil and finance corporations had invested so heavily.

The industry's energy crisis campaign was successful in shaping the federal policy of national energy self-sufficiency and Project Independence, which focused on western coal development. Beginning in the Ford administration, a wave of domestic energy development overrode the environmental protection movement, extending offshore oil drilling, authorizing the Alaska Pipeline, and allowing an increase in natural gas prices. Meeting domestic energy needs remained a primary concern during the presidency of Jimmy Carter. Carter promoted public education for energy conservation and efficiency, on the one hand, while encouraging domestic oil exploration and the growth of the coal, gas, and nuclear industries on the other.

The centerpiece of Carter's energy policy was the creation of a federal Department of Energy, to encourage and organize domestic production of all energy resources, and of the government-owned Synthetic Fuels Corporation. The latter became an arena for explicit corporate and governmental cooperation and support in the launching of financially risky private enterprises.[8] The Synthetic Fuels Corporation as originally proposed was to have $90 billion for loan and price guarantees. Congress later scaled these back to $18 billion, but the race for big subsidies had already begun. The coal gasification project for Mercer County was first in line, as an "experimental" project already asking for support from the Department of Energy. A partisan battle ensued,[9] but in the end, President Ronald Reagan approved the Synfuel Corporation's price supports for synthetic gas and a $1.8 billion loan guarantee (later reduced to $1.47 billion) for building the Mercer County plant, partly as a conciliatory gesture to the Democrats, and also because he too was responsive to the energy lobby, and had restaffed the Synfuels Corporation with men of his own choosing.

Financial support for the coal gasification project was finally authorized in 1983. This represented the culmination of a long struggle to launch the project, which had begun in 1972 on the drawing boards at the Michigan-Wisconsin Pipe Line Company.[10] Because of its questionable economic feasibility, the project failed to attract private investors, and early attempts to win federal support bogged down in Congress. At the suggestion of North Dakota Governor Arthur Link, who wished to avoid being branded a radical environmentalist in an election year, Michigan-Wisconsin invited other gas and utilities companies to join it in a five-member consortium to undertake the project jointly. This group, called the Great Plains Gasification Associates (GPGA), planned to finance construction through a surcharge paid by their regular gas customers. Opponents objected to the proposal on the grounds that consumers should not have to bear the costs of development, but it was finally approved after heated debate before the Federal Energy Regulatory Commission.

Investors considered the Great Plains project risky because it would produce expensive gas in an unstable energy market. With the future of oil prices uncertain, Congress was reluctant to support such a venture. And yet experts claimed the plant was the best and the brightest of the synfuels industry, and valuable at least as a research and development site for meeting the nation's long-range energy needs. This image was promoted by the project's supporters; when the GPGA consortium was formed, in an effort to obtain federal financing, the president of the senior partner, Arthur Seder of American Natural Resources, said: "The project is no longer merely a corporate effort. Now it is more in the nature of a national effort to introduce a totally new form of clean energy. Gasification, we feel, is the most economic and environmentally sound way to use our nation's coal resources" (*Hazen Star* June 8, 1978).

Once the rising market prices and political support of the 1970s had improved their profitability, the nonrenewable resources of the northern Plains and the Southwest became attractive to many investors. What had been sporadic interest in oil drilling, oil shale mining, and coal gasification in Montana, Wyoming, the Four Corners area, and North Dakota suddenly became feasible corporate ventures. The scale of lignite mining operations increased throughout the region, and developers submitted grandiose plans for scores of new mines, coal-fired power stations, and synthetic fuels plants, which included pipelines, transmission lines, railroad spurs, and new roads.

The people of North Dakota first became aware of the grand plans of big utilities and energy corporations for accelerated coal development in 1971, with the release of the *North Central Power Study*. This document was the product of joint efforts by nineteen private utility corporations, six rural electrical cooperatives,[11] several public power districts and municipal power suppliers and the U.S. Department of the Interior's Bureau of Reclamation (Jacobs 1975:10). It recommended no less than forty-two sites throughout the northern Plains region for coal-burning electrical generation plants totalling 209,000 megawatts of capacity. Thirty coal gasification plants were proposed for southwestern North Dakota in 1973, along with plans for several new electricity-generating stations, mines, and expansion of existing facilities in and around Mercer County. These plans signaled the start of a major offensive on the part of energy capital to push at the state level for the exploitation of nonrenewable resources across the northern Plains. The response of state governments varied, but all were subject to mounting pressure to expedite the granting of siting, water, and air permits.

The large national coal companies (many of them big oil subsidiaries) and natural gas pipeline companies pushing these proposals found ready allies within the region. These pro-industry elements included not only the local real estate, banking, and commercial interest groups, but more important, the regional railroads and utilities. The Northern Pacific Railway was anxious to capitalize on its own enormous lignite holdings, as well as for the business of transporting the coal. The electric and gas utilities, including the rural electrical cooperatives, were eager to establish production and distribution linkages with the proposed mines and plants.

Opposition to energy industrialization from environmentalists and farmers also took shape immediately, resulting in heated political struggles between agricultural and other commercial interests throughout the region during the mid-1970s. This opposition was overwhelmed in the Southwestern states, Utah, Colorado, Arizona, and New Mexico, where the industries were restricted very little (Little 1975; Markusen 1980a). In the northern Plains states, the results varied: Wyoming proved to be the most accommodating to the energy interests, and Montana exercised the most control over their activities. North Dakota's response was the outcome of conflict between the powerful energy interests and a few well-placed opponents such as Democratic Governor Link, who urged caution. Representatives from Mercer County were split on how much restraint should be placed on developers, and the result was a moderate level of taxation and regulation somewhere between those set by Montana and by Wyoming (Nace 1978:1).[12]

The North Dakota legislature voted to set the "severance" tax on mining coal at fifty cents per ton, with increases tied to the wholesale price index. This flat rate tax was adopted instead of the percentage-of-value tax supported by the Democrats. The severance money was to be divided according to the following plan: 35 percent to a fund distributed by a coal development impact office to cities, counties, and other political subdivisions that were taxing entities and experiencing the adverse effects of the energy boom; 30 percent to a trust fund to generate income for the state's general fund; 30 percent to the state's general fund directly; and 5 percent to be divided among coal-producing counties in proportion to their contribution to the state's total coal production. Another tax was set on the gross receipts of coal conversion plants.[13] These revenues were to be distributed among affected counties, cities, school districts, and the state's general fund.[14]

Even with these taxes, there was a projected shortfall between tax revenues and the costs of coal development in North Dakota of $29 million by 1983, while 80 percent of the energy would go to consumers outside the state. When a bill was introduced in the North Dakota state legislature in 1979 to lower the severance tax still further, Tax Commissioner Byron Dorgan objected, invoking the popular (and populist) view of local history: "North Dakotans have been exploited for decades by out-of-state interests who want to buy what we produce at fire sale prices" (*Beulah Beacon* March 8, 1979).

Several considerations influenced North Dakota's government response to the coal boom. For many years business interests there had successfully promoted a view of lignite development as the answer to the state's economic woes, and its gradual initial build-up had proved to be relatively benign. Additional elements included the fragmentation of mainstream political opposition within the Democratic Party, the frustration of critical voices by the energy crisis atmosphere, a confusing proliferation of proposals, and the pro-development factions' use of parliamentary tactics, all of which worked against proactive long-term planning.

The dream of developing a lignite-based industrial sector capable of providing stability to North Dakota's agriculturally based economy had been promoted since the 1940s. A series of state-supported agencies[15] envisioned limited electrical generation as the basis for a set of small secondary industries that could use the cheap power to manufacture lignite products. When the use of coal intensified in the 1960s, many saw it as the fulfillment of this vision. A report presented at the 1964 North Dakota Economic Conference expressed hope that a diversified industrial economy would alleviate the state's chronic unemployment and low incomes:

> The economic development of North Dakota will, to an increasing degree, be linked to the increased production of lignite coal. Coupled with this economic development will be a larger per capita income, a better way of

life for North Dakota citizens, and a less fluctuating pattern of economics than a purely agricultural economy can achieve. . . . From a long-range standpoint, it will be highly desirable that as many products manufactured by or from lignite be produced locally as [a more] profitable resource use than is available if the markets and end uses are far away from North Dakota. (Quoted in Nace 1978:34)

The idea that manufacturing would grow up together with power generation was an essential feature of this plan; it was needed to ensure economic stability, since the coal industry is notoriously subject to booms and busts, and to avoid the disadvantages of merely supplying cheap raw materials to other regions. The projected life span of the proposed coal-fired electrical stations was claimed even by proponents to be only thirty to forty years at best, and only a healthy secondary industrial sector could ensure a more steady long-term market for North Dakota's lignite-generated electricity.

Mercer County's past experience with industrialization had been mixed. The construction of the Garrison Hydroelectric Dam in the late 1940s and early 1950s had flooded vast tracts of prime agricultural land along the northern edge of the county.[16] A Hazen man told me how his father lost their farm this way, bought out cheaply by "crooked government agents." According to him, "the people affected never really had a chance to protest the situation; they were much too poor to hire a lawyer, not organized. . . . They had to just grin and bear it." Mineral rights on most of the agricultural land had been sold off to pay taxes during the 1930s, so most farmers and ranchers since then have felt similarly powerless, having little choice but to lease. Others had more positive memories, like this county official: "I was born and raised in this coal country, and in the Great Depression I worked at the Zap mine, as did a lot of others. It was a way for us to pay the bills. Without the mines Beulah and Hazen would not be the prosperous cities they are. Industry kept the towns alive" (quoted in the *Hazen Star* August 26, 1976).

Several small lignite-burning plants had existed previously, including one on Beulah's Main Street, and were an unthreatening aspect of everyday life. Most of the larger power stations constructed in the 1960s were built by rural electrical cooperatives, which were strongly linked to the Democratic Party and enjoyed good relations with the North Dakota Farmers Union and with farm people in general. Basin Electric Power Cooperative, the largest producer of electricity in the region, received a low-interest Rural Electrification Administration loan in 1962 to construct a 200-megawatt plant on the Missouri River near Stanton, in Mercer County; Basin had tripled this plant's capacity by the end of the decade.

United Power Association, a Minnesota-based rural electrical cooperative, had built a similar plant at the same location, and the Minnkota Power Cooperative, one at the nearby town of Center.

These installations were welcomed by most of the local population, and since they were constructed sequentially, the influx of construction and operation work force was not particularly traumatic. In many cases, financially troubled farmers were eager for an opportunity to lease and sell land at good prices, and for the extra income of family members who received employment. This attitude is reflected in the study of the social impact of coal development conducted by a team of sociologists in 1974, which included the area of Stanton in Mercer County. According to their report, the people tended to be complacent about the effects of coal development, and perhaps felt that it offered a brighter future than agriculture:

> Interviewing to date has revealed that pro-development farmers in Stanton are quite typical of persons in this region of North Dakota. They are operating on an economically marginal level and are running small farms for the most part. They do not evince a deep attachment to their land and do not report finding the farming life-style compellingly attractive. Residents are absorbing the effects of the recently constructed power plants and the influx of operations personnel. (Gold et al. 1974:177)

Similarly, another survey conducted in eastern Mercer County in 1975 found that 51.7 percent of respondents said their communities were improving with energy development, while only 10 percent thought they were "going downhill" (Schriner et al. 1976).

But these conclusions are contradicted by a study conducted in 1975 by Mid-Continent Survey of Minneapolis, which found that "the people of North Dakota . . . are not persuaded by the plea of energy corporations that cheap energy should continue to be provided to the American people at the expense of North Dakota air, water, and land" (quoted in *Beulah Beacon* September 28, 1978). Thirty percent of those surveyed thought life would improve with economic growth, but 34 percent said change would be for the worse. The latter were concentrated in southwestern North Dakota where the industrial projects and Mercer County are located.

The dominance of rural electrical cooperatives over investor-owned utilities in the developments of the 1960s was crucial in opening the door for the larger-scale projects of the 1970s. First, the relatively unthreatening nature of their operations lulled the local public into viewing the whole industry as benign. Basin Electric, for example, had earned a good reputation by undertaking pollution control and land reclamation measures even before they were required by law. Even more important, the issue of large-scale coal development, including coal gasification, caused a break in the traditional alliance within the Democratic Party of the cooperatives with the powerful North Dakota Farmers Union. The Farmers Union had opposed the proposals of the 1970s as not being in the interests of farmers. The cooperatives, on the other hand, were vigorous supporters of a greatly expanded energy sector. Since many Farmers Union members were also active in the rural electrical cooperative organizations, the Farmers Union was forced to back down from active opposition. But this split prevented the Democratic minority from presenting a strong opposition to the pro-development Republican majority in the state legislature.

Cooperatives that had constructed coal-fired power stations in the 1960s all planned large projects in the 1970s, at a time when many proposals were also being mounted by investor-owned corporations. By establishing links with the rural electrical cooperatives, corporate energy developers were able to take advantage of their political leverage. This was the case with the Great Plains Gasification Associates, which was able to obtain a water permit for its coal gasification plant to be constructed near Beulah in part because of a deal with Basin Electric Cooperative to make it a joint project; Basin was to locate a large generating station on the same site and sell twenty percent of its power to the gasification plant.

The State Water Commission, headed by Governor Link, received water requests for twelve gasification plants and ten electrical generating plants in 1973 and 1974. This became for a time the only forum in the state capable of limiting the scale, pace, and type of projects to be built, yet the weak opposition to massive development forced the Governor to compromise with the lignite industry early in the permit negotiations. In the absence of a general plan for coal development, the water commission responded to requests on a case-by-case basis. Granting these water permits, however reluctantly, set a precedent that severely weakened the Governor's "go slow" policy, and committed the state to accelerated coal development even before the 1975 legislative session met to consider the state's policy for dealing with the coal industry.

Other circumstances combined to confuse the issue and frustrate the opposition's call for closer study of the harmful potential of such development. Theodore Nace points out that "the various projects undertaken in the 1960s by utilities in the state, long before out-of-state corporations became interested in more intensive development, put critics of strip mining in a bad position, since the practice was already established as a vital part of the state's economy" (1978:37). The public's attitude reduced the pressure for careful and critical examination of potential impacts of industrialization. In any case, with the constant stream of announcements, retractions, and reformulations of project proposals, some of them obviously unrealistic, it was difficult for anyone to be sure exactly what was on the table. The excitement of an apparently imminent economic boom encouraged the optimism of energy boosters, and discussions within the political mainstream did not focus on whether to permit large-scale development, but on the acceptable price for doing so. This attitude is expressed in an editorial published in a local newspaper in the county east of Mercer:

> Something big and wonderful is about to happen to a part of McLean County—initial development of a part of the county's coal fields in the Underwood-Washburn area and generation of electric power. . . . The development of the coal and power industries in the Underwood area, . . . could trigger a reverse in the county's economic and population curve . . . and no sound-thinking person should object to that prospect.
> With environmental standards satisfied, the complex should be nothing but good for the people of this county. Nonetheless, there is this over-riding question: Is North Dakota receiving its proper reward from the mining of coal and generation of power in the state?
> (*McLean County Independent* August 1973)

In this atmosphere, and with the traditionally pro-agricultural Democratic Party split into factions with opposing interests over large-scale coal development, it was not surprising that the 1975 state legislative session saw a resounding victory for the energy lobby (see Jacobs 1975:214–224). Numerous bills intended to protect the environment and the rights of citizens were defeated, such as proposals to require environmental impact statements for all major industrial projects and to allow surface owners who did not control mineral rights the power to veto strip mining of their land. The authority of government to regulate coal development was restricted and diffused over three departments, rather than concentrated in a central planning office as proposed by the Governor. The power of the State Water Commission to attach conditions to water permits was cut back, and the Public Service Commission was charged with overseeing land reclamation and with siting industrial facilities, but denied the power to refuse them a site.

In the end, state agencies approved the construction of three large conversion facilities in Mercer County, where there were already two modern coal-burning electrical generation plants—Basin Electric's and United Power Association's plants near Stanton—and a hydroelectric station at Garrison Dam near Pick City. A consortium of electric utilities headed by Montana-Dakota Utilities would construct a 440-megawatt coal-fired electrical plant on Coyote Creek south of Beulah. The Coyote plant, as it came to be called, was scheduled to start operation in 1981, and would require the strip mining of approximately 158 acres of land per year to feed its burners, plus additional land for storage of its waste of toxic fly ash from incompletely burned coal. Basin Electric Power Cooperative would build a similar two-unit power station next to the Great Plains coal gasification plant in the Antelope Creek valley northwest of the same town. As proposed, this power station was also scheduled to go on line in 1981, and would also use 158 acres of land per year for its mining. Also originally scheduled for completion in 1981, the Great Plains Coal Gasification plant itself, as initially approved for the Michigan-Wisconsin Pipe Line Company, was to have the capacity to produce 250 million cubic feet of synthetic gas per day. This plant would use about five hundred acres of land per year for its mining operations (*Bismarck Tribune* April 16, 1975), and would eventually require an entire township to store over one hundred thousand tons of waste per day, 4 percent of which was to be composed of unknown substances.

Ultimately, the lion's share of the bill for all this development was to be paid by the public, as taxpayers and consumers. Although developers would pay taxes once their projects were operating, local taxpayers would subsidize them during construction, and the companies would, in any case, pass the cost of taxes on to consumers, just as taxpayers subsidize energy development across the nation; the rural electrical cooperatives received low-interest government loans, the gasification project had a federal loan guarantee and price supports, and public utilities benefitted from tax breaks and government investment in their operations.

Although the corporations got most of what they wanted, the deal represented a compromise with the interests of North Dakota localities, and was the result of an established political process that included elected representatives of the people. This last gave the plans legitimacy despite the constraints placed on development opponents, and absolved both the corporations and state organizations from appearing to impose development plans on naive or unwilling citizens. The role of the state in facilitating capital accumulation was thereby obscured, and all attendant problems transmuted from issues of class conflict into mere administrative matters.

Selling Development

An aggressive corporate strategy had achieved conditions acceptable to them from federal and state authorities for exploiting Mercer County's coal. It remained to convince the local people that they had nothing to fear from this prospect. Advertising, public relations and political lobbying were important components in coal developers' strategy for promoting legislation and community attitudes favorable to their interests. They launched sophisticated campaigns in the early 1970s, hiring tenacious lobbyists (who actually outnumbered state legislators in every session from 1975 through the end of the boom) and public relations representatives skilled at presenting a positive, friendly image for the distant and impersonal corporations. The variety of selling points projected in these efforts reflected the industries' need to address a range of concerns among residents in Mercer County, among whom desire for economic growth remained in tension with other values.

To promote public approval of their proposed coal gasification plant, the Michigan-Wisconsin Pipe Line Company sent letters out in 1974 to every Chamber of Commerce in North Dakota, offering to send representatives on request. Within six months, company spokesmen had visited commercial associations in thirty towns, distributing information, presenting slide shows, and responding to questions. One of these public relations officers made a habit of bringing his four-year-old son to these meetings with him to emphasize his "family man" image. The company prepared a film including shots of western North Dakota scenery and people, entitled "Looking Ahead—North Dakota Considers Coal Gasification," for use in such presentations.

Company spokesmen also appeared on eight radio and television stations broadcasting in most of the state (*Bismarck Tribune* August 17, 1974), and Michigan-Wisconsin was also assiduous in its state government lobbying efforts. According to the same news article, "Company personnel have also become regulars at government meetings in the Capitol. They're on hand to listen and make suggestions at state executive and legislative committee meetings during which issues, such as taxation and plant siting, that could affect the project, are discussed." In 1974 such efforts were organized industrywide. Members of the coal industry formed the North Dakota Lignite Council, whose activities included arranging tours of mining and conversion operations for legislators, sending speakers to address civic meetings, and preparing "educational" materials for public distribution.

Perhaps not surprisingly, the top public relations officers often had careers spanning corporate, government, and media employment, and were able to make use of contacts and skills acquired in all these areas. For example, the two point men for the Michigan-Wisconsin community appearance tour mentioned above included one who had worked in communications for Dow Chemical, at the Michigan Secretary of State office, and in the South Dakota Governor's office before joining

Michigan-Wisconsin's parent company. The other was a former radio program director. Similarly, the chief of the Great Plains Gasification Associates' public relations office in Bismarck began his career as a radio news reporter, covering a gubernatorial campaign in Minnesota.

Some of the industries' advertising efforts were aimed at a national audience. Exxon Corporation paid for a seven-page spread in *Newsweek* to promote western strip mining. Ads such as the following appeared in national magazines in the early 1970s: "The clean Western coal is the people's coal. And the people need it . . . now" (quoted in Berg 1977:74). Cartoon booklets promoted the political agenda of the energy lobby. In 1982 the Northwest Orient in-flight magazine ran a sympathetic story quoting only industry public relations spokesmen in praise of the enlightened social planning of Mercer County developers:

> There will certainly be some changes in the rural lifestyle as a result of coal gasification. Yet the company is taking pains to assure that the new industry will marry harmoniously with agriculture, the environment, and the community. The coal plant has been designed to consume many of its own by-products. One by-product, anhydrous ammonia, will supply fertilizer for area farmers; another, coal too fine for gasification, will help generate electricity at a nearby rural electrical cooperative. While surface mining will interrupt the farming of some 370 acres of farmland a year, that land will be continuously reclaimed and the topsoil preserved.
> (*Northwest Orient Passages* March 1982:17)

Within North Dakota, Consolidation Coal Company paid radio stations to keep playing a tune called "Be Proud You Know a Coal Minin' Man!" (Berg 1977:74). Corporate advertising also made use of the "patriotic duty" argument associated with the energy crisis: "It will take nearly four years to build the $2 billion Great Plains project. It will be completed at a time when domestic supplies of oil and natural gas are becoming increasingly hard to find and expensive to produce. And so the project is one promising step in the battle to break the grip of foreign energy suppliers" (GPGA promotional flyer). "We North Dakotans must share with the nation in this grave crisis. . . . We must be generous as we have in the past" (quoted in Berg 1977:74). Several more compelling selling points were played up as well. The most important of these were jobs for North Dakotans and the generalized prosperity said to accompany progress. Other common themes were a nonthreatening posture toward agriculture, stressing practices for reclaiming strip-mined land and the corporations' commitment to "traditional family values" and community responsibility. These themes are illustrated in company pamphlets:

Much has been said about the excellent "quality of life" in North Dakota. But, as a practical matter, it takes jobs, economic stability, and personal income for one to enjoy the amenities that the state has to offer. These needs can be met and our agricultural-based economy complemented through the orderly development of our lignite reserves.
(North American Coal Corporation brochure)

For every permanent job in the lignite industry, another 4.5 jobs are required to provide foods and services, and for every $1 million in expenditures by the lignite industry, approximately 13 direct and 60 secondary employment opportunities are provided for North Dakotans.
(North Dakota Lignite Council "Lignite Facts" brochure)

Basin Electric Power Cooperative believes that a healthy, family-oriented agricultural economy is essential in the production of the nation's food supply and that low-cost electricity is a vital ingredient for economic prosperity and for maintaining the quality of rural life. (Basin brochure)

We are confident that our role in meeting the Nation's challenge for energy independence can be accomplished through the development of North Dakota's lignite reserves in a manner which will be overwhelmingly beneficial to all our citizens. (Robert E. Murray, President of North American Coal Corporation Western Division, in a brochure)

Such displays of respect for the agricultural tradition were belied by the images produced for consumption inside the corporate offices. There, the visual representation shows nothing of any use or value before the proposed developments. The lovingly framed "artists' conceptions" of the gasification plant depict its location as a desolate wasteland of dry and broken terrain, instead of the lush, gently rolling, and fertile farmland it actually was.

In an address to a North Dakota vocational education conference in 1974, the director of Michigan-Wisconsin, when speaking of the planned gasification plant, promised, "For this project the company is committed to hiring North Dakotans on a preferential basis" (*Bismarck Tribune* August 12, 1974). In the same article, the state director of vocational education cited the dramatic growth in state financial support for vocational education and in enrollments: "Students are now making a more realistic choice of future occupations."

Once the price for coal development in North Dakota had been set and decisions reached about which projects were to be permitted, the focus of public relations efforts shifted to the particular communities that would host the projects. Good community relations were essential to the orderly progress of the industrial construction and permitting process. The developers depended on the cooperation of local officials for zoning and construction permits and for housing, water, fire, police, schools, and social services for their employees. While many conflicts arose between the communities and the developers in the boom years, company officers scrupulously maintained the appearance of sympathetic helpfulness, while minimizing the financial responsibility of the corporations.

The public relations strategies employed by the energy corporations in selling development to the people of the county reflected close reading of what most people wanted from it. They wanted jobs and prosperity, not social change, and were encouraged to disregard the contradiction. Regardless of their attitudes toward the energy industry, people in Mercer County saw in the jobs promised by development an opportunity to keep their families together, by preventing the emigration of the young and unemployed, and by providing an opportunity for grown offspring who were living elsewhere to return. Some of these had acquired technical and managerial skills outside the area, and could be eligible for permanent well-paid positions in the new facilities. The companies' public relations efforts led local residents to expect a continuing source of employment from development, while de-emphasizing the financial risks and uncertain future of the boom.

Businessmen, land speculators, and the townspeople in general all subscribed to the traditional capitalist wisdom that progress brings prosperity, at least for those who are alert and astute enough to profit by it. From a local perspective, industrial development represented progress because it entailed more complex technology than agriculture, and would bring upgraded public infrastructure and services, along with population growth, in the towns. The expectation was that it would produce general prosperity as new wealth circulated through the local economy. New businesses would be generated by the workers spending their wages locally, and all would benefit from the services funded by the tax contributions of the energy corporations. Yet although progressivist arguments were certainly persuasive, nevertheless local culture also provided alternative beliefs and values, including those arising from agrarian populism, grassroots labor struggle, and the civic values of community and of Christian religious teaching, all of which offered moral alternatives to the ideology of free enterprise. These contradictory strands had long co-existed in Mercer County, and required of public relations agents a complex strategy not relying merely on an uncritical belief in "progress."

In their efforts to make energy development as palatable as possible to the local communities, Basin and the other corporations used many of the same themes familiar in their statewide campaigns. These included the portrayal of strip mining as compatible with agriculture, stressing the success of their (heavily fertilized) reclamation showpiece plots; optimistic predictions about the growth of secondary industry and service jobs in association with operating the large plants; and the use of patriotic symbols in the Great Plains plant logo—a large numeral "1" decorated in the Stars and Stripes, representing both the claim that this was the nation's first coal gasification project, and the intention of making the United States "number one" in synthetic fuels production, as well as a reminder that to stay first in the world, the United States had to be more independent of imported energy. The symbolic load of their slogan, "Pioneering alternative fuels for America," is unmistakable.

Other elements of their community relations management efforts were keyed into more specifically local concerns. Public statements and printed materials intended for local consumption stressed the corporations' long-term commitment to the well-being and prosperity of the local communities; their generating jobs for local workers and money for the local economy; the importance of well-planned economic growth and community expansion; and the local tradition of industrial activity and its progressive evolution in the future.

> The owners of Coyote [electrical generation station] realize that industries building large facilities must involve themselves in impact mitigation strategies, and through trial and error, meetings and consultations, work together with other industry, government, and local citizens to resolve the issues. Coyote owners are proud of their involvement and appreciative of the assistance and cooperation of the citizens of Mercer County in this process. (Coyote Station brochure)

> In the Beulah area alone, KRCM generates a considerable tax base, in addition to providing an annual payroll of about $2.3 million through mine operations. The average KRCM mine worker earns an annual wage of about $23,000. One of the sad truths about the history of the state of North Dakota is the exportation of its educated youth. A whelm [sic] of job opportunities has opened up in North Dakota with the increased development of coal. (Knife River Coal Mining Company brochure)

> We're not coming in, building a plant and walking away. We've got a responsibility to about 1000 people [to be employed at the gasification plant] when we decided to put the plant here. It's the company's responsibility to make darn sure things in the community are acceptable—more than acceptable—to everyone.
> (GPGA spokesman, quoted in *Beulah Beacon* February 4, 1982)

Industry presentations often played up the local tradition of industrial activity, and its march into the future. The antique coal-hauling cart displayed outside the GPGA administration building at its plant served two functions: to arouse nostalgia and sympathy for the quaint, simple technology of the past and to contrast that with the sleek modernity of the complex, clean, well-ordered plant before them. The theme of progress is similarly employed in photographs of the small and clumsy-looking steam shovels formerly used in local mines juxtaposed with high-quality prints of the sleek modern draglines, and shots of men posing in their giant buckets to set off their size.

The fascination with bigness is played upon when visitors are allowed to tour these industrial facilities. In the power plants, tour guides constantly point out the great power of the forces and equipment at work. Official tours culminate with a visit to the rooftop or the top-story windows, to survey the grand view as if from a castle battlement. In the mines, tour guides encourage guests to appreciate the impressive size of the machinery, lingering in its vicinity and allowing them to climb about on it. When the Beulah Mine held an open house on June 7, 1981, "The biggest attraction was the Queen Bee, KRCM's [Knife River Coal Mining Company] 1570-W dragline. The guests . . . were fascinated by the size of the machine, with its 75-cubic-yard-capacity bucket. . . . Another point of interest was the 120-ton coal haulers. People were able to climb the platform next to the truck and peer into the driver's seat" (*The Digger* June/July 1981).

A homey touch is added by painting such local-sounding names as "Beulah Belle," "Queen O'Buttes," and "Queen Bee" on the sides of the great draglines. Similarly, naming the generating stations Antelope and Coyote, after nearby creeks, lends them a little Western allure. Public relations statements even nodded in the direction of local political traditions of anti-corporation populism by emphasizing their business connections to Basin Electric—a publicly owned rural electrical cooperative.

Basin and Great Plains maintained a joint office building in Beulah, and Basin also had one in Hazen, so as not to offend Hazenites by appearing to favor Beulah. These offices were staffed with full-time public relations personnel who moved their families to Mercer County and made efforts to participate in community affairs. The projection of a friendly, neighborly image was perhaps the single most important feature of the industries' efforts to sell local people on the idea of development. When their employees became members of the local communities, the companies' claim that they truly cared about maintaining air and water quality carried more weight. If they could be perceived as neighbors, industry representatives would also benefit from local traditions of trust, reciprocity, and oral contract—their promises taken at face value. Similarly, public relations communications frequently pointed out that some of their middle-level management employees were from North Dakota and therefore genuinely cared about the problems of environmental pollution and community growing pains. This strategy was explicitly acknowledged by industry officials, who took some pride in its effectiveness. In 1982 the Great Plains public relations director for Mercer County informed me that they had "taken extra special care to be a part of the community" and that the American Natural Gas (ANR subsidiary) President Arthur Seder, whom the local newspapers referred to as "the man who made it [the gasification plant] happen," was "the kind of a guy who really cares about the local people."

The public relations tactics of the mining companies also reflected an implicit recognition of the symbolic importance of presenting their representatives as family men. Land agents sometimes brought their children along when bringing coal and right-of-way leases for farmers to sign. Since most landowners did not control mineral rights on their land and the land could be condemned in many cases anyway, these leases were obligatory. The presence of children served to personalize an unequal and potentially antagonistic encounter. One coal corporation owner formed the habit of dropping by the home of a farmer hostile to the mining activities, bringing his children to give the visit the appearance of a social call, as if they were friendly neighbors instead of enemies.

All of these efforts by developers to secure legality and public confidence in their plans represented the first level of implementation. Gaining a long series of federal and state regulatory approvals and completed financial deals also earned them momentum and a measure of legitimacy. Extending a velvet glove to the people of Mercer County encouraged their acquiescence, even if it did not silence the critics of energy development, many of them ideological populists of the old school, distrustful of all big business and government intentions. It remained for developers to work out the practical details of project implementation with local authorities, who represented the county's own interest groups. Although oppositional rhetoric continued to emphasize class conflict and exploitation, the transformation of these potentially explosive issues into largely administrative problems by the state-level "political process" was essentially complete.

Chapter Five | The Politics of Planning

When the dust had settled after the energy industries had gained their initial regulatory, financial, and permitting arrangements, the citizens of Mercer County were presented with the outcome. This included, in addition to expansion of existing mines, approval for three major new energy-producing plants originally scheduled to be constructed simultaneously and to begin production in 1981 (see Map 3). In other words, they faced the prospect of extremely rapid boomtown growth, with all of its potentially disruptive consequences. Serious conflicts could easily be foreseen—between farmers and encroaching strip mines, between profiteering entrepreneurs and inflation-weary customers, between newcomers and lifelong locals, and between the corporations and the communities. Such conflicts of interest had been transmuted into depersonalized administrative and procedural problems at the federal and state levels, and as this process reached the ground in Mercer County, it continued in the arena of planning for the coming boom. Although it could not contain them completely, planning provided an essential means for masking and channeling the underlying contradictions and conflict inherent in the energy development proposed for Mercer County. It was part of a larger arena in which alliances among larger controlling forces were forged to bring the agendas of disparate but powerful groups into alignment with one another, using both procedural and ideological means to promote a sense of collective goals and partnerships to achieve them.

In order for energy development to proceed smoothly and quickly, efforts to reorganize the environment for the benefit of developers had been presented to the people in Mercer County in terms of the potential advantages to them—as a vehicle for jobs, growth, modernization, and prosperity, to be achieved through a partnership with big capital. The planning process, which became the focus of local political activity by the late 1970s, integrated the goals of capital accumulation and state legitimation by providing convincing documentation for the predicted benefits, on the one hand, and a set of procedures for rationally managing the predicted problems on the other. Since the project's evolution had begun at the highest levels of power and proceeded downward from there, as described in Chapter 4, the more powerful political and economic interests had been able to position themselves to shape the projects, define the planning parameters, and limit their own responsibility for adverse results. This was done while providing a legally delimited space for public participation at the local level. Even though the localities had great potential power to affect the general course of development, given their veto power over land-use decisions, in practice its exercise was constrained both by an institutional apparatus that excluded some forms of resistance and by the ideological power of an alliance for progress purporting to work in the best interests of everyone.

Nonetheless, those to whom development plans were most directly damaging were able to use the system to achieve a measure of compromise and compensation. Elected county officials understood the farmers' distrust of corporate developers, and some were willing to push for protective contingencies on industrial permits. Watchdogs and whistle-blowers among unionized mine workers called public attention to problems in land reclamation practices at the strip mines. In doing so, they were emboldened both by their tradition of confronting management and by the presence of large numbers of fellow union members among the construction force of the new energy facilities. Together with environmental experts and individuals who feared local entities were selling out too cheaply, the opponents of energy industry practices fulfilled a vital mission. Their efforts received ample coverage from local journalists and were a constant annoyance to pro-development officials, yet they helped to safeguard the long-term financial and environmental future of the county. Local opposition was less efficacious on other quality-of-life issues, since official procedures did not leave room for discussion of most nonquantifiable dimensions of local and community life.

The interests, conflicts, and ideologies already current in Mercer County helped to shape responses to the energy boom. Different interest groups emerged with unequal results from their participation in the rational procedures of planning. Their relations were also transformed in the process.

Anticipating Adverse Impacts

Mercer County residents already had had experience with economic and social change, but never on this scale of intensity or with so much demand for an organized response. Development interests, government agencies, and professional planners all insisted that coherent, strictly enforced planning policies were the panacea for avoiding an intolerably chaotic disruption of local community well-being. They argued that since development was arriving in Mercer County later than in other energy boomtowns of the northern Plains, the lessons for planning from their earlier experience could be applied here from the beginning, making for a best-case scenario in Mercer County. The potential negative effects of rapid growth could be anticipated, legislation enacted to mitigate them, and the citizens of the county invited to participate in the process.[1]

During the energy boom, literally hundreds of publications were produced analyzing the impact of energy development on the region. These included theoretical treatments of general planning issues (Markusen 1980b; Rodgers 1976; Summers and Clemente 1976; Yamaguchi and Kuczek 1984), technical models for assessing impact (Cortese and Jones 1976; Dalstead et al. 1974; Markusen 1978), discussions of assessment methodology (Cortese and Jones 1977; Finsterbusch and Wolf 1977), studies of changes associated with rapid industrial growth elsewhere in the region (Carnes and Friesma 1973; Greenstein 1978; Leistritz et al. 1982; Murdock et al. 1982), a wealth of case studies (including Community Service Program 1975; Gilmore and Duff 1974 1975; Gold 1974a; McKeown and Lantz n.d.) and bibliographies compiling all of these studies (Berg 1977; Cortese and Cortese 1978; Miller and Miller 1980).

Despite the abundance of materials, knowledge, and insight gained from this experience, it was shared mainly in academic and professional journals and conferences, and was not readily accessible to the people of Mercer County. This was true even of papers designed to raise questions for public discussion (for example, Christiansen and Clack 1976; Clemente 1975; Nellis 1974; Smith et al. 1976). Only a few publications were aimed at educating the public about the issues and problems of regional energy development (including Berg 1977; Doyle and Reinemer 1979; Jacobs 1975; League of Women Voters 1978), and most of these lacked funds for extensive distribution.

Most of the information available to the Mercer County public about the probable consequences of the proposed energy development came in the formal environmental impact statements commissioned by the developers. These official documents served to set the agenda for public discussion, delimiting the legitimate areas for discussion and negotiation. In overseeing the production of these documents, developers play both the role of advocate and that of evaluator of their own projects. This contradiction is particularly strong in the case of federal coal-leasing impact statements, commissioned by the Bureau of Land Management. Much of the coal development in the west was based on federal coal leases, so the government was itself a major industrial developer.

Since the passage of the National Environmental Policy Act in 1969, such environmental impact documents have been required for all proposed public works developments in the U.S., in order to ensure that environmental concerns are considered during the decision-making process. The law requires that federal agencies responsible for licensing the environmental consequences of large-scale energy projects must include social and economic impacts in their assessments, and that developers are responsible for ameliorating negative social and economic effects (Council on Environmental Quality 1979), but critics charge that the language is imprecise and in practical terms unenforceable. Nevertheless, the public review of environmental impact statements provides an important forum for pressuring industry to accept responsibility for more of the adverse impacts of their projects (Walker et al. 1978); however, most often they are accepted uncritically. As little more than a formality, they provide the spurious appearance of having actually addressed a full range of environmental concerns.

Impact statements are required by law, but the methodology and analysis employed has been largely left up to the developers. The engineers and economists who usually author the documents tend to interpret "environmental" in terms of the physical or natural surroundings, and give scant attention to the social and cultural impacts of a project, although these are often of great importance to the members of the affected community (Friedman 1978). Project recommendations are often supported by economic cost–benefit analyses which simply omit those qualities that are difficult to quantify and monetize, such as aesthetic, emotional, and spiritual values.[2] For example, discussion of the consequences of population growth is often limited to a consideration of additional municipal service needs, and those of economic growth to "vague references to increased tax revenues and employment opportunities" (Berry n.d.:7).

Since developers wish to proceed with their projects as expeditiously as possible, while minimizing their financial responsibility for adverse social and environmental consequences, there is considerable pressure to produce documents that emphasize the positive benefits of the proposed development. In fact, impact assessments are usually conducted late in the decision-making process, after a particular project has already been decided on, and so play no part in the actual formulation of proposed developments but only in their implementation. In the case of Mercer County, where several projects were proposed simultaneously, the practice of filing separate and limited impact statements for each mine expansion and plant facility made it difficult to piece together an overall assessment of their combined effects.

In spite of the wealth of data available from analogous energy boomtowns already developed in the region, the official environmental impact statements for Mercer County projects were typical of their genre in consistently lacking any temporal, comparative, or theoretical consideration of the social changes that were likely to occur. The lack of sociological analysis behind social impact assessments is striking. They tend to assume the existence of "an undifferentiated public interest" (Friesma and Culhane 1976:348), rather than social groups with conflicting interests (Peele 1974:118), who stand to benefit and bear the costs of development unequally. In fact, low-income residents are found to bear the heaviest costs in many projects (Krawetz 1981:18–19; Peterson and Gemmell 1977:381). The values and interests of local business leaders, which tend to coincide with those of the developers, are represented disproportionately over those of the larger community (Berry n.d.:19; White 1977). Impact assessments generally evince an ingenuous acceptance of "economic growth" as a positive benefit, without regard to the nation's historic experience of its human costs, such as loss of community cohesiveness, self-sufficiency, and local autonomy; disruption of family ties and traditional lifeways; and increasing social and economic inequality.

With all their shortcomings, the impact statements represented the most complete assessment carried out on the future environmental and social impacts of energy development in Mercer County. Few of the area's residents read them anyway, preferring to leave this arduous and tedious task to planning specialists and elected officials. The general public relied for its information on newspaper articles, the accounts of those who had visited other boomtowns in the region, and above all on their historical experience with industry in the county, which most saw as environmentally regrettable, but socially benign and economically beneficial.

All local people had a big stake in development, but until the permitting process reached the county level, they had little real opportunity to voice either their concerns or their support. Farmers, miners, and merchants, along with local governmental entities, each had their own interests in identifying what the adverse impacts of boom development would be and working out in advance how to handle them. During this initial period, groups coalesced around planning issues and began to articulate their stands. All of them agreed that the industries should be made to pay for the impacts of their development projects, such as road damage and housing shortages. This early activism was essential in alerting elected officials to many potential problems. As negotiations proceeded among politicians and industry officials over how to define and attribute such negative impacts, and establish procedures for mitigating them, local residents participated in the public debate by writing to their state representatives, speaking out at public meetings, and attracting media coverage. They were also eager to talk to me about their concerns, in hopes that my work would would give them visibility. The following description of the anticipated problems is a composite drawn from many sources and reflects the contested state of knowledge about what to expect from development at this crucial period of project entry.

The harmful environmental consequences of strip mining were of special concern to the agriculturalists. They called attention to several potential problems, including the depletion of groundwater; the questionable feasibility of cropland reclamation; hazards posed by pipelines and transmission lines; air, soil, and water pollution; and damage to land contours affecting water drainage and soil erosion.

Lignite beds are the primary aquifers, or water-bearing strata, in this semi-arid soil. The impact statement for a proposed expansion of mining activity in neighboring Dunn County projected that groundwater levels would be lowered by 33 feet at a distance of one mile from the excavation, and about 7.5 feet at two miles (*Bismarck Tribune* September 17, 1974). The experience of farmers living in the vicinity of existing strip mines in Mercer County indicated that these effects would be exacerbated by hilly terrain, and they were concerned about receiving compensation if their wells went dry.

Many questions were raised about the reclamation of mined-out land for farming. In his response to a draft environmental impact statement for proposed federal coal leasing in North Dakota, Governor Link questioned the wisdom of hasty expansion of strip mining on (among others) environmental grounds: "It assumes adequate land reclamation to be an established fact, but it has yet to be demonstrated on arid and semi-arid western lands. While some revegetation has been accomplished in North Dakota, no revegetated area has yet been subjected to sustained grazing or farming activities" (*Bismarck Tribune* August 22, 1974).

The fragility of this grassland environment and the unequal power of agriculturalists and energy corporations are both illustrated by the experience of ranchers with oil exploration activities in the dry rangeland of western North Dakota and Montana. Here, a typical ranch consists of a series of connected draws or little grassy valleys. Heavy drilling vehicles driving over this land even a few times was found to create a devegetated track and a dust coating carried by wind throughout the valley system. Dust-covered grass ceases to grow and cattle refuse to eat it, so what was a very profitable ranch the year before can be rendered useless. Efforts to collect damages in these cases failed.

In an effort to allay the fears of local farmers, land reclamation test plots were prepared in Mercer County. Where the original subsoil and topsoil were put back, the initial results were acceptable for pasturage, but required heavy inputs of fertilizer to produce crops at anything like normal levels. And whatever the technical success of land reclamation, there remained the problem of enforcement. Existing mines in the county were already many years behind on their reclamation schedules, and the Public Service Commission—charged with enforcement—had little credibility among farmers.

Gas and water pipelines and electrical transmission wires posed additional nuisances and hazards for the farmers whose land they crossed. Farmers were concerned that pipelines be buried deeply enough so that they would not be struck by machinery when working the fields, and also that the earth displaced by the pipelines be redistributed in such a manner that drainage would not be adversely affected. They also wished the electrical transmission lines to follow section lines rather than cutting across their fields. This was in order to avoid the inconvenience of farming around the towers, and also because they would obstruct sprinkler irrigation.

Industry spokesmen insisted that the high voltage electrical transmission wires posed no health threat to livestock or humans, despite growing evidence of a cancer risk, since little energy was lost from them. Farmers countered this claim by staging demonstrations in which a fluorescent light bulb spontaneously glowed when held up by a man standing beneath the wires. Industry claims that the wires did not interfere with radio and television reception were similarly refuted by experience. Perhaps the most far-fetched attempt to sell the idea of transmission towers to farmers was the suggestion that they would provide shade for livestock. As one farmer scoffed, "Will they put up awnings on them or what?" In the face of the inconvenience and hazards posed by these installations on farm land, farmers complained that they were being asked to sacrifice too much for the dubious benefit of the nation that "needed their coal." One farmer's answer summed up their general response: "I'm not *that* patriotic!"

Other concerns about expanded mining included its effect on

wildlife (and hunting), the aesthetic spoiling of the landscape, and the immorality of removing good agricultural land from production. Farmers who would be forced to lease land to the mines worried that they would not receive compensation for the crops they would otherwise have raised.

Because coal conversion plants were a newer phenomenon here, and with a less familiar and more rapidly changing technology, no one was quite sure what sort of environmental pollution to expect. This was particularly true of the gasification plant, which was to be the first of its kind on the continent. As is generally the case with new technologies, the rate of technological development far exceeded the rate of discovery of its possible harmful effects. A county public health officer expressed some nervousness in saying to me, "We are the experimental animals."

Coal-burning plants had already been identified as a primary source of acid rain, which had severely damaged lakes and vegetation in eastern Canada and the northeastern United States. There, rain acidity levels had increased between a hundred and a thousand times previous levels between 1954 and 1974. A study by the American Lung Association also warned of potential respiratory problems from coal-burning air pollution (*Bismarck Tribune* August 31, 1974). This problem was exacerbated by the use of pollution control devices that merely removed solid particles while releasing gases such as sulphur dioxide and nitrogen oxides into the atmosphere. These quickly degrade to sulfuric acids in the absence of neutralizing solid particles. Developers promised that new plants would employ the most advanced technology for smokestack "scrubbers" to remove nearly all toxic substances from their emissions. The toxins thus removed would have to be disposed of locally in other ways, however, so this advance actually intensified the toxic waste problem for the local people.

Industry hailed western coal as having a relatively low sulphur content as compared with eastern coal, but other studies showed that when taken as a function of its energy-producing potential rather than its weight (in order to adjust for its relatively high water content), western coal actually had *higher* sulphur levels (Jacobs 1975:101).[3] While acid rain caused by plant emissions did not pose a problem locally, since the soil was, if anything, too alkaline, there were potential downwind problems and the effects of other emissions were largely unknown. Burning coal was known to release carbon dioxide into the atmosphere, which, scientists were beginning to warn, contributed to the problem of global warming.

Significant reductions in air quality were predicted in the official environmental impact statements. Mercer County air had Class II protection status for the prevention of pollution levels that will adversely affect the public health. However, proximity to the Badlands National Park and its Class I air protection status, for prevention of significant deterioration, including visibility, put a lid on emissions allowable in Mercer County. Reductions in visibility were prohibited in Class I regions by the Clean Air Act, so the industries sought revisions that would allow reclassification of the park's air status to allow further pollution. It was hoped that the Antelope Valley electrical generating station and gasification plant would be relatively clean facilities, but the Coyote plant built in the late 1970s by itself produced half of the area's allowable pollution increment.[4]

An environmental group raised questions about the extent of possibly harmful trace elements in the area's coal reserve, most of which were not covered by existing government regulations; the elements would be released from the plants as either solid, liquid, or air emissions. A study by the Mitre Corporation[5] estimated that a commercial coal gasification plant using North Dakota lignite would emit in one year 28 million pounds of arsenic, 2 million pounds of cadmium, 20 million pounds of lead, 108 million pounds of manganese, and 400,000 pounds of mercury (*Dakota Counsel* 5[6] 1982:7). Hearing this, local stockmen remembered the death of cattle in the 1960s near the town of Bowman in southwestern North Dakota, due to molybdenum contamination from a coal-using uranium plant. According to an impact statement prepared for a proposed gasification plant in neighboring Dunn County, coal samples showed elevated levels of arsenic and mercury in the lignite. Yet this impact statement went so far as to state that, "Considering the amount of coal that will eventually be mined (approximately 12.9 million tons yearly for one plant), no conclusions can possibly be drawn pertaining to the location and concentration of trace elements in the coal from known or existing data" (*Bismarck Tribune* June 14, 1974).

Concerns were raised in Mercer County about the large amounts of fly ash and sludge containing such toxins, which would require additional land for storage and from here could pollute ground and surface water by leakage. In fact, the Great Plains consortium applied for a permit to bury 110,000 tons of fly ash per day, 4 percent of which would be an unknown substance. Because of the Antelope Valley Station's proposed sophisticated scrubbing devices designed to reduce air pollution, there were fears that the plant's solid wastes would contain particularly high levels of soluble salts and toxic elements. Eventually, storing the waste from the Antelope Valley Station and the Great Plains plant would require an entire township, and even then could not be reliably contained.

As for the probable social and economic impacts of energy development in Mercer County, less detailed information was available, in part because these aspects typically receive only sketchy attention in official environmental impact statements, and also because of the industries' systematic attempts to downplay these consequences and to avoid financial responsibility for them. Nevertheless, it was obvious that providing public services for the increased population, many of them temporary construction workers and their families, and managing the rapid expansion of retail businesses and residential developments, would entail heavy financial and organizational burdens for local governments. Major upgrading and expansion of roads, schools, and police, and of fire, water, and sewer services would be needed long before the increased tax base could help to pay for them.

In 1970, there were six towns in Mercer County which, together with the agricultural families scattered over the countryside, had a combined population of 6,175. According to 1978 energy work force projections prepared by industry officials, this number could be expected to increase to a peak of 12,580 in 1981 (it actually reached 14,359 in 1983). In addition to creating acute housing shortages, studies of energy boomtowns across the region indicated that such population expansion was associated with increased rates of crime, alcoholism, spouse and child abuse, and mental depression. Public services such as education, fire protection, law enforcement, and water and sewer services were overburdened as well (Albrecht 1978; Burdge and Johnson 1977; Dixon 1978; Freudenberg 1979; Little 1977; Murdock and Leistritz 1979; Wolf 1975).

Although attempts to assess the specific impacts on Mercer County public services and finances were less detailed than the environmental impact studies, they did reveal serious problems. A 1974 report detailed some of the expected social and economic effects of the proposed Great Plains gasification plant. According to this report, which based its calculations on what proved to be lower than actual imported construction work force figures, the county would require some thirteen hundred new housing units, only four hundred of them permanent. Necessary improvements to the local transportation system included a new railroad spur, a gas pipeline, modernized safety facilities at the Beulah airport, repairs and alterations to about seventy-four miles of existing roads (costing about $3.6 million), in addition to intersection traffic control devices. The county's schools would require between seventeen and thirty-eight new classrooms, only two to fourteen of them permanently, costing up to $900,000. Needed expansion of medical care facilities included thirteen to twenty-one more beds at the Hazen Hospital (at a cost of $1.1 million), and additional staff, including three or four more physicians and a dentist. Only one additional physician would be needed permanently, however (*Bismarck Tribune* September 25, 1974:12). According to this report, Beulah and Hazen would also require three to four additional police officers during plant construction, and firefighters would need increased water supplies. Sanitary landfill facilities would have to be expanded. All of the towns would need improved municipal water supply facilities, and Beulah would need significant expansion of its wastewater treatment facilities.

Official reports of this sort invariably focused on critical shortfalls in physical infrastructure and municipal services. While these were certainly important concerns, they neglected other social concerns raised in studies of energy boomtowns across the region, such as shortages in mental health services, youth and senior citizen services, staffing for local government, recreational facilities, vocational rehabilitation, and employment services (Clemente and Summers 1973; Davenport and Davenport 1979, 1980; Denver Research Institute 1979; Uhlman 1978).

All of these problems would be due in part to sheer increase in numbers, but their impact would be disproportionately greater because of the condition of the towns prior to the development growth. Mercer County's towns were typical of other impacted communities in the region in that they were small in size, located more than one hundred miles from any urban metropolitan center, and had a low tax base and a large proportion of senior citizens, due to limited employment opportunities and consequent outmigration of youth. Most existing community facilities were operating at nearly full capacity, and there were few resources available to meet the human service needs of even the pre-impact population, other than those traditionally provided by family, friends, neighbors, and churches.

The expected population growth also threatened to disrupt community life in Mercer County. Conflict between newcomers and long-term local residents was endemic in the other energy boomtowns of the 1970s (Graber 1974; Jirovec 1979:80; Massey 1978; Tremblay et al. 1981). The more fearful anticipated a wave of crime, prostitution, and youth drug abuse as a result of the presence of the construction work force. In addition to the prospect of being overwhelmed by strangers and having to accommodate to new residents' different values and lifestyles, residents of Mercer County were concerned about outsiders taking the jobs that locals considered rightfully theirs.

All of these problems were expected to be provoked by the expansion of the energy industries, whose legal responsibilities were more narrowly defined and not responsive to challenge at the local level. The prospect of energy development offered opportunities for economic growth and modernization, the longed-for goals of small town boosters, but these would clearly come at a high price—a price to be paid in ways that no one could truly imagine or anticipate.

Preparing for the Boom | Faced with an urgent array of boomtown planning issues and big-city social problems, the people of this relatively isolated rural county had little chance to contemplate the larger structural conflicts also inherent in the process of economic transformation. Instead of designing and promoting community development plans inspired by local needs, those responsible for plannning in the county found themselves reacting to big developers' initatives on a piecemeal basis, spending more energy seeking redress according to received formulae for damage already done than in proactive efforts. In doing so, they not only worked within existing legal and procedural forms, but also followed the mandate of their constituency, since most in Mercer County supported at least some coal development, so long as industry paid its way. Focusing the energies of local officials on reacting to a multitude of specific problems also worked to channel conflict over development into an administrative arena, where it was largely disarmed and more easily managed.

Local efforts to meet planning challenges were also limited by the fact that the fundamental decisions about how much and what kind of development to allow had already been made by higher authorities. Federal agencies, the state legislature, the energy corporations, and public utilities cooperatives had already negotiated and formalized the financial arrangements, environmental protection measures, and state building, water, and air permits before approaching county and city officials with their applications for local permits. This top-down procedure had the effect of avoiding confrontation with local opposition until after the big plans were cut and dried, and the proposed projects had acquired an unstoppable momentum.

The possibilities of preventing adverse environmental, social, and economic disruption caused by industrial development through government regulation are always affected by the prevailing political climate. Big developers continually seek to streamline and rationalize the regulatory process so as to avoid dealing with the concerns of local residents (see Heiman 1988; Walker et al. 1978). Environmental controls were a particular target for efforts to combat progressive legislation during the 1970s. According to the anti-regulatory ideological formulation, "Government and obstructionist zealots [are] the cause of our economic problems" (Walker et al. 1978:48). In the case of the energy industry, the policies of the federal Environmental Protection Agency (EPA) were pro-development. When the regional EPA administrator visited Mercer County in 1978, he praised the cooperation between industry and local government, and declared: "Our purpose is to work for energy development in an environmentally sound way" (*The Common* August 17, 1978:1).

The permissive climate for coal-mining companies was brought to public attention by a group of whistle-blowing miners at the Indian Head Mine near Zap, who raised doubts about the state Public Service Commission's enforcement of land reclamation regulations. In 1976 five workers at this North American Coal Company mine filed formal charges of reclamation fraud against the company, thus notifying the Commission in a way that could not be ignored. Among the violations documented in the charges were failure to remove, store, and respread topsoil according to rule, long-term neglect of reclamation in areas not visible from the roads, and a rather spectacular alleged hoax during the Governor's visit to inspect reclamation efforts, in which, the workers claimed, the company hired men to drive around with empty seeders pretending to plant reclaimed land with prairie grasses. Although the Commission was faced with sworn statements accusing North American of these and other reclamation violations, the corporation's efforts to discredit the whistle-blowers may have influenced the Public Service Commission to find the corporations guilty of bending, but not of breaking, the law. That is, in spite of substantial evidence of a systematic and long-term pattern of violations and fraud, North American was determined to have broken the regulations "unintentionally" and received what amounted to a slap on the wrist. The company was ordered to hire reclamation specialists and to begin a reclamation education program at the mine. In defense of the Commission's ruling, it must be added that the law left them little choice. Since 1975, they were legally barred from fining or closing down violators, supposedly because of the negative repercussions this might have for the general public.

According to Indian Head miners in 1985, North American's abuses had continued thereafter without interruption. They were particularly concerned about lax reclamation enforcement on public lands administered by the federal Bureau of Land Management. One of them commented: "Every time the mining company goes onto state and federal land, it is a green light to destroy everything. The PSC [Public Service Commission] does minimal enforcement, and there are no farmers to complain." The watchdog efforts appeared to pay off in the long term, however, as reclamation quality and PSC oversight improved in the late 1980s to a point where few complaints remained.

The formal apparatus for planning the energy development in the county was installed by the state and supported by the investors. The procedures for land use and permit granting were determined by law, and a government agency funded professional planners to draw up the comprehensive plans. "Impact" was legally defined and measures to mitigate it were agreed upon by corporate and governmental authorities outside the county. The most significant measures taken by the state legislature to mitigate the impact of development were imposing special taxes on the extraction and conversion of coal and the creating of an Energy Impact Office, as described in Chapter 4. This office was funded by a portion of severance and conversion taxes, and was charged with evaluating grant and loan applications from affected political subdivisions and with disbursing funds to a selected group of impact-related projects each year. These measures aimed at reclaiming for the impacted communities some portion of the capital gained from resource exploitation, and were passed over the objections of the energy lobby. These funds did much in the long run to rescue Mercer County from financial ruin.

The Energy Impact Office (originally named the Coal Impact Office) was an unusual governmental entity. A single director evaluated the grant applications for specific projects from impacted counties and political subdivisions such as school, police, water, and fire districts. This official supervised the allocation of more funds than any other person in state government, and was therefore frequently accorded the title of "the most powerful man in North Dakota." Having a single director certainly meant quicker decisions and potentially greater responsiveness to local needs, but it also increased the risk of corruption and personal bias in allocation decisions.

The major development projects, which most local people supported in some form, were already decided upon. But it was still an open question just how much the local communities would be able to benefit from their partnership with the industries, and the political jockeying among interest groups was intense. The big construction projects were presented as accomplished facts to local officials; they were left to work out the details of additional road, pipeline, railway, and transmission line construction, to cope with the population boom, and to mediate relations among industrial personnel, real estate developers, chambers of commerce, construction workers, miners, farmers, local homeowners, the newcomers and old-timers, and shoppers objecting to rising prices at the supermarket.

Dazzling corporate portrayals of the benefits of development and growth did not wholly succeed in drowning out the voices of caution from environmentalists, planners, and Governor Link, nor did they cause the people of Mercer County to lose sight of their own visions of what they wished to gain from development. Different groups participated in the process of change in different ways, and judged the outcome according to its degree of correspondence with their own desires.

Farmers, whose lands were threatened by strip mining and whose special status as the economic foundation of the local economy was challenged, were themselves divided. The Farmers Union continued to honor the post-Depression Democratic Party alliance with the rural electrical cooperatives, despite the cooperatives' current involvement in joint projects with energy corporations. In defiance of this alliance, some farmers formed a countywide association to protect their rights against encroachment by the new industries. While some actively opposed the use of their lands for industrial purposes, on the grounds that it represented permanent destruction of a valuable patrimony and renewable resource, others were glad of a chance to retire on their income from coal leases. This split among the farmers reflects their ideological ambivalence, discussed in Chapter 3. Some saw themselves mainly as business entrepreneurs who could profit from energy development, while others identified themselves as stewards of the land, with a moral commitment to the farming way of life. The latter included some anti-corporationists opposed to any nonagricultural use of the land.

The local miners, of course, were sympathetic to the expansion of the coal industry, since it meant more employment for them; yet they quickly realized that it was not an unmixed blessing. Under the new environmental laws, one-third of mining jobs were in land reclamation, and since the corporations were reluctant to keep the expensive reclamation process on schedule, miners pushing for reclamation enforcement formed an uneasy alliance with pro-reclamation environmentalists who were opposed to strip mining altogether. The miners' unions came under increased pressure, since the new mines and facilities were to be run with nonunion labor.

The vision of the small town business class was most in tune with that presented by the industrial preachers of prosperity. This group had historically looked to economic growth and urbanization as both a survival strategy in competition with neighboring towns and to validate assertions of superior community status and worthiness. Most were eager to turn their backs on the agricultural market, which represented to them the unstable and debt-ridden past, and to embrace industrial growth as the promising wave of the economic future.

In the initial excitement of the energy boom, many local residents attempted to participate in the planning process, yet their efforts took place largely within an institutional framework organized by the most powerful interests—the government agencies and large energy businesses which were developing the area. A county planning and zoning commission was established, with advisory powers to the County Commission. The federal Department of Energy funded an Energy Development Board, staffed with planning experts, to develop growth management plans and become a rural "energy conservation laboratory" to evaluate new ways of utilizing coal by-products. As Ted Kapas, a federal Energy Research and Development Administration official, remarked "It's not often that proper planning can start on the ground floor of a community" (*Hazen Star* March 31, 1977).

The tradition of distrusting outsiders remained strong, however, and some locals were less than thrilled. A County Commissioner objected, "We know our problems without anyone coming in and telling us what they are" (*Hazen Star* August 4, 1977). When out-of-state consultants were cut from the Energy Development Board's budget after a year of operation, the change was greeted with "celebration." A senior staff planner explained, "We've found it's best to get things back to the people here. Outside studies, for example, aren't accepted here as the local ones are" (*Beulah Beacon* November 16, 1978).

During its brief period of operation, the Energy Development Board staff successfully encouraged the citizens of Mercer County to take planning seriously, and promoted the use of systematic regulations and procedures. At this time professional city planners were hired by the two largest towns. Basin Electric Cooperative, one of the main industrial players, established a Mercer County Impact Alleviation Task Force (the Task Force, for short). This was a voluntary association of concerned citizens whose task it was to identify impact-related problems and inform the authorities about them. The Task Force also served as a forum for the energy industries to disseminate information and to practice their public relations skills. Most of the major energy businesses active in the county joined forces to form the Inter-industry Technical Assistance Team (ITAT) to provide the public with estimates for the projects' construction schedules and expected impacts. ITAT produced a series of informative reports summarizing the results of their statistical analyses, with plenty of illustrative graphics and quantitative projections on work force characteristics, available housing, Energy Impact Office grants and loans received, and so on.

The elected governmental bodies charged with actually making the zoning and permit decisions were the County Commission, which ruled on most of the major industrial permits, and the Town Councils, responsible for overseeing the expansion of residential, retail, and small manufacturing areas. Each considered recommendations from their respective planning and zoning commissions, but themselves had final decision-making authority. Throughout most of the boom period, the three-member County Commission was an experienced, pro-development team that tended to evaluate the county's interest in financial terms. They were primarily interested in making what they called "good business" decisions for the county as a whole. The Town Councils, particularly those of the larger towns, were mainly staffed by prominent businessmen, who sought civic prosperity through growth and competition with neighboring towns for new immigrants and businesses. These community boosters generally saw their interests as being in harmony with those of industry.

The Coal Conversion Counties association, a pro-development lobbying organization representing the impacted communities, had a similarly paradoxical relationship with the energy developers—desiring industrialization for the sake of increased tax revenues precisely that feature of development the corporations sought to minimize. The Coal Conversion Counties originated with the Mercer County Task Force and defied a ruling by the state attorney general, Allan Olson (who later became governor of the state), by hiring a lobbyist.

The local business communities were well represented in their towns' planning and zoning commissions and town councils, from which most farmers were excluded by place of residence. Of all the local interest groups, farmers were the most threatened by industrial development. All of the mines and plants were built on formerly agricultural land, and there was little recourse for those who resisted having their land mined or crossed by pipelines or high voltage power lines, since the Public Service Commission in most cases could simply condemn the property. Not all farmers and ranchers opposed the development—many benefitted financially from coal leases and off-farm employment—yet one significant opposition group was formed, the Mercer County Landowners' Association.

This was a grassroots organization, including renters and leasers of farm and ranch land as well as landowners, dedicated to representing the interests of agriculturalists in their relations with industry and government. It functioned rather like a union local, within a regional environmentalist and agriculturalist organization of Resource Councils. The Dakota Resource Council (based in Dickinson, North Dakota) and the Mercer County Landowners Association (MCLA) monitored the activities of industries and government agencies and articulated the interests of the agricultural opposition at public hearings, to the press, and to other farmers.

Of all the organizations mentioned so far, this is the only one that existed outside of the institutional framework for planning. The Landowners Association lacked the legal status of governmental agencies and the economic power of pro-development lobbies. The group achieved some success as a gadfly at public hearings, but government and corporate officials soon learned that little real power lay under the farmers' blustering and threatening rhetoric. While they had to take seriously the statements of its constituent individuals in official procedural settings, decision makers adopted a tolerant reserve in dealing with the Landowners Association as a group. As one County Commissioner blithely commented, "We just ignore them."

Building a base of support for farmers and ranchers concerned with environmental impacts was made difficult by the reluctance of most of them to devote time and energy to organized collective action. Some one hundred twenty people did join the MCLA, but expanding the membership throughout the county was difficult, in part because of the highly localized nature of acute conflicts with industry over land reclamation, water shortages, and noxious odors.

Similar problems plagued the Energy Development Board and the Task Force, which elected officials saw as interfering in their work. The Development Board, which had never related much to local concerns, was disbanded after the Carter Administration ended, and the Task Force limped along with a declining membership. As participants realized the institutional powerlessness of this citizens' advisory committee—legally barred even from lobbying—they lost interest in the organization. As one local official put it to me, "It came down to politics. People found they couldn't change the system."

The significance of this statement lies in its recognition of the futility of the efforts of private citizens to influence planning decisions directly. The "system" he refered to was the legally sanctioned framework of bureaucratic governmental authorities and the corporate experts supplying them with legitimate information and assurances of cooperation. It is significant that although the Inter-industry Technical Assistance Team, like the Energy Development Board and the Task Force, lacked formal legal powers, this agent of the big developers succeeded in monopolizing the business of providing impact projection figures by outcompeting state planning agencies and private consultants. Their figures, which proved to be reasonably accurate, were used by the Energy Impact Office, financiers, housing developers, professional planners, and all of the legally constituted planning bodies in the county. This service earned the industries a reputation for cooperation and a strong lobbying voice with the County Commission.

The formal planning apparatus thus worked to exclude anti-development private individuals and their associations from the most important level of decision making. Actually, there was no planning to be done at all, in the sense of assessing community needs and designing development strategies to meet them. Rather, the corporation boards of directors had decided to implement particular industrial projects to serve their own interests, and they saw the rest as a process of removing obstacles to this specific course of development. This pattern of top-down implementation also characterized the formulation of the legal definition of energy impact and the measures agreed upon by government and corporate officials to ameliorate its negative consequences for the people affected.

Despite the limits on popular involvement in the development planning process, publicity had generated great excitement in Mercer County. As the permit process reached the county level, local people had their first opportunity to voice both their concerns and their approval. Public hearings were packed with both enthusiastic opponents and supporters of development, as well as others merely eager for information. Protest over corporate plans was most radical and outspoken in these early meetings, where shouting matches erupted between MCLA activists and local officials they accused of complicity with energy industry interests. Even outside the arena of permit hearings—where individuals and properties were at issue in concrete ways—initial public interest in planning issues and problems was also high. Dozens participated in the first Task Force meetings and industry-sponsored planning field trips to showcase towns in Wyoming, such as Wheatland (how to handle boom growth) and Gillette (how not to). This public enthusiasm for participating in the planning process was only dampened when financial negotiations delayed the gasification project for almost three years. As public interest in planning waned, both industry and local government officials did not disguise their relief at being freer to their jobs without what they saw as the cumbersome presence of amateur overseers.

In its broadest sense, development "impact" refers to the consequences of constructing and operating proposed projects. Impact mitigation efforts attempted to charge industry for the direct (and sometimes indirect) costs of development. People in Mercer County saw this as a fairness issue: There was widespread consensus among them that they were sacrificing quality of life for the sake of development, and that industry should at least be made to "pay its own way." Yet the legal definition of "impact" limited the kind of community projects which could be funded through the Energy Impact Office. State legislation specifically excluded social programs, counseling, and "secondary impact" generally from Energy Impact Office assistance, allowing only basic governmental service needs caused by "direct impact." Funding requests for social service personnel and programs were systematically turned down, ostensibly because they were excluded by the mandate of the Office, but also because of continuing pressure from the energy lobby to avoid being held financially responsible for this kind of impact.

The coal taxes and Energy Impact Office arrangement did not represent an ideal means of forcing industry to pay the costs of site selection and development. They helped direct money to where the impacts were greatest, but failed to give local communities any measure of bargaining power with the developers. Since the new plants and mines were not taxed while under construction, local governments saw direct industry financing as a means of closing the temporal gap between their outlays on improvements and the large projected tax revenues once the facilities were operational. Instead, this indirect financial scheme merely enabled them to apply for compensation for damages, with the administrative costs borne by the taxpayers (Markusen and Glasmeier n.d.). The costs to industry were not dependent on the amount of adverse impact created, and in any case were passed on to consumers in the form of slightly higher electric and gas bills.

The most potentially powerful mitigation mechanism for the people of Mercer County was the local permit process and siting controls. The procedures employed there required (at least nominally) a full disclosure of environmental, social, and economic disruptions, and included public hearings where individuals and officials could express their concerns and question the firm's presentation. These hearings provided a setting for serious bargaining and could be used by local jurisdictions and interest groups to force industry to bear more of the costs of development by negotiating conditions on permit and siting approvals. The Landowners Association, with the assistance of the Dakota Resource Council, regularly helped impacted farmers to prepare substantive questions and testimony aimed at securing enforceable protective contingencies. Yet, even here, the industries successfully resisted attempts to force them to provide direct financing for impact mitigation efforts.

Complex negotiations over rezoning land for the gasification plant in 1976 revealed how greatly local decision makers were intimidated by the prospect of losing the project altogether. The plant was still awaiting the results of its application for federal financing and wanted the permit to support its claim of already having invested so much it would be wasteful to stop the project at this point. Delegations of Hazen and Beulah businessmen also lobbied for immediate rezoning so that the municipal improvement projects they had already undertaken in expectation of the gasification project could receive money from the Energy Impact Office. The towns had been encouraged by government planners to begin preparing for the boom in advance: Beulah was already facing $3.25 million in payments over the coming two years.

Meanwhile, representatives of the Mercer County Landowners Association urged delay until the county received assurances of impact mitigation money, either from the Impact Office or front-end financing directly from the company. The spokesperson for the Landowners Association denounced the idea that county taxpayers should subsidize industry by paying for any of the impact mitigation: "We owe these people nothing" (*Hazen Star* August 12, 1976:1).

To make matters worse, the proposed plant site was highly unsuitable. Because of a Public Service Commission rule against siting energy facilities on top of recoverable coal reserves, the developers had chosen a coal-free spot in the center of a large, cloverleaf shaped bed of strippable lignite they had leased for fuel. This happened to be the site of the best aquifer in the county—marshy ground with gravel beds—a poor choice from both the environmental and engineering viewpoint.

By the time the agreement was finally approved, a year and a half after hearings had begun, the county planning and zoning commission had yielded to industry on several land use conditions, including weakened compliance with air quality standards and no front-end financing on road improvements needed for plant construction, thereby forfeiting their bargaining power. Some of the commissioners had actually suggested dropping all the conditions (including such essentials as deep-well injection of waste), in order to pressure the state legislature to provide adequate funds to mitigate county impact problems. An opponent of such unilateral disarmament protested: "This is our only handle on development, our only leverage on the state" (*Hazen Star* December 9, 1976:3).

Additional years of experience in dealing with the industries were important for local officials to learn how to exercise their power more effectively. The numerous zoning requests by industries in 1979 and 1980 provided the County Commission and County planning and zoning commission with some leverage in their demands for financial assistance to help pay the costs of development. Estimating that 75 percent of community social service programs were directly due to energy impact, a planning commissioner threatened to deny a zoning request if the gasification partners refused to help out. In the case of Coteau Properties' rezoning request for their Freedom Mine, the County Commission went beyond threats and delayed the application several months while demanding that the corporation work out a satisfactory agreement with affected landowners concerned about surface damage and road rerouting. The company wished to give only verbal assurances, promising to work out the details later, but an adamant County Commissioner suggested that "maybe the farmers would be a helluva lot more satisfied if it's done now." Another delivered a lecture on rearranging their priorities: "Here the coal companies have always worked with the landowners to resolve their differences, and Coteau had better learn" (*Beulah Beacon* March 6, 1980:3).

Such tough stands in support of local interests were not the rule, however. The chair of the county planning and zoning commission (staffed mainly by farmers and ranchers) in 1979 explained the difficulties of representing his constituents' interests, given the superior legal expertise of the corporations, with their staffs of specialists "able to find any loophole in zoning ordinance and state law. . . . The planning commission was leaning more to industry but not intentionally. As a commission, we try to make an intelligent decision based on what is presented in our own research, and sometimes a gut feeling. But with their resources they can do whatever can be done" (*Beulah Beacon* August 23, 1979:1). Another planning commissioner explained to me: "There's been impact mitigation conditions written into all the leases and so on from early on. But the conditions were worded in a vague way, maybe. At the time, industry said they were adequate and expressed goodwill and all, but it has turned out that they could weasel out of some of it."

Local officials saw themselves as staunchly representing their communities' interests in relations with the industries, a view with some support among their constituencies. A County Commissioner described to me how they had delayed a crucial rezoning decision to accommodate local interests: "We want to do what makes sense economically . . . but like when someone doesn't want something rezoned, we delayed six months one time because one local guy wasn't happy with his settlement. We held off till Great Plains made a deal about relocating him, even though speed was of the essence for the decision, in terms of economics."

Over the years of boom expansion, day-to-day decisions of planning and zoning boards became the focus of conflict over how to conduct social life in small communities. Those conforming to legal regulations that demanded uniform standard procedures encountered continual low-level resistance from individuals who resented what they saw as an imposition by meddling outsiders. The town of Golden Valley did not even have official city limits until 1978, when its first zoning document was drafted, and yet newly hired professional planners emphasized the importance of strictly following a general plan. They cautioned that once one began to take personal considerations into account and bend the rules, the situation would quickly get out of control. Strict enforcement was impossible in such communities, however, where it was perceived as unjust and tyrannical by those used to developing their own property in any way they wished.

For example, because of small lot sizes, special variances to the zoning ordinances were frequently necessary when town residents wished to build additions onto their houses. It was a requirement for such variances that all the neighbors approve of the change. In the past, this agreement had been a verbal one, but the new process required that the applicant get the neighbors to sign a document. This change formalized the procedure and heightened the seriousness of the request. An elderly man objected to this practice at a public meeting, saying it was "unfair to pit neighbor against neighbor." On another occasion, a man lamented what he saw as the consequences of local authorities' unreasonable demands for zoning change procedures: "Me and him used to be the best of neighbors. We'd always stop and talk whenever we met and all, but now he'll hardly say 'hi' to me anymore. It's not good when you bring a third party in like this."

There was little support among the local population for the comprehensive plan or for the legal formalisms of planning procedure. Systematic development planning was seen by many locals as one aspect of a general intrusion by outsiders, and its enforcement evoked the strong insiders-versus-outsiders conflict characteristic of the boom years. This perception was in part due to the fact that many of the most prominent pro-zoning figures actually were newcomers to the area. The Energy Development Board, which was an important vehicle for rationalizing the planning process, was seen by most as an alien organization, staffed by overeducated experts from outside the area. These attitudes also sprang from the traditional populist view of industrial development, as just another case of powerful big business from outside trying to profit at the expense of the little guy, and somehow in league with outside experts coming in and trying to tell the local people what they should do about it.

The idea of conforming to universalistic planning regulations was also at odds with the individualistic farm background of the majority of the county's adults. Rural residents here were accustomed to doing whatever they pleased on their own land, and resented any intrusion of outside authority, particularly in the area of land use. As one old-timer explained, "They're used to building whatever buildings they want; when they move into town, they don't realize the importance of zoning laws, neighbors' complaints, and those kind of legal technicalities." A local official opposed to increasing regulation of construction to cope with a rising number of building permits argued on this basis: "The farmers get quite upset about building codes. They're very reluctant to go along with an inspector. To deal with a farmer is very different than a city resident" (*Hazen Star* May 10, 1979).

In spite of this resistance, even lifelong locals serving as public officials felt pressured to systematize their decision making, and spoke of their planning responsibilities in the administrative idiom of "managing" development. One of them explained to me: "It used to be that the town council didn't consider the letter of the law much; they ran the town pretty much as they pleased. Thirty or forty years ago, they didn't consider people's constitutional rights. They had to learn to read ordinances and to follow them." Mercer County men also found it hard to conform to the concept of group leadership, such as that required of the county planning commission. Cooperation was difficult not only because of their "farmer-individualism," but also because the local image of leadership corresponded more to that of strongly imposed paternal authority rather than a model of consensus building.

Because the professional planning practice of following standard rules was associated with the powerful and the educated, and supported by an official institutional structure, it was imbued with superior status and legitimacy. Even those real estate developers, businessmen, and farmers more comfortable with a personalized, case-by-case approach were forced to work within the bureaucratic framework, to at least pay lip service to its ideals, and to mimic its professional rhetoric. As the procedurally legitimate operating style, it pre-empted conflict with development opponents whose arguments were framed in other language—moralistic and personal, rather than legalistic and "rational."

The conflict between bureaucratic and personal styles is obvious, particularly when we consider that proponents of both were attempting to work together on planning commissions. Difficulties arose particularly from the psychological contradiction of imposing standard regulations on a small scale face-to-face community. The mayor of one small town explained to me that although he recognized the necessity of "following the book nowadays, without making exceptions, to avoid ending up looking like Gillette, Wyoming [a nightmare of uncontrolled boom growth], it can be really hard to say 'no' to a long lifetime friend." Another local observer explained the problem of regulating rural nonfarm residence permits this way: "Let's say we grew up together; went through school together; I've known you for thirty years. And you say you aren't going to junk the place up, just have a nice place and run some horses. Now, your word is as good as gold to me, because I know you. But you can't do that with newcomers, and it isn't really fair to have one set of rules for one and another set of rules for the other."

The contradictions were exemplified in the case of one county employee, who was hired as the Public Works Director, but was also expected to fulfill the function of land use administrator, as well. As his colleague explained to me, "It's hard for him to go out to someone's farm and help them with some engineering project and then to turn around and say no to him over a land use request. He can't be effective as a planner, make decisions for the public good instead of individual interest, because of his personal involvement with the people on other grounds."

In the past, boosterism had been the primary method employed by community leaders to promote the survival and growth of their towns. Since frontier days, when these rural settlements first rose on their economically shaky foundations, building and sustaining the towns depended on the efforts of business entrepreneurs to cultivate civic pride and confidence in the area's capacity to sustain continued development. In more recent years, small rural communities in danger of dying out were even exhorted to boosterism by the government. In a 1979 report, a U.S. Department of Agricultural economist admonished those small towns and hamlets wishing to reverse the trend of declining population that they "require a strong willingness to survive on the part of the community, capable leadership, considerable community pride, and a willingness of the citizens to work together for community projects" (quoted in *The Common* October 18, 1979).

During the energy boom, the deliberately boastful optimism of booster rhetoric remained important in representing the community to outsiders, as in this statement made to me by a local mayor when I asked how the new people were changing the area:

> More new people than there is old! Well, those people, a lot of very educated people, coming in, . . . and it hasn't been all bad. We've got a lot of things that have happened in the communities, very positive. We've got excellent school systems in the area. Good swimming pools, new grass green golf course, tennis courts, parks; we've been able to bring in, for example, a lifelong learning center, where we're bringing college courses in the area. We've got athletic programs that we've never heard of before. . . . And these are the type of things that the smaller you are, the less you have of. Senior Citizens got a new center. We've got new churches built all over the area. Compared to big cities we're still a dot on the prairie, but we're pretty good compared to other little towns that have got no industry. And they're fast dying . . . with the agrarian society as bad as it is, where we're not: We've got businesses coming in all the time.

Although boosterism continued to be useful in community public relations, it became entirely superseded by grantsmanship in public financing for the improvements mentioned by the mayor. In order to win grants and loans from the Energy Impact Office, local officials were required to write highly formalized proposals, demonstrating the need for the project, its impact-relatedness, and a carefully elaborated budget. The competition for money was fierce, and encouraged the development of highly professional planning skills. Local government officials and those working in a variety of service programs traded advice on grantsmanship, including what points to emphasize, the structure of funding agencies, and the problem of educating the public about the need for additional local taxes.

The professionalization of planning and community development efforts helped to provide order during a potentially chaotic period of rapid growth. But it also worked to limit the participation of local residents in decision making. In practice, only those who were either elected officials or skilled at presenting their case in the bureaucratically appropriate moment and manner could exercise influence on the outcomes.

Alliance for Progress Much of the process by which developers implemented their plans in Mercer County can be interpreted as hegemonic, in the sense that both their dominance and general public acquiescence in it derived not from overt repression or violence (except in the case of occasional confrontations with organized labor) but rather from the pre-existing national institutional and ideological forms historically shaped by bourgeois cultural leadership. The eagerness of local pro-development interests to realize their vision of progress and economic stability was matched by the developers' need for local cooperation to project their power in Mercer County. The resulting "micro-hegemony" forging alliances with local pro-development interests and promoted favorable attitudes in the general public. From the initial stages of selling people on the idea of an energy boom, through the endless dance of permit granting, to the final arrangements on work force housing, both the industries and local pro-development interests were concerned with creating partnerships for development and harmonies of interest to bridge and supersede underlying conflicts.

Of course, there were limits to the success of such efforts, and the persisting resistance to this micro-hegemony will be discussed in later chapters. The problem of building a sense of shared interest in energy development on the local level was made more complex for developers by the diversity of interest groups present, with their already well-formed political orientations and conflicts. In this context, powerful development interests from outside the county sought to forstall critical debate by replacing it with ideological forms of consensus[6]—a vision of grand harmonies of interest in the common pursuit of progress—specifically through the institutional arena of official planning. There the rational discourse of modernization was accepted as more authoritative and legitimate than local populist forms of expression. Such inequalities operated as a property of the system despite the goodwill and democratic intentions of many individual office holders. Planning remained, not a community-based process in which a full range of local voices could participate on equal terms, but more a project-driven effort to legitimize and implement the plans of outsiders, while securing for impacted constituents whatever safeguards and restitution could be achieved within its institutional bounds.

Of basic importance in the process of consensus building is the concept of progress, shared by all of the parties involved. The cultural heritage of European thought includes an understanding of the overall scheme of social history as one of gradual, incremental, and unilinear change, a progressive unfolding of inherent potential destined to result in ever more perfect social orders, of which the technologically advanced modern societies of the economically developed world would represent the culmination. According to the version incorporated into free-market thinking, orderly development is believed to be generated by individuals and individual business enterprises, pursuing their own unbridled interests. The "fittest" survive, while the "unseen hand" maintains the system in dynamic stability.

The linkage of events in Mercer County with the idea of social progress was an obvious one, promoted as much by local boosterism as by corporate public relations efforts. This conceptual frame encouraged people to accept the immediate negative impacts in hopes that the long-term results would be beneficial, and it also provided a means for coming to terms with their lack of control over the course of change. The image of economic development as an unstoppable progressive process was frequently invoked by people in Mercer County at moments of frustration or resignation, with statements such as these: "The present energy development is just like when the farmers came here and kicked the Indians off the land. Now industry is kicking the farmers off. It's like evolution"; "What happens will happen, and we have no say in it"; "I guess other places have had to go through it"; "The development is inevitable"; and even, "There's no stopping it! People have their destiny spelled out for them." To some extent, these are factual statements about a reality of relative powerlessness, but to the extent that they reflect an understanding of industrial development as a grand and inexorable process, they invoke the ideology of progress as an argument for non-action.

Efforts to promote a sense of collective goals shared by both developers and the Mercer County public were aided by the nearly universal acceptance of the basic logic and premises of capitalist thought and social organization. Like other Americans, Mercer County residents grew up with the familiar concept of private enterprise as the route to jobs, growth, modernity, and prosperity. They were also predisposed to accept as legitimate the legal procedures privileging ownership and exploitative rights to natural resources over the interests of others sharing the same environment. The late-twentieth-century forms of agrarian populism and labor unionism with which they were familiar, although these provided important wellsprings for oppositional thinking, did not radically challenge the basis of capitalism but were themselves the result of a long history of accommodation to its dominant terms.

The practice of planning during the course of the energy boom consolidated the dominance of local elites, and strengthened their alliance with developers as a group, including energy firms, real estate promoters, and other entrepreneurs. Many of the most prominent planning figures were newcomers to the area, and brought with them a technocratic commitment to "management" and "efficiency," and a reverence for strict zoning as the key to rational development. Their ideal of community development was essentially the bourgeois model of the planning profession, which stresses the preservation of property values, residential class segregation, and smooth traffic flow between living, work, and shopping areas.[7] The focus of their efforts in Mercer County was on paving central streets, expanding basic services, and facilitating the industrial commuting traffic. Trailer homes, rental apartments, and single family houses, which previously had been in mixed neighborhoods, were strictly segregated in new housing developments, according to the newly drawn up universal planning guidelines. Further class segregation was accomplished by having a uniform lot size within developments, some designed for low incomes and others as wealthy enclaves. At the urging of professional planners and local business leaders anxious to attract the "better sort" of new residents, planning and zoning commissions undertook to clear up what they referred to as "junky-looking" properties in the towns, where residents were using their yards, in the rural farmstead manner, as outdoor storage areas, rather than as the status display gardens of the urban middle class. The residents who were the strongest advocates of strict zoning tended to be the best paid newcomers, whose interest in protecting their property values owed as much to urban cultural norms as it did to strictly economic calculation.

Securing the cooperation of local elites was important to developers, but they also needed to build more extensive coalitions of public support, and pursued a multitude of specific measures aimed at enhancing the sense of participation by Mercer County citizens in the public activities of industry. Involving local residents in development activities, either as members of a citizens' advisory association or through leasing their land, served to give many more friends and relatives a stake in development, and so to dampen opposition.[8] Similarly, there was strategic value in hiring some local people to work in the energy industries, even if few had the requisite skills and experience. On occasion this fact was expressed openly, as when one public relations man informed me that it was "only a matter of time until the local farmers lose their suspicion of the mining companies. A big factor is that they can see family members getting jobs there and not having to leave." By sponsoring community informational meetings, tea parties, tours, and field trips, corporate representatives strove to make the general public feel that they too were taking part in the great events shaping a more prosperous and progressive future.

Planning and permit granting, with their measure of local participation, served as a central vehicle for depoliticizing the process of uneven development and making it appear both acceptably democratic and in the interests of the county as a whole. Its ethos of economic rationality prompted city and county officials to evaluate plans mainly in financial terms, and to see their first duty as making good business decisions for the people. Through a variety of means, some of them institutionalized in official procedures and some of them the result of simply allowing existing inequalities to assert themselves in the planning context, most public participation in the planning process was quietly diverted onto powerless sidetracks. While paying lip service to the democratic ideal of public participation, those in positions of real power allowed it to sink under the weight of its own contrived futility.

Over the years, the participation of local residents at permit and zoning hearings waned. As curiosity wore off and wholesale opposition bowed to the inevitable, it became common for only those most directly interested in particular cases to show up. The difficulties of working against the developers had become quite clear: There was little institutional scope for individuals by themselves to affect the decisions of government or big business, and working effectively within the system required bureaucratic skills and resources beyond the reach of ordinary people. Many of those whose opposition to industrial development remained steadfast became burned out and frustrated over a decade of largely fruitless struggle. Those who continued to contest the dominant line—that energy development in this form was good for the county—gradually dwindled in number, and came to sound shrill and irrational in contrast to the smooth reasonableness of those working for what came to be accepted as the foundation of a more secure economic future. Even so, those who had worked to safeguard local interests and curb industry excesses had succeeded in achieving a compromise that Mercer County could live with.

Chapter Six | Living with Development

Government and industry officials carried out elaborate preparations for managing the energy boom and Mercer County residents thought they knew what to expect. Yet the realities of boomtown living brought many unexpected developments and disappointments for local residents. In the period just prior to the energy boom the local economy had been in decline, and many welcomed the prospect of expanded industrial development for the sake of the jobs they hoped it would provide for their families and friends. Local residents expected it to provide a continuing source of employment without transforming their way of life in other ways.

People also expected that progress would bring prosperity, since industrial development would bring more paved roads, better public services, and population growth in the towns. According to pro-development publicity, prosperity would trickle down as the boom created jobs in new businesses generated by the workers' spending their earnings locally, and through the tax contributions of the energy corporations. This new wealth would circulate through the local economy in the form of wages and public services, so that everyone would benefit.

And yet, when the boom began, things did not work out quite as expected. Few permanent jobs went to local residents, and only a minority profited from the boom, while inflation and tax hikes increased the financial burden on the majority. The communities were overwhelmed by thousands of migratory workers, becoming almost unrecognizable to those who had lived in them all their lives. Local authorities undertook improvements in streets, recreational facilities, and other city services, but meanwhile the tenor of public life became increasingly impersonal and bureaucratic. Even after the temporary construction workers had left and the new permanent industrial employees arrived, social transformations in community life continued as the new industries became more integrated into Mercer County society.

These changes were continuously interpreted and commented on by local residents, in terms of the range of values and beliefs that were locally meaningful. New experiences also heightened Mercer County residents' awareness of tensions and contradictions among these values, encouraging their reinterpretation as well.

The Construction Work Force

From 1978 through 1984, the people of Mercer County were host to a construction work force of outsiders, who numbered 5,854 at its peak in 1983.[1] This number was greater than the combined population of the county's towns before the energy boom (see Table 2). About half of these temporary workers commuted daily or weekly from other parts of the state, while the rest resettled in Beulah, Hazen, and Zap (Inter-industry Technical Assistance Team 1984:5–7). A few hundred of them came with their wives and children to live in mobile home courts or in the new housing additions and apartments burgeoning on the edge of town. The majority, however, came and lived in the area as "bachelors"—unmarried men or men who had left their families in another state.

Half of these temporary workers were North Dakotans, but only 9.6 percent were already residents of Mercer County (Inter-industry Technical Assistance Team 1984:8). Of the rest, the largest proportion from any single state was from Minnesota (12.7 percent), with the balance coming from Montana, South Dakota, Colorado, Wyoming, and even farther afield. The Minnesota contingent was so large because of industrial decline in that state's Iron Range region and a recession in its metropolitan centers.

These workers were specialized construction craftsmen—pipefitters, ironworkers, boilermakers, insulators, carpenters, and electricians—who earned their living by migrating from one major construction site to another, following a series of temporary jobs across the western United States. One girl of eleven, living in a trailer court with her family, told me that although they had originally lived in Sioux Falls, South Dakota, she could remember twenty-one moves since then. It was not unusual for these families to move an average of four or five times a year.

Specialized construction workers feel ambivalent about their itinerant lifestyle. Some enjoy the novelty of travel and get itchy feet at regular jobs, "I get tired of working in one place too long and like to

Table 2 | **Mercer County Population Distribution, 1960–1983**

	1960	1970	1979	1980	1983
Beulah	1,318	1,344	2,311	2,908	6,035
Golden Valley	286	235	276	287	377
Hazen	1,222	1,240	2,199	2,365	3,351
Pick City	101	119	156	182	264
Stanton	409	517	614	623	801
Zap	339	271	347	511	625
Town Total	3,675	3,726	5,903	6,876	11,453
Rural Total	3,130	2,449	2,379	2,528	2,906
Mercer Co. Total	6,805	6,175	8,282	9,404	14,359

Source: U.S. Census, 1960, 1970, 1980; special censuses commissioned by county entities, 1979, 1983.

move on to somewhere new." Most, however, pursue it out of economic necessity and not because they lack roots in a specific home place. One sixty-two-year-old welder from northern Minnesota explained: "I've been following the rainbow all my life, but I still haven't found the treasure. Back home . . . I just love it there—in a year I'm going to retire, and I can't wait! When it gets down below forty degrees outside, I'll just throw another log on the fire and sit tight!"

The family life of the construction work force was often tenuous, and for some it disappeared altogether. Those who came alone, leaving their families behind in Minnesota, Wisconsin, or farther away, suffered from the separation, feeling isolated and lonely after working hours. Although a few enjoyed a semblance of home life in households where they rented rooms, usually with elderly widows, the daily lives of most were reduced to a routine of work, relaxing with the other solitary workers in the bars and company dining hall, and sleeping in hotel rooms or the dormitories provided by the company. At best, they managed to set up temporary renter households of friends and workmates, but even these arrangements could not dispel the loneliness and dissatisfaction of living far from their loved ones. Many of the "bachelors" were married adults—reluctantly absent husbands and fathers. They sent money home to support their families, but the infrequency of home visits left them feeling estranged and distant from their wives and children. This separation was perhaps even more difficult for the wives left behind to care for homes and children and in many cases to hold down jobs of their own.

There was not enough housing available to absorb the construction work force, and so Basin Electric and the Coyote project partners built a large and well-equipped complex just outside Beulah—near enough town for the men to patronize its businesses, but far enough away to minimize the disruption from their presence. This Bachelor Quarters housing or "BQ," as it came to be known, was later purchased by Great Plains to house the gasification work force. It consisted of barracks-like dormitories, a dining hall, recreational facilities, and a twenty-five-pad recreational vehicle park with water, sewer, and electricity hook-ups. Workers had the option of living and eating at the BQ in lieu of a twenty-dollars-a-day subsistence pay for room and board on their own. In 1982, six hundred men were living there, and more barracks were under construction. At the peak of the boom in the summer of 1983, the BQ had thirty employees of its own and housed twelve hundred workers.

Many chose to live at the BQ dormitories for its convenience. It was close to the work site; they could come home, shower, run downtown for a couple of beers, come back for supper, hang around with their workmates, watch television, and sleep—all without having to interact with the local people, apart from an obliging bartender. For these men, life revolved around the job, and they kept company with their fellow workers twenty-four hours a day, keeping to this monotonous round for the sake of the Friday paycheck.

This was precisely the lifestyle that designers of the camp had hoped to create. A Basin official bragged about how impressed other corporations were with its effect on worker productivity, explaining:

> You take a guy and you bring him in and you house him well and you feed him well and he's going to be a productive worker. If your worker doesn't have an adequate place to live, he's going to live in the bar. And if you are drunk every night you're not worth a damn the next day working. . . . We fed for one hour, and if you weren't there you didn't eat. They were giving up their sub [subsistence pay] for that. . . . If you're giving up something for it, you're gonna be darn well sure you are there to eat. We fed from five to six, and they got off of work at four. Well, they only had time for a couple of beers in the bar. . . . It was an all-you-can-eat situation, and when you are totally fed up on food there's no way you are going to go out drinking. . . . It kept the problems down.

The construction workers who came with their families had an easier time of it emotionally, but their situation was also far from comfortable. Most of these owned mobile homes and carried their homes with them—an important element of stability and continuity in their nomadic lives. The family life of these migrants was dominated by the husband's search for lucrative but elusive and ephemeral construction jobs. To avoid the husband's periodic separation from the rest of the family, they sacrificed living in a home place to follow him about from town to town. Living together in tight quarters, almost without other support networks, and under the constant threat of unemployment, these families were severely stressed.

The trailer courts of Mercer County at this time were little more than transient encampments. The new courts where construction families lived had been set up on short notice, and initially lacked the amenities of other residential additions, such as sidewalks, paved streets, parks, or vegetation. In the trailer court where I lived in 1978, the mobile homes were set up on concrete blocks on the raw red dirt, which tracked everywhere in muddy or dusty profusion, depending on the weather. There was an uncommitted, temporary feel to life there, and little sense of community. Some men might gather to pitch horseshoes of an evening, or a couple of women join forces for canning, but most families stuck to themselves.

The trailers themselves offered unreliable shelter. In some cases they were not even secured to the ground—in defiance of both state law and the destructive force of the high winds and tornadoes that regularly strike North Dakota in the summertime. One night the trailer across the street from mine burned to the ground in half an hour after being struck by lightning. One experienced trailer resident gave me a friendly warning, "These things got real bad wiring. If you ever smell smoke, get out as fast as you can, the nearest door or window. Don't try to save anything—you got three minutes before it's a fireball." Another stormy night brought winds that shook the metal roofs until they roared like thunder, and sent a dozen of the trailers smashing and rolling and spewing their contents across the neighborhood. Even after this calamity, when I remarked upon the danger, dirt, and monotony of these living conditions, construction wives spoke of their determination to bear it for the sake of keeping their families together and food on the table: "Well, we're just out here for a while. . . . It's not so bad; we're making good money and it's just another two months. You get used to where you just don't worry about it. Just do our time, and then get the hell out of here!"

Life in the construction workers' trailer courts was not all bad, of course. In the later years of the boom, the landscaping and city services improved. Those who had stayed for a year or more began to make friends locally, and a tentative community life emerged, segregated from that of the host towns.[2] Little lawns appeared, with flower beds, children's wading pools and tricycles, a barbecue grill for weekend cookouts. The mobile home itself provided a comforting element of continuity to the family—no matter where in the country they happened to be, they were always right at home inside it. One young man who grew up in a migrant construction family explained: "The trailer was nice. It was tough to be always in a new school, to always be an outsider, but year after year I always slept in my same room at night." Neighbors were not always total strangers, either. Since workers skilled in particular crafts were needed during specific phases of large construction projects, their families often encountered one another at site after site. The turnover at trailer courts was high, the personnel shifting with the construction phases, and so neighborhoods of families who always worked during a particular phase disintegrated during lay-offs and reassembled again at other sites many times.

The history of the Kempel family illustrates the unsettled life style of even the most stable of construction families. When Maria and Carl were first married, they lived on a farm in the northern part of the state. After they lost their farm in the early 1960s, Carl was able to join the carpenters' trade union and work on constructing the first modern power plants in Mercer County, near Stanton, and then on the Coyote plant south of Beulah. With some ten consecutive years of almost full employment for Carl, and part-time work as a cook for Maria, the Kempels were able to buy a house in Beulah. Meanwhile, their three children grew up, married, and moved away so that only one daughter remained in the state, within weekly visiting distance.

Then came a long period of unemployment, and the Kempels left Mercer County for construction jobs in Montana, meanwhile renting their house out to a new plant manager. When the work dried up in Montana, they returned, but remained unemployed, living in a recreational vehicle on the rental income from their house. When carpenters were needed at the gasification plant construction site, Carl and Maria were able to move back into their home. They rented rooms to two boarders—a carpenter and a pipefitter who had left their families behind in distant towns. Together, they shared a pseudo-family life, eating meals together and spending evenings together like a family. Carl was laid off again in 1984, and Maria took a job working the night shift at a convenience store.

Elderly widows on fixed incomes found an opportunity both to earn a little extra money and relieve their own loneliness by providing room and board to workers. Eva, with whom I stayed for several months, housed a succession of boarders. First there was George, a plant supervisor, who stayed for eighteen months, and made only occasional visits home to his wife in Wisconsin. His wife corresponded with Eva, sent her simple gifts, and thanked her for taking good care of her husband. When I stayed with her, Eva treated me like a granddaughter, and enjoyed introducing me as such to her friends. Later, Ed moved in—a tall, blond Minnesota Finn—and his friend Bert convinced Eva to let him sleep on a cot in the basement. Bert was also a Minnesotan, but shorter and darker, presumably a genetic legacy from a Chinese grandfather who had cooked in a big hotel in Bismarck. They were both millwrights at the gasification project, and belonged to the carpenters' union.

Ed liked to fish and hunt, while Bert was intellectual and spent his spare time engaged in an obscure project in the basement, involving the comparison of various Greek translations of the original Bible. Both of them were married, in their forties, and working to support wives and children back home. Ed made the trek home most weekends (a twelve-hour bus trip each way) partly at Eva's insistence. She frequently reminded him that his wife, who worked full time as a nurse, needed his help with their four teenage boys. Bert rarely went home; this job had been preceded by a long period of unemployment, and since he and his wife had lost their house, she had moved in with her parents.

After Ed and Bert were laid off, Mickey moved into Eva's house for a while. This big, slow-moving Norwegian was barely twenty, and had left his parents' home in Walhalla, North Dakota, on the promise of help from a family friend in finding work. Mickey's job search was unsuccessful, except for a short stint on a clean-up crew, and he eventually returned to Walhalla discouraged.

To those who did find construction work at the Great Plains gasification plant, it was obvious they were part of something historic. The largest construction site in North America, "Great Plains" sprawled over two sections of land, and was adjoined by the Antelope Valley power station and the Freedom mine, both also under construction. Every morning, and in changing shifts throughout the day, long lines of pick-up trucks and cars of all descriptions converged at the turnoff north of Beulah, as the work force made the dusty trek to the industrial complex. Kaiser Engineering was the main contractor at Great Plains, but work was organized through a complex structure of hundreds of subcontractors, sub-subcontractors and even sub-sub-subcontractors. Despite extensive record-keeping efforts, Kaiser could never be sure how many people were working on the site at a given time.

In a work site humming and buzzing like a giant beehive, several thousand men of various trades pursued a confusing array of tasks, interweaving across a landscape resembling a veritable city of scaffolding, warehouses, pipelines, crushers, cranes, cooling ponds, boilers, fences, tanks, towers, trucks, cars, forklifts, three-wheelers, men on foot, men with blueprints, men looking busy, men taking a break in a quiet corner, men rushing about on diverse errands.

This was exciting, as even the most jaded craftsmen admitted, but working conditions depressed their morale. The construction was a union job, yet because of work shortages nationwide and the right-to-work laws in North Dakota, the Great Plains workers had relatively disadvantageous "catalectic" contracts. Negotiated by their international union leadership, these contracts included wage rates almost 20 percent below union scale, no travel pay, with overtime work at only time-and-a-half instead of double-time pay, no coffee breaks, and no right to strike. When an electricians' local defied this agreement in 1982, picketing in support of striking workers on another site, they were summarily fired. Workers complained of callous, top-heavy management, incompetent supervision, wastefulness, and poor quality control. These claims were not without basis; when the plant's German designers came to check on things in 1983, they were appalled to find an entire train of the plant constructed in reverse sequence. Most workers struggled to do their best despite the unfavorable circumstances, but for others, their discontent translated into goofing off, stealing tools, and even outright sabotage.[3] A warehouse worker ruefully remarked: "There's been so many wrenches thrown down the pipes it will be a miracle if this thing ever works."

On the weekend, the family men in the work force went off to their loved ones, travelling up to fifteen hours to get home. The younger bachelors, however, sought company closer to hand. Since few unattached women were to be found, the bachelors mostly just gathered in the bars to drink. A woman braving these night spots might find herself the only female in a crowd of one hundred or more, and would never lack for dance partners. Some local parents took the precaution of locking their teenage daughters in at night to prevent them from fraternizing with the men. With such a captive clientele, it is not surprising that prostitutes and "exotic dancers" arrived to work the raunchier bars. Many of these camp followers came down from Canada, and at one point an enterprising nightclub owner was bringing a busload in every weekend.

Other local bars frequented by the "construction crowd" offered a more light-hearted atmosphere. The River Rat, the Blind Pig, and the Zap Inn (named for that famous event in Zap's history, the Zap-In) were fun places to relax and kid around, where a few of the more adventurous local young people mingled freely with their temporary neighbors. On a typical warm summer evening in Zap, for example, the streets buzzing pleasantly with kids on bikes and people strolling along, I joined the crowd at the Zap Inn. The place was filling up with men and an occasional woman in their twenties and thirties, attracted by an intriguing poster announcing a men's wet T-shirt contest ("ERA for Men!"). The friendly and boisterous atmosphere contrasted with the usual Mercer County barroom reserve, and indeed few of the clientele were locals. When one young fellow, a stranger with a mustache and pony tail, leaned over the counter to get some change, someone protested loudly, "Get that hairy body out of my drink!" The stranger was taken aback, but it turned out to be a joke, and a minute later, the "offended" fellow and his pals were digging through their pockets to offer him spare change for the phone, asking in a friendly manner, "Have you got enough?"

As the evening progressed, the T-shirt contest never materialized, but there were more public displays of wit and humor. At one point, a man came in with a bandage over one eye under a pair of glasses, having apparently suffered some recent injury. He had made light of the condition, however, by attaching a toy teddy-bear eye—the kind with the loose black pupil that moves when shaken—over the bandage, for a strikingly bizarre effect. His friend announced to the room at large, "Bill lost an eye today. But he got a new one!" This brought general hilarity, and was only one of several pranks that evening.

A little mixing with locals could happen in places like this, but only a few of the workers really made friends with long-standing residents or socialized with them in their off-hours—attending sporting events, eating out, or going to the lake for fishing, swimming, and boating. For those who found the bar life tiresome or offensive, there remained little choice but to remain lonely sojourners, their social life on hold while they worked on the job.

Insiders and Outsiders

Long-time residents of Mercer County blamed the temporary construction work force for the towns' problems, including traffic, inflation in food and housing prices, and an increase in petty crime—which local fears exaggerated into a crime wave. High school officials complained of increased alcohol and drug use among teen-agers, speculating about pushers among the work force and the rougher sort of youngster from their families. Locals complained about the "riff-raff" in the trailer courts. Controversy erupted over prostitution and exotic dancing, and they were banned in the towns.

Most of these fears focussed on the so-called bachelor workers, who were the most disturbing element. Local people were afraid of the construction workers, and disliked their rough ways and alien life styles. One woman expressed her insecurities this way:

All these changes around here are scary. Some people are afraid to go out at night, you know. . . . A lot of these new workers—with that long hair and dressed the way they do—they look kind of like *criminals* to us. People are afraid they are maniacs or on drugs or something. . . . We're just not used to those kinds of people. And you know, your neighbors are not so friendly any more. The other night we heard something at the door—it took an hour and a half for the police to get there. We would have been dead!

In an outraged letter to the editor of a local weekly newspaper, another lifelong County resident blamed the construction workers for a wide range of social ills:

Personally, and having lived here all my life, and having farmed in this area for the past 35 years, I am sorry that we ever "made it possible" for them to build these plants here. We had a beautiful community before this impact began; now it has gotten to be a regular jungle; you have to stand in line most of the time to get groceries, whatever services you do need, if you can get them, you WAIT! All the trash that comes with progress has invaded our community, and there are drug problems, battered wives, exotic dancers, and you name it. For the very few who do benefit from it, I think we are paying a mighty high price! It has gotten to be a regular Sodom and Gomorrah!

Mercer County public opinion subjected temporary construction residents to negative stereotyping, despite the fact that most of the outsiders were from neighboring regions and their behavior conformed to local standards of morality. At the county fair, for example, a pair of local women were praising a lovely entry in the flower arranging contest. They were surprised to hear from another woman, one of the judges, that the artist was a temporary resident living in a trailer court. The judge remarked, "Most of those construction wives just take to drinking all the time 'cause they've got nothing else to do, but this one is different."

Long-term Mercer County residents did their best to carry on their normal lives and ignore the presence of strangers. These efforts were aided by the physical separation of the newcomer neighborhoods from the older parts of town, and the fact that the two groups socialized mainly among themselves; but many local residents were edgy. This showed, for example, when a workers' truck turned into a crosswalk as a local woman and I were crossing the street. The pick-up did not actually come close to hitting us, yet my fellow pedestrian broke her dignified public reserve to cry out testily, "Doesn't he know that's illegal? I guess it doesn't matter any more *what* the law is!" And then, embarrassed that I, also an outsider, had witnessed this ill-mannered outburst, she added, "Isn't the weather nice today?"

In town on a sunny workday morning, one could almost believe that the calm and uneventful days of yore had never gone. With the work force out of sight, the strangers' presence was remote. But on rainy days, with construction work called off, Beulah seethed with activity. The noise and bustle on Main Street made leaving a store like stepping onto a construction site. Young men crowded into the K & J Bar, "where the light of day is never seen," their sullen merrymaking all but drowned out by the jukebox and traffic noise. Across the street, the Kozy Korner Kafe was full of small groups of women and smaller groups of men, spending an hour over their coffee and quiet talk. No kidding or laughter here, despite the workers' friendly attempts to draw out the stony-faced teen-age waitresses.

The fact that so many jobs were going to outsiders lay at the heart of local resentment against them. Most in Mercer County had supported the industrial expansion because of the promise of good jobs for their family members and friends. Following the typical boomtown pattern reported by Bluestone and Harrison (1982:89), however, few of the local people were qualified for the better-paying construction jobs. These were among the highest-paying jobs in the county, and most of them went to highly skilled outsiders. Skilled construction craftsmen were making twelve to fifteen dollars an hour, if only for a temporary period, and those in even the lowest-paid technical jobs at the gasification plant started with a salary of $25,000 to $30,000 a year.[4] Most of the increase in employment for local residents came in the expanded service economy at the minimum wage level. Those in Mercer County who had been led to expect more high-paying industrial jobs for themselves were disappointed to see strangers benefitting from the county's sacrifices.

The workers considered this resentment unfair. They countered the accusation that they were taking jobs away from local people with the following arguments: "The locals want the jobs from the outsiders, but I went through *training* to be an ironworker. . . . If they want the jobs, they gotta go and get the training." "It doesn't make any difference [where you are from] because it is all union anyway. And lots of North Dakotans are getting jobs in Minnesota, so it's a trade-off. What I don't like is local farmers who get jobs at the plant. They have another way to make a living. They should let some unemployed guy get the job." This particular complaint against farmers seeking off-farm income was shared by others in Mercer County, as in the following bitter diatribe, also sent to the newspaper:

Our local people should have jobs before bringing others in from God knows where. I can see skilled labor, but when it comes to plain labor it is crazy.... Also the farmers are plain hogs they farm and grab jobs more than they can handle, and run their earnings through farm expenses, short changing the man that has to work for a living to feed his family on only one pay check. Working man has no tax exemption for work expenses farmers has all [sic]. But our living expenses are all alike.

People in Mercer County were disappointed in their hopes that the fat paychecks of construction workers would mean money pouring into the local economy. Most of the men had been out of work for many months, and had left their families behind in other parts of the country. As one bank manager ruefully observed, "We do a huge money order business." Workers spent some money on housing, food, and entertainment, but most were intent on saving every penny they could to send home to support their families and pay off old debts. Even among those whose families had migrated to the area with them, few were interested in spending their paychecks, preferring to save earnings against future periods of unemployment.

Those newcomers who came as families were less threatening than the single men, but they constituted a separate community, which exacerbated class segregation in town. Their ties to the outside remained stronger than to their new and temporary home. For many, this was simply one more stop on a lifelong migration from one construction site to another. Their friendships were mainly among similar households and few of them made efforts to integrate themselves into local society.

In 1982 the new permanent workers began training for their jobs as engineers, technicians, supervisors, and managers. Some seven hundred were hired to run the gasification plant alone, almost all from outside the area. These permanent employees and their families came from all over the country, generally from urban areas like Detroit or Gary, and even from overseas. The industries offered high salaries and attractive housing and financing benefits as a compensation to these upper middle class urbanites for having to move to a place they considered a remote backwater of civilization. These workers were welcomed by local elites who had shunned their blue collar colleagues. An elderly resident exclaimed: "The ones coming in now are a whole different class of people. I didn't want to have those other ones in my house—some bulldozer driver—but these new ones are fine."

These high-paying plant operation positions were the coveted plums of the energy boom. Only a few went to native sons of Mercer County, and Joe was among the lucky ones. When he was hired as a trainee at a power plant, Joe was in his thirties and had served in the

Navy, where he had gained experience working in engine rooms. He claimed that his fellow trainees had no previous experience with machines and that many more locals could have been hired. Joe was working as an operator in the control room, a darkened chamber high up in the side of the plant wall, lined with banks of instrument panels, winking lights, and video screens. He found the work dull, except that the control room had become a hangout where employees gathered in their free time to talk. Still, he was pleased with the job; it had allowed him to move back near his friends and his ailing father. He had bought a farmhouse near the plant, but spent most of his free time in town.

Like the construction workers, the families of the permanent work force also moved into new neighborhoods. Many rented housing initially, before choosing where to buy a home, but they did not rent in the same neighborhoods as the temporary workers. The housing choices made by this group reflected their high salaries and urban tastes. Most moved into the large, expensive tract homes rapidly assembled in new, treeless developments. The most upscale of these, the Murray Estates addition, included two-acre "ranchette" lots on a rolling hillside south of Beulah. Its bucolic image was designed to appeal to the aristocratic pretensions of the executive class, and yet the spaciousness and privacy was also attractive to retired farmers and other local people who saw it as a convenient place to live close to town and still be able to keep a horse or a large garden, that is, to use the land as one does on a farm.

This mix of residents, with their different attitudes towards land use and its symbolism, made for a series of conflicts. In 1984, for example, one local resident built a large steel building to house his collection of antique cars, touching off a controversy that split the neighborhood cleanly into two camps—the newcomers versus the locals. The newcomers had moved there because it was a prestigious place with a country-club atmosphere representing exclusivity and elite aesthetic standards. To them, the garage was a trashy eyesore, signifying lower class values and aesthetics, and they brought a lawsuit claiming that its construction violated the neighborhood covenant, if not the zoning ordinances. The long-term locals had different ideas of what the subdivision was all about. To them, the large lots meant just more space—somewhere they could keep a tractor or livestock as a hobby, or grow a little hay. To them, the newcomers' complaints seemed unneighborly, snobby, and more than a little strange. The old-timers responded to the charge that the steel building was ugly by pointing out the same failing in some of the domestic architectural monstrosities of the newcomers. In the end, the locals won in district court, and the steel garage stayed put.

Attracted by the beauty of the Mercer Country countryside, another segment of the permanent newcomers chose to live outside of the towns altogether, establishing previously rare rural nonfarm residences by buying farm or ranch land and either moving into the existing house or constructing a new one on the premises. County zoning ordinances expressly forbid persons not engaged in agriculture to reside on agricultural land, and so each case required a specific variance granted by the County Commission to rezone the place from agricultural to residential use. Over the boom years, some two hundred fifty rural non-farm residences were reluctantly permitted by the Commission, over the objections of many local residents.

Towns sought to discourage the practice because of the loss to their own tax base, the school districts because of the additional costs of providing bus services to new homes beyond existing routes, and agriculturalists because it took good land out of production, further reducing the supply of this scarce commodity. Young farmers waiting to inherit land were especially horrified at the infuriating possibility of their parents selling off land for a rural non-farm. These new rural residents, about half of whom were actually returned locals who had acquired urban tastes and skills, sought the calm, bucolic charm of country living. While the farmers did not lack such aesthetic appreciation for the land, to them it was also a source of livelihood, and they resented the intrusion and high-handed manner of these would-be country squires. One wrote this response to a local newspaper-sponsored opinion survey:[5]

> A lot of these new people are building in the rural areas—they demand roads to their homes, bus service for their school kids . . . and so many other things that have been beyond our fondest dreams so far. Who do they think they are? Many have just come in and "taken over" without really contributing anything—just taking whatever they can get in salaries, recreation for their families, etc. Salaries have gone sky-high in our schools, places of business and all over simply because the power plants and related businesses are paying those higher salaries.

In-migrants found themselves socially ostracized. Early in my research, a Minnesotan worker went so far as to offer me this advice: "People here don't like us. If they find out you're an outsider, they won't talk to you. Just tell them you are from someplace. Just look on a North Dakota map and pick out some small town . . . then they'll tell you anything." Another worker complained, "The locals blame the workers for everything, for the high prices in the grocery store. They think it's their [the workers'] fault, because they can see them."

Disparaging remarks by the mayor of Beulah about the migrant workers' trailer courts and their noisy dogs prompted this defense in a letter to the editor:

> As a construction wife, I must apologize for being in your midst. We did not study a map of the country and decide that this was such a great place we wanted to live here. We were SENT here. Of course, we are glad to have some means of earning money to pay our mortgage installments, utilities, taxes, insurance, yard care, etc. for our home.... It is also nice to eat regularly. My husband welcomes the challenge of construction work and building something worthwhile under adverse conditions.
>
> It is not easy to leave one's spacious home, family members and good friends to travel to some strange place, there to exist in a sardine can jammed with other little people-containers into a cheerless complex policed by glum guards. Nevertheless, ... the people who live here try to be considerate of one another, the children are exceptionally good, and a lot of formerly good watchdogs have been thoroughly squelched.
>
> If it were not for construction workers who are willing to give up most of what average people hold dear, this country could not have developed industrially as it did. Your area would have a continuance of the population decline that was the bane of N.D. for years. Many of the local young people would be forced to migrate somewhere else in search of decent jobs. Now industry calls for more services, and the local business people should ask themselves who helps provide their paychecks. Taxes on new industry provide benefits for all residents.
>
> And as for the local people envying the construction people for their good wages, ask the natives how much they would be willing to give up for better wages and how they would like to pay for two households and duplicate taxation.
>
> In addition to apologizing for being here, I would like to thank the local people for being, on the whole, so friendly and helpful. ND has a lot of hard working, decent people; and the state is a credit to the nation.
>
> Please remember—construction workers are people too. And in a town that rolls up the sidewalks long before the sun goes down and buttons up tightly on Sunday, an outsider can be bored and lonely.
>
> (*Beulah Beacon* June 29, 1979)

Those who hoped to make Mercer County their new permanent home were especially pained by the hostility of lifelong residents: "They wouldn't accept you as a local if you begged with your dying breath. I'm not interested in getting into politics here (I don't have the money for *that*!) but they don't even accept you into social life"; "They get together on the street and talk together in whatever their language is, and they're probably saying something about you."

The city planning and zoning process was important for both

expressing and managing the insider-outsider conflict. In building the Bachelor Quarters, industry assisted in the segregation of the temporary work force. Other efforts to exclude them from towns took the form of failing to provide trailer parks and other amenities for them, or enforcing zoning ordinances to exclude unwanted recreational vehicle campers. The segregation of industrial populations within small rural communities is a historical pattern in Mercer County, as throughout the United States. Poor coal miners were relegated to the "Dog Town" slum and company shantytowns in the early years there, much as the recent construction workers were ghettoized into marginal trailer parks. This segregation of rural industrial workers was not simply due to their occupational status, but also to their arrival as a group of outsiders whom the town was not prepared to assimilate. In his account of small town American life in the early twentieth century, Douglass notes that when many outsiders come at once, "they are quickly formed into an almost impenetrable clan on the town's outskirts" (Douglass 1919:84).

Although their numbers contributed to such residential marginalization in Mercer County over the energy boom years, its classist motivations were also clearly expressed. When a zoning variance was requested to develop a trailer court well outside of town next to a garbage landfill site, one supporter argued that right next to the dump seemed like "the perfect place to put mobile home parks." When the county public health officer protested, citing the comprehensive development plan and public health risks, the same supporter insisted: "But the towns don't want them!"

Such efforts to exclude working class newcomers were opposed by business people who hoped for the workers' trade, and by open-hearted residents who felt it was their towns' duty to provide a place to live. Planning experts insisted that new developments be contiguous with the existing town centers rather than in scattered satellites or strung out along the road, and yet the result was still the relegation of outsiders to the social as well as geographical margins of community life.

Estrangement and Regulation

The changing economic organization of Mercer County produced changes in community life that have come to be recognized as symptomatic of industrial development. Social philosophers such as Karl Marx, Émile Durkheim, and Max Weber, observing the transformation of European life with the rise of modern industry, developed concepts that help us understand the nature of these ongoing processes of social change today. While these theorists differed profoundly in analyzing the relation of modern social change to developments in the political economy, their descriptions of the resulting estrangement and regulation in everyday life all have important applications to conditions in Mercer County.

As a humanist philosopher, Marx found capitalist industrialism to be alienating in that it engendered conditions in which people cease relating to one another as human beings in political and economic affairs, and instead treat each other as objects and production factors, with needs that are secondary to those of the market.[6] He criticized the rise of a system demanding profit maximizing and competition for estranging people from one another—for the systematic decline of human solidarity and sympathy. Although Mercer County has been part of an industrialized civilization for more than a century (and its people heirs to a much longer capitalist tradition) the energy boom brought new and intensified forms of social estrangement, particularly in heightened class differentiation, competition between groups for employment, and the developers' treatment of people's needs as subordinate to those of energy production. The people—both employees and local residents—were expected to adjust their lives to the changing energy market, rather than vice versa.

Durkheim, the French sociologist, was concerned with a differently conceived problem of declining social solidarity in modern society.[7] His approach emphasized the importance of consensual moral norms in providing the means by which members of a society orient themselves. Together with the cohesion produced through functional interdependence, they provide the organization and integration needed for a well-adjusted and satisfying life in modern society. The lack of such integration—a state of normlessness—he called "anomie."[8] While twentieth-century United States society could hardly be described as lacking in conflict, both in terms of interests and in terms of values, anomic conditions became particularly intense in Mercer County during the energy boom. It was a stressful situation of tumultuous social change, with changing norms and social relations; the effects were felt by newcomers and lifelong locals alike.

Other changes in public life that, like alienation and anomie, are long-term trends symptomatic of industrialization were already present in Mercer County; but they were intensified during the boom years, fitting a pattern described by Max Weber (1946, ch. 8), and later elaborated by sociologist C. Wright Mills in his analysis of the rise of the modern American middle class. A German sociologist writing late in the nineteenth century, Weber decried what he saw as a pervasive trend in industrializing Western civilization towards depersonalizing human relations, with its consequent limits on individual freedom. He found evidence for this trend, which he called "rationalization," in the systematization of many areas of social life according to universalistic rules, formalized authority, efficient production, and oppressive routine. He noted the rise of bureaucracy, which he saw as a rationalized form of social organization. Bureaucracies are themselves devoted to impersonal ends, and consist of a hierarchy of roles (appointed offices) with differential powers and responsibilities, and a system of normative rules that are explicitly defined in writing. These roles and rules apply universalistically to all persons by category rather than reflecting personal relationships or individual bias; decisions are thus predictable, a matter of following policies set by those exercising centralized control at the top. Combining aspects of both Marx and Weber's perspectives, C. Wright Mills, in *White Collar* (1951, Part I), documented the twentieth-century rise of American bureaucracies and the rationalization of public life in the United States, coinciding with the rise of monopoly capitalism and the decline of the small town economy based on family enterprise and competitive rivalry in intimate communities.

This configuration of changes that accompanied the industrial modernization of the United States included growing depersonalizing of social relations, rising class differentiation and segregation, and the bureaucratization of broad scope of daily life this has been a central theme in community studies of twentieth-century American life. In his historical study of Springfield, Massachusetts, Michael Frisch (1972) characterizes the overall shift from "experiential" community (which members viewed in relatively direct, personal, and informal terms) to a more abstract modality of social identification. Elements of this pattern of change, noted in Robert and Helen Lynd's studies of "Middletown" (1929, 1937), also characterized industrializing Mercer County. These include an increase in conspicuous consumption and the display of expensive possessions as status symbols, greater bureaucratization of relations between the business and working classes, and the decline in local autonomy. The Lynds attributed the growing political apathy of Middletown residents to the increasing isolation of families and the estrangement of neighborhoods and social classes. In Mercer County, too, social differentiation grew with a loss of community closeness, while political power became increasingly concentrated in absentee corporate ownership and its local client elite. In their studies of social change in "Yankee City," Lloyd Warner and his associates also noted the repercussions of increasingly centralized absentee control over community affairs (1941–1949). They documented the rise of a new elite, whose status was signaled by conspicuous wealth and membership in exclusive voluntary associations. As in Mercer County, many aspects of civic life in Yankee City became infused with the impersonal urban style imposed by the dominant national institutions.[9]

The character of community life I observed was profoundly affected by the energy boom. Although preboom civic life (as described in Chapter 3) was far from being a bucolic idyll, local residents experienced the boom as bringing unwelcome and disorienting changes in their quiet little towns, and complained about greed, theft, having to lock doors, not knowing their neighbors, and their loss of control over local affairs. The presence of so many newcomers itself did much to undermine the intimacy of small town living. In a town filled with strangers, whole new neighborhoods, and new classes and kinds of people, the old-line Mercer County people lost the sense of the familiar that had characterized their public life before the boom. People expressed this loss with statements like, "It used to be around here that you knew everybody and their kids and all, but not any more"; "Now there are so many strangers around, you don't even bother to be curious about them"; "At first the impact wasn't so great, people were able to absorb it all right. It was good for economic life, some new ideas, some new faces—kind of got us out of a rut. But lately, there's just been *too much*. You walk down the street and don't know everybody; you go to church and don't know everybody."

The urbanizing of Mercer County resulted in the social displacement of its farmers and ranchers. Agriculturalists coming to town no longer found it full of old friends and familiar faces. They no longer felt at home there; where they once had gathered to linger over coffee or throw dice for rounds of beer, now they felt crowded out by strangers. Increasingly, they shifted their leisure socializing to towns further west, where the energy boom was less in evidence. This movement created, incidentally, a minor business boom in Dodge, the next town west of Golden Valley, where Ruby's Bar, once the only one in town, was joined by two other drinking places.

Older residents, who found the loss of community closeness hardest to bear, complained of the growing social alienation among neighbors:

> You don't socialize with your neighbors any more. It used to be they would come over to your house and all, and you would take the kids to play with their kids. Now you go to a social club or to the lake. You don't even know their kids any more.

> It's a different lifestyle than being a farmer. The farmer knew his neighbor, and *he* knew *his* neighbor, and *he* knew the next one. It was like that. Now you would hardly know who that is, your neighbor.

It's not like in the early days. When the [German-Russian] immigrants came in it wasn't just empty. They had to go in wherever there was room for them to. And once they were there, why, the others got to know them, and it didn't matter if that was what your neighbor was; whoever it was, you *neighbored*. But not any more. Now they [the newcomers] just ignore you.

The decline of the traditional wedding dance is indicative of this shift away from the intimate, personal, face-to-face community, with its idiom of family relations, to a more bureaucratic, rationalized, and impersonal one. Mercer County wedding dances had been ceremonial celebrations of community unity. They were all-night parties with an open invitation that followed a more exclusive wedding ceremony and dinner. They were well-attended by people of all ages from all over the county. The wedding itself was a family ritual, in which new kinship ties were established. The dance was an occasion for the public celebration of the family event, and a reaffirmation of the relatedness of all community members. Fewer wedding dances were held during the boom years, and their atmosphere of family closeness was threatened by a flood of outsiders. A farmer related his experience: "We used to have dances here in the barn until some guy nearly died. It was during the construction, and all these rough people came that we didn't know who invited them.... I didn't like to throw them out.... There was a fight early in the morning when we were already sleeping. Then we were out milking and somebody came and said there's a man in the barn almost dead!... We decided to have no more dances here."

There was a widespread feeling that boom development was lowering the quality of life in Mercer County towns, particularly in Beulah, where the majority of temporary workers and their families were housed. The frontier strategy of growth for survival, and liberal ideology linking progress, growth, and prosperity remained compelling, however, and civic leaders continued to encourage new residents to settle in their town. The explanation given by one planner was frankly monetary: "We want as high an increase [in population] as possible, because it means *money*. Every person here is worth about thirty-five dollars from severance and conversion taxes!... We also get revenue-sharing money, so it amounts to almost one hundred dollars a head.... In the short term, more people cost the community, but in the long term property taxes catch up and growth benefits the community."

The changes were a challenge to the community ideology of egalitarianism and neighborliness posed by the deepening involvement of the corporations in local affairs. The local ideal of community viewed it metaphorically as a great family unified by a spiritual bond and a common interest. Despite the presence of conflict and inequality, community members are considered to be susceptible to claims of moral responsibility for fellow members, according to an ideal of fair play and reciprocity. Good neighbors are not only helpful, but can be trusted to conform (more or less) to this ideal of public behavior.

Industrial public relations strategists took advantage of the relatively personalisitic tradition still present in Mercer County in efforts to present the corporations as community members, and the industries as simply another interest group on a par with others in local politics. This pose was most successful in the early years of the boom, especially with those inexperienced in dealing with corporate officials. Having accepted the corporations' claims to insider status, however, the people of Mercer County expected them to honor an implicit social contract—to act as good neighbors and deal in good faith, without taking unfair advantage as judged by local standards of community morality.

Experience taught Mercer County residents that economic relations with outside capital are far from equal, that the corporations' verbal effusions about their commitment to the well-being of local communities were sometimes contradicted by their deeds. Through a process which a local pundit referred to as "breed a better bureaucrat," county officials learned not to trust verbal assurances from the industries, and to get all agreements formalized in writing. Much was promised, but only legally binding contracts were honored by the corporations.

Local residents sometimes learned the hard way that companies employed legalistic, rather than moralistic, ethics. As one farm widow related in response to the newspaper's opinion survey, she was no match for the intricacies of mineral leasing:

> The NACCO [North American Coal Corp.], I had believed them. As many others did, I believed it was $5.00 per acre. I would get 2 cents a ton. It sounded good. Afterwards I went to the lawyer, which I should have done to begin with. I gave away my coal. They will ruin my topsoil. Restore? It can never be restored to its originality again. . . . One day [an agent] came, representing the Exxon Oil Company. I did call my lawyer about leasing over the telephone. . . . I believed I got $20.00 an acre and the [income from every] 6th barrel. I told my neighbor about it. The next day another man was sent to my neighbor, representing Exxon. He wound up with a 7-year lease and the 8th barrel. . . . Then these fellows say you can have uranium or any other [mineral] such as sulphur, etc., but they have it all under their lease. A month later another company came in paying $50.00 per acre. A month or so later I had a dream my husband spoke to me in a dream and said, "Be careful with your resources. I have no more to give

you. . . ." The Coal Companies nor the Oil Companies are not honest. Look at what is being done to our water. Pretty soon we will be like Arabia, we will pay more for water than for gas.

Local standards of economic morality were thus challenged as legalistic ethics became accepted as an alternative norm to personalistic ideals of how people should treat one another. Perhaps the greatest threat came not so much from relations with the energy corporations, which Mercer County natives could, after all, place in the historically familiar category of "outside capitalist interests," but rather from within the community itself. The boom offered many opportunities for profiteering by entrepreneurial individuals among the local population, and the influx of outsiders meant the presence of large numbers of people whom many locals felt no particular obligation to treat well and fairly. These strangers were considered fair game.

A Beulah Chamber of Commerce official and manager of a local real estate company defended the inflated prices of rental housing by arguing that it was justifiable to fleece well-paid "sheep" and by denying the presence of economic distress in the community: "The people employed at the various power plants in the area are making a salary where they can afford to pay high rent or to build a new home. . . . The people who have been living in Beulah for the past ten or twenty years should be situated now and shouldn't have to worry about renting or housing" (*Beulah Beacon* September 29, 1977).

A former supermarket employee commented several years later on her part in the boom-time inflation: "Everybody who came up here got raped. They were marking things up at [a supermarket] by 55 percent. I know, because I was the one marking the shit up. A normal mark-up is like 12 to 15 percent. I really don't think it was right, but if I was in business, I'd probably want to take advantage too."

Those who were either not in a position to take advantage of the situation or chose not to do so, denounced the "greed" of those who did. Most in Mercer County did not mind this too much, as long as it was only the highly paid outsiders who were overcharged, but in some cases everybody had to pay the inflated prices. This was decried as an unneighborly assault on the pocketbooks of fellow community members. A local housewife complained about rising prices at the supermarket: "I hope they'll get some competition going on now to bring them down, but it doesn't seem to be happening. There's something evil going on, seems like there's deals among the businessmen—it's *greed*."

A working class man expressed himself even more vehemently in a response to the local newspaper opinion survey: "I think Mercer County has had enough energy development. The businessmen all like

Living with Development | 171

the business but the people see otherwise. It's nice to have a little competition in the area but the local businesses are ripping off us local folks also. So as I see it turns out the rich get richer and the poor get poorer." An elderly lady mused over coffee: "It's the greed of people nowadays that's so bad. And the people with more money complain more. Some people you just can't fill! The owners of new houses complain, but they are making so much more than others. They are a lucky few."

Another symptom of depersonalized public life in a town full of strangers was the decline of verbal agreements and informal dispute resolution among community members. Conflicts that would formerly have either been resolved by the parties without formal intervention or simply allowed to continue unresolved were now much more likely to be submitted to bureaucratic procedures. The police reported an increase in calling the authorities in matters of dispute and petty crime, and more people were signing formal complaints instead of dropping the matter after contacting the police. This trend was encouraged by the police; in 1977 Hazen's police chief had bemoaned the problem of "people not wishing to file a complaint. . . . [They] want to complain but they don't want to press charges or possibly hurt someone. Now we've adopted a policy of 'no complaint, no police action'" (*Hazen Star* February 24, 1977). During the energy boom the county social services board likewise noted an upsurge in neighbors reporting cases of family violence, whereas in the past most had hesitated to interfere. A long-term resident explained the change this way: "Like if your neighbor's dog starts using your lawn for a bathroom—before, you would either go pound on his door and complain, or else decide to put up with it for the sake of good relations. But now . . . if you don't even know or care about your neighbor, you might just call the cops instead. People might still not like to call about their neighbor, but they sure are quick to complain about illegally parked R.V.s, and all the dogs barking in the trailer parks."

The energy boom brought a new emphasis on law and order to what had been a more relaxed and friendly police force. Lifelong locals were outraged at being treated by civil authorities according to the same rules as the unreliable outsiders. A farmer recounted to me with righteous indignation what happened when his seventeen-year-old hired man was arrested for driving a borrowed motorcycle without a license and attempting to flee when police tried to stop him:

> I got a call from the courthouse at 1:00 a.m. that they had him and wanted three hundred dollars bail. So I went all the way over to Stanton [about 25 miles from his farm] and when I got there they wouldn't let me write a

check. It was Friday night and there was no way for me to get cash, the banks were closed. But the officer said too many construction workers wrote bad checks to bail out their buddies, see, so the judge said now they won't take any more checks from anybody. Not even a local! I couldn't believe it—I've known those guys all my life and what do they think, I'm going to run off and leave my farm? Next day was Saturday. I couldn't get the cash because the banks are closed then . . . and because I had to work all day 'cause it was harvest time. Same thing Sunday. That kid had to sit in jail three days, till Monday morning! Because of impact.

A similar formalization took place in the style of enforcing social values and public morality. For example, in 1949, when a group of teen-agers began gathering after school to smoke cigarettes at a store in Beulah, the problem was discussed at a meeting of the commercial club (forerunner of the Chamber of Commerce) and successfully resolved through personal influence:

> The "hang out" was up for "grabs" at one commercial meeting, but no one wanted to be responsible for taking direct action. For them to go directly to the "hang out" operator would cause hard feelings. To go to the parents would cause even harder feelings. The law seemed helpless in the situation. Finally it was decided that the proprietor should be cautioned, in a nice way of course. It was never a matter of record what happened. Undoubtedly, many of the teenage smokers . . . never did know why their favorite haunt got so law-abiding in a hurry back in 1949.
> (*Beulah, North Dakota* 1964:11)

Solving problems in that small, intimate community required delicacy and judiciously applied informal social pressure. In the 1980s, when teen-age smoking (and drinking) again became a problem, the school superintendent did not hesitate to contact parents and police officials, and lobbied vociferously for a substance abuse counselor to be added to the school staff to provide expert assistance. He instituted a peer counseling program in the school, and follow-up therapy sessions with the offenders' families, conducted by professionals.

As a new generation of urban-oriented business entrepreneurs took control of Main Street, there was a shift away from reliance upon unpaid family workers toward increasingly impersonal and bureaucratized employer–employee relations in local businesses. Many more national franchises opened, such as Dairy Queen and Pizza Hut, where management practices were subject to universalistic determination. Locally owned businesses adopted similar regulations. One retailer boasted: "We have a formula for managing the store, and we try to stick with it consistently." Some businessmen also adopted bureaucratic

Living with Development | 173

personnel management practices, not without encountering protest. Employees complained that formalized work rules were not only unfriendly, but unnecessary in such small businesses, but employers were glad of the disciplinary advantage of being able to point to a printed rule in cases of infraction.

The flavor of customer relations also changed. Credit was not extended to blue collar newcomers, and some of the new businesses refused it even to lifelong residents. The owner of a clothing store, himself a relatively recent newcomer to the area, made no secret of his discriminatory policy: "We don't give credit to construction people. The regular locals get credit. Those construction guys come in here or their wives and want to know why they can't have it. . . . I've got the song and dance down now for refusing credit."

Businessmen placed more emphasis on advertising and public relations, and encouraged the practice of greeting customers with a standard smile and rote friendly phrase. In earlier days, a stranger entering a small town business was most likely to receive mutely impassive service, while encountering the half-curious, half-hostile gaze of local customers. But now, it was "service with a smile," a nametag, and a semblance of personal warmth and interest, while the other customers were used to the sight of strangers, and were quite likely to be strangers themselves.

Families in all parts of Mercer County society had difficulties coping with this period of rapid industrialization. The tumultuous experience of community estrangement, depersonalization, and increasing reliance on systematic formalisms coincided with dramatic shifts in the economic organization of family life. The growth of industrial and service jobs for those who would otherwise have had to leave the area increased the proportion of households living by wage work rather than self-employment and unpaid family labor. As early as 1970, 20 percent of the county's labor force worked as miners, and another 45 percent in other wage and salary jobs. By 1980, this total of 65 percent had risen to 79.5 percent of the labor force working outside of family enterprise (U.S. Census 1970, 1980).

For the rapidly growing number of families living by wage and salary jobs rather than from a family farm or business, earning a living was no longer a cooperative, coordinated effort of a family working together under paternal direction. The basis of nuclear family households as production units, and their importance as a social and cultural institution, was also challenged by the presence of new and differently constituted outsider households and the large number of unattached and semi-attached working men temporarily residing in their communities. In a successful application for a family violence specialist to be added to their staff, the county social service board cited a significant rise in family stress-related cases due to the industrial boom. The board noted a 114 percent increase in their Aid to Families with Dependent Children (AFDC) caseload from June 1976 to July 1980, when the county's population had increased by only about 30 percent. The average AFDC statewide increase in North Dakota during this time was only 5.2 percent. The rate of juvenile court activity in the county in 1980 was four times higher than earlier; the rate of child abuse and neglect cases was 225 percent higher than would have been expected based on population alone (*Family Violence Specialist* 1981). The battered women's shelter established in 1979 reported an unusually high 103 cases between March 1979 and February 1980, when the population of the county averaged 8,843.

Even these high rates do not reflect the full extent of domestic malaise. In Mercer County people generally avoided exposing private family problems to public authorities, and out in the countryside there were few neighbors to report them, even should they feel it was their business to do so. According to a Lutheran pastor recruited to Mercer County expressly to counsel families under stress in the development boom, the newcomers were most likely to seek help from social services, while long-term local residents went to the church if they could overcome their shame enough to seek help at all. According to him: "Most of the wife beatings and child abuse I see is among the long-term locals, just from the stress of all the changes."

The expansion of local job opportunities, even if mostly in the minimum-wage services, had potential for accelerating changes in the family's authority and role structure (see Blood and Hamblin 1958). Although the number of off-farm jobs was never as great as pro-development interests had implied or predicted, the presence of more economic opportunities for young people freed many from the necessity of choosing between working in the family enterprise and emigrating. This weakened the power of the older generation to command the economic cooperation of grown offspring. The following case illustrates this trend: An aging farmer applied to the county planning and zoning commission for permission to park his grown son's trailer on his farmstead, an act that required a zoning variance, since his son did not earn his living primarily as a farmer. Family quarrels are usually pursued in private, but this old man complained vehemently at the public hearing that he had been unable to convince his son to take over the farm, although he had browbeaten him into taking over the cattle operation. The son worked at the gasification plant, and preferred this job to farming.

Women had always participated in the labor force in Mercer

County, but the practice was viewed chiefly as a hard-times strategy to boost low household incomes. The newly expanded service sector meant more employment opportunities for women. Most of these were low-wage jobs, but local women appreciated even the small measure of economic independence they afforded. In the past, unmarried women other than widows were rare here. With little opportunity for them to make a living on their own, young women normally either married or emigrated after high school. By the 1980s, a new generation had come of age that was more tolerant of female employment and viewed paternal dominance at home as anachronistic. In young families with two wage-earning parents, the roles of husband and wife were more congruent than complementary. Unmarried women no longer had to emigrate or marry in order to support themselves. Women also began taking a more powerful part in community life as business entrepreneurs, journalists, planning commissioners, and even a police chief.

Incorporating the Corporations

As the construction phase of industrial development drew to a close in the mid-1980s, public attention shifted to the thousands of newly hired permanent plant employees and their families who hoped to make Mercer County their new home. Local residents had welcomed the arrival of the permanent work force, and considered their presence less disruptive than that of the temporary workers. Local residents expected that this group would be incorporated into existing patterns and institutions of community life, just as the occasional newcomers had been assimilated in the past. This new wave of immigrants, however, could not be absorbed without changing existing social and economic relations in fundamental ways. Indeed, these had already been transformed by the complex of changes accompanying industrialization already described. The process of assimilating the newcomers also produced increasing social differentiation, urbanization, and homogenizing acculturation within the mainstream of American mass society.

Assembling a permanent work force to operate the new facilities was a major undertaking. While experienced personnel could be transferred from other mines and power plants to the new ones in Mercer County, the coal gasification facility was the first of its kind in the country. It required a new corporate structure, built from scratch, and extensive personnel training at all levels. The opportunity to work with this new technology, as well as the impressive financial incentives offered by Great Plains, attracted some seven hundred thousand applicants for the seven hundred permanent job openings there. The vast majority of those hired were from urban industrial centers outside of North Dakota, although a few were local people who had earlier emigrated and acquired industrial and management skills outside of Mercer County. With starting salaries for newly trained technicians running at $30,000 a year, these people were among the most prosperous in the area.

The population boom had brought about a corresponding expansion in the health, education, and other professional service fields, and so the permanent newcomers included, in addition to the industrial operating personnel, an expanded class of urban-trained professionals. These new doctors, lawyers, teachers, nurses, social welfare workers, civil engineers, laboratory technicians, counselors, city planners, and so on were mostly young (in their thirties and forties), with urban tastes and orientation. Other newcomers included those who had come to open new businesses or buy out old ones on Main Street or in the new commercial strips along the highway.

The consensus among local residents was that these people would eventually be assimilated into the existing communities, and residents approved of the efforts of some to gain insider status through purchasing homes, joining churches, and supporting their adopted community at sports events. In fact, this group was so numerous and independent that much of their integration would necessarily take place on their own terms, rather than those of lifelong residents of Mercer County. Many of them, particularly those highest up in the corporate structure, had no serious intention of assimilating in any case, feeling quite comfortable with their uprooted status. Their attitude was like that of other members of the "mobile managerial class" described by anthropologist John Dorst as "most at home in a postmodern environment of transportable, anonymous experience" (1989:44–45). In any case, local people did not feel threatened by the upper class newcomers; white collar workers did not evoke the almost criminal image of the construction boom "riff-raff" in local eyes, but they remained socially alien to all but the local elite.

The lack of fit between the melting pot rhetoric and the undeniable reality of social differentiation at both ends of the class spectrum is reflected in this rather confused statement by a local public official, in response to my question about how the presence of so many newcomers was affecting the atmosphere of the community and how long it would take to absorb them:

> We're learning a lot, in the community. We're expected to provide different recreational facilities. Different types of people are coming in. Where we were basically a German community, we're now pretty well

mixed, from all segments of the population. But they are all blending in very good with the community. . . . They're joining the organizations and the churches. There's a certain segment of the population that is Mormons, so they formed their own church. It's been good for the community. It's offered our children more in school, because [of] the demand from other people [who] have come in . . . [for] more things for the community.

Long-term Mercer County residents used the word "newcomer" rather than "outsider" to describe those who planned to relocate permanently and become a part of their adopted community. This term connoted a positive attitude toward these particular immigrants, and they were only called "outsiders" when locals wished to express disapproval or hostility toward them. Unlike the outsiders of the construction boom, these permanent newcomers were considered socially redeemable, and capable of someday becoming insiders, or "locals." In the mid-1980s, there were more or less three categories of people at different stages in this process: the locals, who had been there since before the industrial developments of the 1970s, the established newcomers who had arrived during the 1970s and had already moved into significant community leadership positions, and the newest newcomers, who had not yet gained full acceptance and were still excluded from leadership offices.

The process of gaining insider status required some effort on the part of the newcomer. Property ownership was an important prerequisite, since the purchase of a home, business, or other investment signified a long-term commitment and belief in the future of the community. By this means, newcomers could instantly acquire some substance, respectability, and a voice in community affairs. Rural American society has never been tolerant of single women, and marriage and motherhood were particularly important to newcomer women for gaining acceptance in Mercer County. Voluntary associations served as important vehicles for integration, since church attendance signals moral values and community service is a highly appreciated contribution. Membership in such smaller-scale "communities" also provided relationships with key locals that could lead to building broader networks in the insider society. Many newcomers joined associations such as the Jaycees, sports leagues, and the Eagles Club both for the recreational opportunities and to mix with the locals. The golf clubs of Hazen and Beulah were favorites of the more prosperous newcomer joiners, who constituted about one-third of their total membership in 1984.

Linda's case illustrates highly successful assimilation into insider status by a woman. Originally from South Dakota, with a degree in political science from the University of Minnesota, Linda first came to Mercer County in the early 1970s as a social services caseworker. She married an electrician who had been living there since the early 1960s and was already an insider. Linda first met her neighbors, then accepted an opportunity to lead a Girl Scout troop. She joined a homemakers club, taught church school, and served as a substitute teacher at the school. Becoming increasingly involved in community affairs, Linda was elected to her Town Council in Stanton, and later to the County planning and zoning commission, the only woman to serve on this twelve-person panel. She served for several years before resigning in protest over what she saw as the haphazard planning policies and sexism of her colleagues. But her professional career had advanced meanwhile, and Linda became a regional director of social services, guiding the agency through the throes of computerization. Linda's advice on how to become accepted in the community?: "Get involved, join things, offer to help. Get to know people and offer your services. I don't think people even remember that I am an outsider!"

Men's careers of assimilation followed broadly similar lines. When Craig came to Beulah in the late 1970s to buy out a clothing store, the town welcomed the energetic young entrepreneur. Coming from a small North Dakota town himself, he knew how to operate: "The thing is to get involved; you only get out of a town what you put into it." Craig volunteered his time generously on projects sponsored by the Chamber of Commerce, and by the end of his first year, Craig was elected president of the Chamber, a time-consuming position shunned by more established businessmen. After a short time, Craig married another newcomer; his wife worked at the hospital and was active in the Jaycettes. By 1984 Craig had become a successful and established pillar of Main Street, and a well-known character about town.

Mercer County's class system was transformed by the energy boom, not least by the establishment of a new upper stratum of highly paid and prestigious families. If the temporary work force had represented a new pariah class, the corporate managers and supervisors constituted a new elite—an elite that appeared suddenly, created out of whole cloth and without historical connections to other local classes. These members of the "mobile managerial class," settling in the larger towns of Beulah and Hazen, made little attempt to assimilate through community service, and remained for the most part uncomfortably superimposed upon the pre-existing social relations. Their livelihoods were tied to corporations with a national or transnational scope of operations; protected from possible failure of Mercer County plants by generous "golden parachute" contracts, this class did not share in the economic interdependence so basic to organic community life. Local history and tradition had little meaning or relevance for them, except as a romanticized image of a generic "Plains frontier." As a rule, they had little notion of how to relate to local farmers or older townspeople, and little interest in their lives and concerns. As a relatively independent group, they sought to re-create their lifestyle and social position in the urban centers where they had previously lived.

Many of the new elite families built weekend homes on Lake Sakakawea, but while in town the golf clubs became a favorite center of their social activity. The Hazen Golf Club, for example, served as a sort of country club for industry executives and their wives. Its president was usually elected from their ranks, and the "Great Plains ladies" formed their own club within the Club. It also served as an arena for connecting with the local elite; the Club sponsored a "meet the GPGA [Great Plains Gasification Associates] management" party, to which all members were invited. Employees of Basin Electric were also active at the Club, particularly on the board of directors. Their contributions helped make the Golf Club a classy urban-style showpiece.

The golf clubs of Hazen and Beulah had first been built with volunteer labor by local folks who played golf for entertainment. Their unpretentiousness was exemplified in their sponsorship of an annual Winter Golf Tournament, a tongue-in-cheek affair resulting in innumerable lost golf balls and freezing hilarity as players bundled in snowsuits stumbled through the hip-deep drifts. Both clubs had nine-hole courses and aspired to full-sized eighteen-hole links with fine sod surfacing. During the 1980s, Energy Impact Office money became available and both clubs sought separate funding for improvements. Since support was only available for the cooperative development of full-sized links to be shared by neighboring small towns, the two clubs abandoned this effort and undertook improvements independently, at great effort and expense.

The road to cosmopolitan splendor for the golf clubs was not always a smooth one. On one occasion the Hazen Club needed a new bridge over a picturesque creek. In the past such maintenance had been undertaken by groups of volunteer members donating their work and materials, but this time a newcomer member, who happened to be a high-ranking corporate executive, offered to "take care of it" himself, and get it done for free. He used materials from the plant construction and company engineers to design the bridge. As one amused local Club member recounted: "You could have driven a tank over the thing. Then the damn thing was too heavy to move into place without a crane, so he borrowed one from the plant at night, a little one he could mount on a truck. It really damaged the grass, and he got caught anyway and we had to pay for the materials. . . . The whole thing ended up costing the Golf Club thousands of dollars."

Built with the new elites and visiting industrial dignitaries in mind, Beulah's Best Western Hotel opening in 1979 brought new heights of normative urban luxury and sophistication. Its restaurant was expensive and served *haute cuisine* by local standards, and in its dimly lit cocktail lounge, crowded with bulky modern tables and black leatherette upholstery, while listening to a slinky sequined singer in heavy makeup crooning out a peppy version of "Blue Bayou," one could forget the small town surroundings and imagine oneself in any American city. Even here, though, there remained traces of a family-run business around the edges, with children playing in the lobby and running errands to the guest rooms, and old friends dropping by for a cup of coffee behind the check-out desk.

The new elite of corporate management and young urban professionals were trend setters in the shift to urban tastes and status display through conspicuous consumption, and yet their role in the county's urbanization was superficial. Urban ambitions had been a fundamental ingredient of small town boosterism in Mercer County from the beginning, and local town residents had welcomed the arrival of such amenities as a public swimming pool, tennis courts, a new movie theater, more restaurants, and mainstream franchises such as Dairy Queen and Pizza Hut. Ever since the automobile and paved highways had made frequent travel to the Bismarck-Mandan metropolitan area feasible, Mercer County residents had been enthusiastic city visitors. Even before the cosmopolitan infusion of the energy boom, they regularly made the trip for special shopping, professional services, or even just a night on the town. The entertainment available in Mercer County itself held little charm for the large numbers of young, well-heeled newcomers, and the Friday night trickle of city-bound traffic increased to a flood by 1984.

The energy boom made it possible for the larger towns to realize some of their urban ambitions, taking on more of the anonymous and generic look of American suburbs and shopping strips, but it also brought about the social displacement of farmers and ranchers. The business people of the larger towns no longer depended on rural trade, and were caught up in the fervor of development. With their population swollen with newcomers, towns gained importance at the expense of the countryside, and townspeople turned their attention away from the farmers, whom they now considered old-fashioned and anachronistic, and towards the city, pursuing its sophistication and modernity.

For better or worse, the energy boom had transformed life in Mercer County and above all in its newly urbanized centers, Beulah and Hazen. Evaluating and coping with these changes magnified for Mercer County the tensions between the desire for economic growth and the other values that this goal seemed to contradict.

Chapter Seven

Patterns of Power: Changes in Political Economy

Political and economic life in Mercer County changed over the course of the energy boom. The well-established interest groups of the previous political economic order—agriculture, business, and labor—maneuvered for position in a fluid situation, and each sought to influence the course of economic development. In the process of industrialization, however, these classes were themselves transformed. Development did not affect the county evenly; in pursuit of their own interests, the corporations sought to establish particular relationships with the different local interest groups and vice versa. The result was a structural reshaping of Mercer County's political economy corresponding to its expanded role as an energy supplier.

The conflicts, rivalries, and alliances of the boom years often formed around old social structural fault lines, and actors employed goals, rhetoric, and organizational strategies developed in earlier local experience. These struggles, however, now took shape within a new power structure, one which the industries could dominate. The ever-increasing direct involvement of the government in support of industry was an overt counterpoint to the power provided the corporations by a legal, ethical, and institutional framework that gave industry and its camp followers (such as real estate developers and business entrepreneurs) significant advantages.

The Eclipse of Agriculture

The interests of the growing industrial sector were most directly in conflict with those of farmers, both because of the threat to crop land posed by strip mining and the challenge to the agriculturalists' special status as the economic foundation of the local economy. This position had already been damaged by the long-term structural problems faced by agriculture nationwide. The industrial boom in Mercer County accelerated the marginalizing of farmers, and the declining power of the agricultural class was apparent both in their relations with townspeople and with the industries.

In the past, the prosperity of town and country in Mercer County had been closely linked. As the number of farmers declined in the first half of the century, so did the number of local commercial centers. Where there were once fifteen small towns in Mercer County, there were only six in 1970, and two of these were nearly extinct. Had it not been for the presence of an already expanding coal mining industry, the population decline might have continued through the 1970s and 1980s, as it did in other counties in western North Dakota lacking industrial income.

This linkage of town and country's fortunes was weakened by the growth of industry. Changes in town versus rural populations in Mercer County before and during the energy boom give an indication of the rising power and importance of towns over the countryside (see Table 2, p. 151). While the total population grew from 6,805 in 1960 to a peak of 14,359 in 1983, the rural population actually declined from 3,130 to 2,909. Before rapid industrialization, agricultural families accounted for almost half of the county's population, while at its height they represented just over one-fifth. It has long been noted by rural sociologists in the United States (e.g., Douglass 1919; Miller 1928; Taylor 1933) that its small towns look to the city for their model, and abandon their character as service centers for farmers when a chance arises for urbanization. The business people of the larger towns of Mercer County no longer depended on the farmers' trade, and were caught up in the fervor of industrial development. They were eager to turn their backs on the countryside, and to be liberated from dependence on uncertain agricultural income.

This redoubled orientation of towns away from the countryside exacerbated old antagonisms, but, in the new struggle over the benefits of economic growth, the business class of the growing towns had a clear advantage. With the political and economic power of the agricultural community declining, it became less of a force to be reckoned with. Before the growth of industry, Mercer County's agriculturalists and townspeople formed an integrated social and economic system, in which personnel moved easily from one group to the other, and were economically interdependent. While the interests of town and country dwellers had always been somewhat antagonistic, and their relations strained at times, the division had previously been mitigated by the cross-cutting bonds of kinship, friendship, and shared culture. The urbanizing forces of the energy boom severed the bonds of town dependence on the countryside, and also cut the agriculturalists adrift culturally. The new generation of townspeople had less knowledge of and sympathy with the lives and concerns of farmers. This was especially true of the new class of urban-trained professionals who were moving into positions of leadership and influence in town and county government.

Agriculturalists were well aware of their eroding political position and resentful when development policies made their interests secondary to those of townspeople. When the local newspaper survey mentioned in Chapter 6 invited comment on the energy impacts, the following response typified the complaints of rural residents:

> Take a look in any direction from Hazen and you see many homes that are not farms. When there won't be any school buses because of the cost, the farms will still be here! The school is broke, period. More taxes! Our rural roads are really getting in bad shape. Money! What happens if we have a bad winter? Money! Now the best part: the type of people moving into Hazen and Beulah. I for one was for slow development. Now I hope the people come by the droves, the more, the better: Hazen and Beulah have it coming. Then one day everyone will find out there isn't any money to pay for the development and all hell will break loose! I wonder who will stay around? You have any idea?

Town and country were split over the kind of projects to be undertaken with the money available from the Energy Impact Office. The towns took the lion's share, while the concerns of agriculturalists over roads, reclamation, groundwater, and air quality dwindled in political significance. Rural residents complained bitterly that the impact aid was going disproportionately to benefit the townspeople, despite the fact that farmers were suffering at least as much, if not more, of the adverse economic effects of development, as in this survey response:

> I believe that the county is getting a nice sum of money for impact, but, it seems that so many of these new people coming in, and even some of the original residents, seem to feel that they can demand just about anything that comes to their mind, and they will get it! Let's be reasonable, people! Such things as covered skating rinks and water on the golf course and all these other frills that these people have been demanding should be paid for by the few that are using them! It is ironic that we, who have lived and farmed this land, and who will be giving up our livelihood so they can extract coal for these plants and get the impact funds from our coal fields, are still hobbling to town over gravel roads that are so full of holes, while

our city folk, who live on black-top all week long, and then, for a nice long weekend choose to go to the lake, have blacktop way down to the waters' edge! How selfish can you get? I think that we have a very legitimate gripe when we feel it is about time some of this impact money is used to blacktop the main roads leading to the towns of Mercer County, and not using about every cent for the benefit of those who dwell in the city, and have so much time to "play around."

Another put it more succinctly: "Politics Politics Politics. This is farm and ranch country. I don't like the two words *Coal Country*."

Although their influence in town politics had never been very great, the agricultural class had, in the past, wielded considerable power with the county government. This level of local government burgeoned with the industrial boom; in 1979 its budget saw a one-year increase of 49 percent ($1.6 million increase), and it continued to grow every year during the boom. The County Commission was responsible for decisions regarding rural land use, road maintenance, and other items of particular concern to farmers and ranchers. As long as they remained a large proportion of the voting population, agriculturalists were assured of electing members from their own ranks to fill these important posts, or at least of continuing to be a primary constituency whose interests would be promoted by the commission. This also changed with the energy boom, when developers' interests in rural land use began to compete seriously with, and even overshadow, those of agriculturalists.

According to the Dakota Resource Council, the umbrella organization for county landowners' associations and environmentalist groups, the problem was not limited to the Mercer County Commission. In 1979 they charged that the State Public Service Commission was "more concerned about the demands of the energy industry than the concerns of the people of this state" (*Hazen Star* June 7, 1979:3) and charged that the Commission had changed its procedures to limit the information available to landowners and tenants affected by energy facilities. These changes included the elimination not only of advance mailings to them, but also of the publication of notices with legal descriptions of the land and who was to be affected, and of their mandatory review process. The result was that many individuals found themselves having to work out their own relations with the corporations, with variable success, while an overworked core of activists at the Landowners Association and the Dakota Resource Council provided information and legal assistance.

Some of the companies maintained good reputations for fair dealing with the farmers and ranchers, and appreciated the Landowners Association's efforts. On occasion, however, industry and its subcontractors used the individualistic approach to gain an advantage over the uninformed. This occurred in the case of a transmission line to link Basin's Antelope Valley Station to the power grid at Hebron, North Dakota. Landowners along the route were entitled to compensation for the easement and for each transmission tower, and the contractor began contacting them at the Hebron end of the line, where people had less experience with industry. When the Mercer County Landowners Association began contacting affected landowners, they found that some had sold out for as little as $300 per tower setting, while those who used the advice of attorneys provided by the Dakota Resource Council got $10,000 per setting. Even after the MCLA organized an association of affected landowners along the transmission route, Basin refused to negotiate with them collectively, and continued its policy of making separate compensation agreements with each individual.

The experiences of farmers and ranchers varied a great deal. Some were delighted at the prospect of income from leases and off-farm employment. One exclaimed: "The only thing I regret is that I won't live long enough to enjoy the money! I wish they'd hurry up and mine where I leased it." Others, however, felt forced to lease their land unwillingly, and mourned the loss of their homes and fields.

The case of one rural neighborhood south of Beulah illustrates this mixed experience. The first major leasing in this area took place in the 1930s and 1940s. At that time, many leased their minerals never thinking that mining would actually come to pass. The second wave of leasing took place in the late 1970s, and was not accomplished so hastily as the first. Landowners got together and spent over a year drawing up the contract with the Knife River Coal Mining Company, and got a much better deal. On that occasion, most of the farmers in the neighborhood leased only a portion of their landholdings, and used the money to pay off debt on the rest. A few retired and moved away permanently, further depopulating the countryside.

In the mid-1980s, the neighborhood again came under pressure to lease. This time, Knife River wanted more land than ever for their advancing strip mine. In most cases the entire landholdings, including the site of the homes and out-buildings, were required for efficient operation of the mine. Knife River held neighborhood meetings to explain the situation, although the farmers' legal rights were far from clear.

One farmer explained the reluctance and confusion felt by the landowners of the neighborhood:

> Knife River is mining on some of our land, and they want to mine the rest—all around here. Several of our neighbors don't want to lease any

more either, but the mining company puts lots of pressure on to lease. We've got all the money we wanted out of it already. Older people don't want the money, just a placid life on their own land. . . . The reclamation appears to take a long time, and, well, we would just rather not lease right near and right where the house is, and the long fields just west down the road. . . .

I don't know if we will be able to hold out, though. The mineral rights to the land close to the house are federally owned, and the new regulations are not clear about if the surface owner's agreement is needed to lease it. The home quarter is already surrounded by leased land, so it will be terrible anyway during the mining—right in the middle of a mine! That's why Knife River wants our land so badly, so they won't have to mine around it. But I just can't stand to see it happen; I'll probably have to just leave when the mine comes, move away to someplace, because I just can't stand to see it.

In cases where the surface owner's agreement was necessary for a valid lease, it was possible for a landowner to refuse the mine. A farmer in the same neighborhood described such a case nearby:

[One of my neighbors] wouldn't lease, so they mined around him. He just didn't want to give up his land, and they tried and tried but couldn't make him do it. But after he died his kids leased. They had to pay estate tax on his unmined coal. It's like the Indian Treaties. People don't want to give [the land] up but end up losing it anyway over the generations. The coal company deals fair, but they think differently than farmers. People here don't want to lease—they wish the coal wasn't here at all.

In another case, south of Zap, a farmer claimed to have been tricked into signing a lease, and unsuccessfully went to court to prevent the mining of her land. According to her son, who farmed the operation, "If they ever did mine on her land, she'd be a millionaire. But we're used to our way of life. It's not the money we're after. We'd feel best if they just packed up and left" (*Hazen Star* March 31, 1977:3).

The growing troubles of the agricultural economy gave many farmers mixed feelings about industrial development of prime agricultural land. Good crop prices tied to booming export markets in the 1970s had encouraged ambitious agriculturalists to expand operations and modernize equipment. Public policy contributed to the borrowing fervor by lowering production constraints designed to support prices, and U.S. Secretary of Agriculture Earl Butz exhorted farmers to plant every possible acre (Strange 1988:18). Easy credit and rising land values made farmland seem like a good investment, and competition for it kept pushing values higher. By the late 1970s, however, production had far exceeded demand, and falling export prices slashed the incomes of heavily indebted farmers. The stage was set for a new wave of bankruptcies and foreclosures in the 1980s. For farmers caught in this financial bind, the growth of industry offered the welcome relief of off-farm employment in the mines and growing service jobs and of income from coal leases. This was but the sugarcoating of a bitter pill, however, since the coal-based industries expanded at the cost of destroying agricultural land. While some farmers actively opposed the use of their lands for industrial purposes, others were glad of a chance to cut their losses and retire on the income from coal leases.

The presence of relatively high-paying energy jobs contributed to a tight labor market for farm operators used to hiring help. During the years of rapid job expansion, men who used to work at farm labor could get industrial jobs, while high-school boys and retired men who formerly did part-time farm work could get higher wages in town. One farm operator explained how he tried to adjust: "I can't afford to pay the same as energy jobs, but my hired help gets other benefits: I pay for his housing and utilities, he gets free meat off the ranch and his own pen in the feedlot. If he wants to stay, he can lease some of my land. . . . But I've had to change my operation with labor costs so high. I quit raising hogs and milking cows because they take too much labor time."

The great quantities of land now being devoted to industrial uses disrupted agricultural production in several ways. The reclamation of strip-mined land was more than a decade behind schedule in remote parts of the county not visited by regulatory enforcement agents. Some of those living near mines reported a drop in the water table, and some wells went completely dry. Although the mine corporations denied responsibility publicly, in at least one case they paid for a new well, an indirect acknowledgment of responsibility. A letter responding to the newspaper-sponsored survey lists a series of complaints typical of many landowners' grievances:

> The coal company and electric company make it miserable for people living in the neighborhood. The electric wire should have been put underground. The coal company don't get the land leveled off. I was interested in a land mine, about eight years ago, and it isn't leveled off yet. They shouldn't be forced to stockpile four feet of topsoil, we don't have this much topsoil. Two feet or less would be plenty. I blame [the] Public Service Commission for this—I suppose they don't have men that know conditions. Also, the coal company destroyed my fence by not giving me enough time to remove it, [and] also drove across my land with heavy machinery and made it hard to put up.

Another responded with a stronger statement, expressing the opinions of most farmers:

> I think "they" (ANG [American Natural Gas], Basin Electric, North American Coal) should pay all the bills they create—city and rural. We have heard much of the city's side but did you know that they won't even pay the farmer for his land damages—loss of production due to coal mining activities? I own few [sic] coal but have a lot on my lands. So it will be dug. I asked for 8 cents/ton for what coal I own. . . . Plus I asked for land damage—loss of production payments *or* what the leases provide, whichever is higher. I have been refused thus far my greedy ugly farmer request. We farmers always want so much. We must be refused (I am writing now with irony).
>
> When they leased my neighbor's land, they told him he'll get 2 million dollars if mining commences. Now it's going to be 80,000. He can't make a living on that over the time period the land is out [of production]. He was forced to relocate.
>
> They are quicker to relocate farmers than to pay them actual damages. Maybe they'd sooner relocate Beulah, Hazen, Zap, Golden Valley, etc. It's for power. A play for power. And the more they get the less they need to do to make things right, impact-wise.

With complaints of this sort on the rise, the mining companies began taking greater pains with their public image and landowner relations. Coteau Properties, a new mining subsidiary of North American Coal, hired a local miner to be in charge of landowner relations. He explained his job this way: "I just keep things running smooth with the landowners for the mine. Say they send people out onto people's land a lot to drill for coal, to test for it and so on, and sometimes the landowners get pissed off. Things used to be a lot worse, before they hired me to take care of it. You see they know me, I'm a local, was a miner for eighteen years. . . . Now they can just call me up if they have a gripe. They're not so suspicious and nervous about development anymore."

If landowners had learned what to expect from coal development, they were also becoming well-versed in the technicalities of enforcing land reclamation and pollution control regulations. The Dakota Resource Council provided local agriculturalists with legal and environmental expertise, and was influential in bringing the largely urban intellectual environmentalist movement to rural North Dakota. As one Council worker explained: "Before, ecology was seen as something that city people do to rural people. . . . and so you got ranchers burning Robert Redford in effigy and things like that. Now things have changed, with the coal mining and reclamation problems, and the environmentalist movement in North Dakota has a more local identity, something rural people are involved in."

Over time, those farm operators who were the most active watchdogs on development activities gained the experience and expertise to confront industry agents at legal and procedural hearings with self-assurance and well-planned questioning. They learned to demand specific and binding responses on a host of essential details for every action affecting their land, such as coal testing, pipeline installation, and nearby mining and reclamation. Corporate agents, accustomed to having their vague assurances accepted, fumed in frustration at permit hearings in the early 1980s, as well-coached farmers pressed them on fence repair, restoration of original land drainage contours, and maintenance contingencies.

The ambivalence with which farmers regarded industry was characterized by a profound suspicion of big outside capital. This, together with a moralistic rhetorical style and a cooperative organizing strategy, was the legacy of the agrarian populist movement. The farmers' economic goals were individualistic—survival for each independent enterprise. They did not see cooperation as intrinsically desirable, but as a survival strategy for countering the power of big capital. Only when many were threatened by an acute and concrete common problem did farmers who normally compete with each other band together in localized grassroots protest and self-help associations.

The rhetoric typical of agrarian anti-industry activists in the region rearticulated the old populist themes, blaming big outsider corporations and uncaring government, and praising the moral superiority of the hard-working family farming way of life over that of "city slickers." In this modern example of populist moral rhetoric, a western North Dakota journalist invokes the roots of agrarian democratic socialism:

> The Northern Plains remain largely . . . a region of husbandmen raising food to feed a world—despite the industrialization, urbanization, and commercialization of the rest of the United States. The Northern Plains are a last frontier, the remnant of Thomas Jefferson's vision of America. . . . Who will own what land is left when industrialization is completed, when the coal resource is used up? Will the individuals survive as freeholders, tilling their own ground? Or will corporations operate as landlords and food producers and use individuals as labor for their companies' profit? (Jacobs 1975:277–279)

In an appeal to its members to support lobbying efforts to prevent the state legislature from weakening air pollution standards, a Dakota

Resource Council activist calls upon an ideologically compelling and politically legitimating depiction of family farming as a "way of life" (not just a way of making a living):

> I have spent the whole of my fifty-six years in North Dakota and hope to spend a few more. Forty of those years have been spent making a living for myself and my family which I had hoped could some day take over my ranch and continue our way of life if they so desired. My two sons have now taken over my ranch and are struggling to make a living on it. My fondest hope for them is that they will be able to continue to have a few undisturbed acres to farm and ranch and the fresh air that was our heritage from our fathers. (*Dakota Counsel* 1982 5[4]:2)

Moralistic argumentation in support of the family farming lifestyle emphasized the positive values of working hard to make an honest living on the land without exploiting others or accepting handouts. It claimed the farmers to be the primary producers of local income, which had sustained the small town economy. It referred to their social contribution in producing cheap food for an ungrateful nation, and claimed the moral superiority of keeping good farmland in production, as opposed to other land uses.

Populist rhetoric was a time-honored tradition in North Dakota politics, and it was also a reflection of genuine agrarian values. Even so, it was largely ineffective in gaining the sympathy of large corporations and their urban-oriented agents. The interpretation offered by this Tenneco official discounts it entirely: "I don't buy this 'wanting to preserve their way of life' thing that the landowners say. The farmer is really only interested in what he can get out of it. When they don't own their own coal, they fuss 'cause all they get out of it is a wrecked pasture, but when they own it, and can make a lot of money out of it, they're in a hurry to sell. Then they say, 'Here, you can take the first bite with the dragline right out of the kitchen table.' "

There was some historical basis for sympathy between agriculturalists and coal miners, because many of the latter were recruited from farms and because both found themselves in conflict with big capital. Although the two occupations are based on conflicting uses of the land, the expansion of mining activities in the 1980s brought about a tactical alliance between them over the issue of enforcing land reclamation laws. This cooperation was limited to a few activists from each group, however, and did not represent a widespread community of interest. When asked about the farmer–labor alliance, most agriculturalists judged that there really was none to speak of. Although one or two miners regularly attended meetings of the Mercer County Landowners

Association, active cooperation was limited. As one farmer explained: "They're not really on the same wavelength [as we are]."

Pressing as the problems posed by industry were to Mercer County farmers, the spreading farm crisis of the 1980s sapped their efforts and diverted their attention. During the boom period of rising land values and farm expansion in the 1970s most young and undercapitalized would-be farmers had been unable to begin operating. In the ensuing bust, accompanied in this part of the country by a debilitating drought, those young farmers who had managed to begin were the most vulnerable and the first to sell out. The result was further consolidation as conditions took their toll on the younger generation and on an aging population of farm operators more concerned with the retirement deals offered by coal leases than with fighting the mining companies.

The Expansion of Business | These years of declining agricultural power and prestige were boom years for the business communities of Mercer County. Expanding populations and more industrial customers supported an increasing number and variety of local businesses and professional offices, as indicated by the numbers of commercial telephone listings (see Table 3). These numbers indicate that the construction of Mercer County's first electrical plants during the 1970s near Stanton gave a boost to the business communities of that town and of nearby Hazen, while those of Beulah and Golden Valley actually declined between 1962 and 1972. The energy boom of the 1970s and early 1980s, however, brought extremely rapid growth to Hazen and especially to Beulah. While most of the smaller towns' businesses also expanded, they grew at a slower rate, and the result has been an increased differentiation of the communities into small and large, with the latter becoming increasingly urbanized.

As might be expected, different types of businesses expanded at different rates. In both Beulah and Hazen, most of the business expansion came in the areas of industrial contracting and services; real estate and housing; and building contracting and supplies, including home furnishings. Taken as a group, these "boom businesses" grew 650 percent between 1962 and 1985. Similarly, Hazen's "boom businesses" (those in the group listed above) grew 450 percent over the same period. Growth rates in areas other than the "boom businesses" between 1962 and 1985 totaled only 210 percent for Beulah and 100 percent for Hazen.[1] Agriculture-related businesses did not expand at all, and actually declined in Hazen.

Before the energy boom, most of the established businesses in the

Table 3 | Mercer County Commercial Telephone Listings, 1962–1985

	1962	1972	1977	1982	1985
Beulah	71	70	100	180	211
Golden Valley	12	9	10	11	12
Hazen	65	81	101	142	164
Pick City	*	*	4	9	13
Stanton	9	21	26	33	31
Zap	7	11	12	12	16

Source: West River Telephone Directories.
*Town not listed.

towns were operated by families—everything from bars to banks, furniture stores to funeral parlors. These family businesses depended mainly on the historically shrinking agricultural trade. This limited income prescribed the use of unpaid family labor, and inhibited business expansion. With the boom development came new opportunities and new competitive pressures, which some of the older business families were ill-equipped to meet.

The growth of absentee ownership is a common symptom of industrialization in small American towns, and its social effects have been documented by the classic community studies. While the most important instance in Mercer County was that of the large energy corporations that owned the industries and controlled the new economy, this process was also at work among the towns' retail merchants. Prior to the energy boom, even the largest property owners tended to live in the county, and the two most important banks in the county were local family enterprises. By the early 1980s, however, increasing numbers of new businesses were owned by individuals who did not live in the county, but hired local managers to run them. More national chain stores opened here too, owned by out-of-state corporations. As a result of these trends, by the mid-1980s the family was no longer the typical unit of ownership and production in the business class of Mercer County.

There was money to be made by businesses in a booming local economy, and this fact attracted more national retail companies and outside entrepreneurs. Local businesses that were not in a position to expand and improve their premises were pushed aside by more aggressive newcomers. As one local businessman remarked ruefully, "You either have to go along with it—grow and modernize—or go out of business." The family bakery in Hazen, for example, was unable to compete with the new supermarket bakery prices, and closed its doors in 1980. Some who invested in store expansion and remodeling in anticipation of the boom were forced to leave when the gasification plant was delayed for three years. Others chose to sell out rather than confront the new demands of a changing clientele. A man who left the insurance business explained his reasons: "I thought that after thirty years in insurance I should be able to sit back and run it without any trouble. You know, I should be able to relax, and know what to do about everything that came along. . . . But when this development—all these strangers coming in with their problems, new problems I had to deal with. . . . I *resented* it, so I sold the business."

Vigorous young entrepreneurs from outside the area bought out existing businesses and opened new ones of all types. According to figures publicized by the Inter-industry Technical Assistance Team, 450 families had moved into Mercer County by December 1981 to set up service businesses. This trend resulted in a revolution of ownership of the retail businesses in the county. By 1984, a new generation of newcomers owned some 80 percent of the businesses in the larger towns.[2] Older businessmen had been comfortable with the slower pace of life before the boom, but these new young entrepreneurs were in a hurry to make money. To do this, it was necessary to expand and compete. Although some of these newcomers believed in the traditional family business as an ideal, most were too young to have grown children to help out, and the new, modernized enterprises were too large for a couple to run by themselves. Instead, they hired their clerks, waitresses, and other unskilled labor from the county's large pool of unemployed and underemployed people, which included both long-term residents and newcomers from construction worker families.

New alliances emerged among the powerful interest groups. In the new context there were improved opportunities for ambitious leaders in business and politics to advance their careers through cooperation among themselves rather than by maintaining good relations with a political following or constituency. Important political figures in Beulah and Hazen were either employed by the industries (or had family members who were), owned businesses patronized by industry, or land that they hoped to develop.

The changing relationship among the local business and political leaders, outside developers, and the energy corporations was nowhere more apparent than in the case of real estate in the larger towns of Hazen and Beulah. With populations increasing two to three times during the 1970s and early 1980s, there was a high demand for residential and commercial development. Real estate became a focus of financial investment and policy interest.

There were three kinds of real estate investors in the towns, each with different links to local power bases. The first type consisted of local people who either happened to own strategically located land for development, or were local businessmen and building contractors who decided to enter the realty market. Members of this group worked through the chambers of commerce and local governments as insiders. As community members, they also benefitted from long-established personal ties, and as prominent civic figures, some local developers even served in elected positions on town councils and planning and zoning commissions.

The second type consisted of "outside" developers and real estate brokers—those who were not long-term community members, but bought property and in some cases themselves built housing on it for speculation. Many of these outside developers were based in Dickinson, North Dakota, the urban center of the oil boom of a decade earlier. With oil development on the wane, they moved their focus of activity to Mercer County. Beulah received most of their attentions, since this was the name associated in the outwide world with the gasification plant. Outside developers usually hired someone from the region to live in Mercer County to serve as a local contact. This was an astute business strategy, since the most effective way of dealing with the people in Mercer County was on the basis of one local person to another; these local representatives sought to deal informally as quasi-insiders with the genuine locals on a day-to-day basis.

The third type of real estate investors were the energy corporations themselves. Their acquisition of residential real estate was presented to the public as a means for assisting local communities in handling the population boom while protecting them from big outside developers. Some of their properties fit this depiction, such as the Bachelor Quarters in Beulah. In other cases, their investments seemed more politically motivated than genuinely helpful. This occurred, for example, when Great Plains and Basin bought a huge tract in north Hazen, and later sold off parts of it to local developers who made a very substantial profit from it. This deal not only won influential friends for industry in that town, but also smoothed the feathers of those in Hazen who claimed that their rival community, Beulah, was receiving disproportionately more corporate attention.

Although the energy corporations were mainly interested in influencing county-level politics, they acquired a position of influence in the towns as well by becoming major local property owners. Corporate plans for developing their residential properties became a central issue in their relations with local governments. In 1980, the Beulah town council negotiated with Great Plains over the Bachelor Quarters site, insisting that park areas be included in the plans. Facing a united council, the developers finally relented. The land owned by Great Plains and Basin in Hazen also became a bone of contention. They had bought it early as a hedge against inflation, and wished to put FHA-601 low-income housing on the site. Some local officials, at least one of whom was a developer himself, expressed concern that this might hinder the construction of more expensive housing for the well-paid permanent newcomers they preferred.

Other real estate developers wielded considerable influence in local politics during the boom years. A county land use official himself worked part time as a realtor for a local company. Many town council members were involved in local real estate developments in one way or another, and the interests of developers were volubly expressed and rarely opposed at planning and zoning meetings. Developers were active opponents of special assessments on property they were trying to sell, and supported local government efforts to get federal housing programs to finance home construction.

The case of a particularly aggressive realtor illustrates the influence of this interest group. She was behind numerous attempts to rezone properties to her commercial advantage, and in a notorious case was even successful in getting a variance to put two houses on a single lot in order to sell more property. Despite her reputation as a greedy and unscrupulous operator, this realtor was elected chair of a town's planning and zoning commission in the early 1980s. She only resigned after a local newspaper publicly denounced the flagrant conflict of interest. The case did not end there, however, since the person who took over the post also occupied a strategic position in the development business. Her husband was the vice president and heir apparent to the presidency of the largest bank in town. This was a family-owned corporation involved in financing and insuring local real estate development. At the time she gained the position as planning and zoning chair, she announced herself to be an independent thinker, uninfluenced by the interests of her husband's family, yet she was shortly thereafter permitted for the first time to buy stock in the family's corporation and began to attend the all-family shareholders' meetings. The conflict of interest remained, although she took care not to practice bias in her official role.

The town councils and chambers of commerce in the larger towns were mainly staffed by industrial employees and members of the business elite who stood to gain by industrial growth. In Hazen, all but one of the town's council members in 1982 were power plant employees, including the council chairman, a failed businessman hired by Basin Electric after his election.[3] Stanton's council was also dominated by energy employees: four of the five members worked at the two nearby power plants; the other worked for the county. Nearly all of the members of the Beulah council, including the mayor, were businessmen, and several were engaged in some real estate sales and development. Another member, whose father was a powerful County Commissioner, had a white collar job at a new nonunion mine, and his wife worked for Great Plains.

Business leaders embraced development and sought to promote the expansion of their communities. The towns competed among themselves in cultivating advantageous relationships with the corporations, applying for grants and loans to finance their expansion, and advertising their communities to prospective customers, investors, and new residents. The drive for expansion and upgrading of local infrastructure and facilities was fueled by several forces in addition to the pressure of increasing population. These included the growth-and-modernization mentality of traditional boosterism; the need of each town in competition with the others to enhance its attractiveness to the potential settlers who represented the stability of future tax bases; and, finally, the availability of funds for projects that had long been wished for. Grants to Mercer County political entities from 1975 to 1984 totaled $37,023,197, mostly from the Energy Impact Office. This sum did not cover all their financing needs, however; loans over the same period from the coal severance tax trust fund amounted to $5,079,000.

In addition to grantsmanship, the business class continued to use the traditional techniques of civic boosting to promote their communities. Increasingly close ties between the energy corporations and the local chambers of commerce were apparent in their cooperation in producing and distributing community promotional materials. These included informational pamphlets for prospective new residents, who were also corporate employees.

Beulah's advertising emphasized an urban and industrial image designed to inspire confidence in the town's economic future as well as the modern conveniences of the present. A billboard at the city limits announced: "Welcome to Beulah. Lignite Capital of the World. Largest City in Mercer County. Over 100 Businesses to Serve You." Hazen's Chamber of Commerce adopted a different advertising strategy for their town, promoting a bucolic, small town image designed to appeal to the more urbane and sophisticated permanent newcomers seeking a tranquil respite from what Hazen's business and social leaders liked to characterize as the rough and ready construction atmosphere of Beulah. Their billboard read: "Welcome to Hazen. Greener and Cleaner. A Friendly FAMILY Community." A brochure designed to attract new residents included such statements as, "People working together for mutual benefit is characteristic of Hazen," "More and more young couples with young families have chosen Hazen as a home. Many benefits await the newcomer. . . . Nice, friendly people will make the move easier," and "Best of all, Hazen offers its services in a relaxed and friendly manner. New people quickly become neighbors."

The majority of townspeople were not in a position to benefit financially from the boom. Those who did not own businesses or property to develop were resentful about having to pay special tax assessments for expanding city services, and suspected retailers of collaborating to keep prices high. Responses to the newspaper-sponsored opinion survey mentioned earlier expressed this point of view: "The effect of the boom has not been that great, many are able to make a comfortable living off it, but only a few entrepreneurs have gotten rich off the boom—developers and contractors." "I think the informal structure of money here is very close knit. There must be secret agreements because there's so little price competition. There at the SuperValu and the Jack 'N' Jill [they] have the same prices." "I have seen nothing good about Industry coming to Mercer County; everything so far has been done for the good of a very few, and the rest of the county residents are paying for it in higher taxes, higher food prices, crowded facilities in churches, schools, hospitals, etc. A few are filling their pockets and the rest of us are paying for it!"

The emerging differentiation among the towns was the result not of one-directional development producing a rural–urban continuum such as that described by Robert Redfield in rural Mexico (1941). Rather, it occurred with their simultaneous reshaping into more or less economically specialized communities as a combined result of corporate policy and the efforts of local business and political leaders. Three of Mercer County's six towns were within the orbit of extensive energy development. Stanton had been the center of the industrial boom of the 1960s, and Beulah that of the late 1970s and early 1980s. Hazen, situated between them, shared in both booms. By the mid-1980s, however, it was clear that the two largest towns were growing much faster, and that Stanton was already declining again.

Zap remained fairly stable as a working class town of coal miners and retired farmers. This town had never been of much interest to energy boom developers, who prefered to invest in the larger towns. Zap's labor-oriented political leadership had also avoided giving special considerations to developers—over the objections of its business community. Even so, two sizable trailer park additions were built to house construction migrants and low-income residents, and the town council made efforts to attract permanent workers, though not of the upper management stratum. Golden Valley, meanwhile, continued its long decline, almost forgotten by the rest in their pursuit of progress and development. With little new housing available other than one small trailer court, Golden Valley hoped to garner some of the agricultural business that had fled Hazen and Beulah. Almost completely dependent on the farm income of the surrounding countryside, its streets seemed lonely and deserted in comparison to those of the other towns. Pick City, which had its origin as a work force encampment during the construction of the Garrison Dam, had also languished for many years on the brink of extinction. Its revival in the 1980s was due to the rise of the new upper class in Beulah and Hazen, a group with enough disposable income and leisure time to build weekend vacation cabins on the lake. Pick City became a tourist and vacation supply center, with bait and tackle shops, gas stations, convenience stores, and a lively watering hole near the hydroelectric station called the Dam Bar—its motto, "The Best Dam Bar by a Dam Site."

The Weakening Position of Labor

During the booming industrial growth in Mercer County in the late 1970s and early 1980s, there was a deterioration of the local power of industrial labor as a class. This was accomplished through a concerted corporate and government effort to promote nonunion facilities and ideology, and to defeat the unions' efforts to maintain the contract conditions and levels of organization they had struggled so long to achieve. Labor's attempts to confront industrial management in Mercer County had been met historically with some ambivalence in the wider community, and yet the community basis for labor organizing and consciousness had been a vital factor in building the local union movement. Now, with business interests more powerful than ever in the local political economy, and with many industrial workers coming in from outside the area, this community basis was weakened.

The erosion of labor's power was due to many factors. Unions were fighting for survival in the 1980s on a national scale. Workers and labor relations experts alike have cited the firing of the striking PATCO air traffic controllers by President Reagan in 1981 as a watershed event marking the beginning of a new anti-union offensive on the part of business and government. Between 1980 and 1985, the unionized proportion of the national work force dropped from an estimated 21.4 percent to about 19 percent. Under the Reagan administration, the National Labor Relations Board systematically worked to limit union contract privileges and labor participation in management decisions, and to complicate the local union election process (Clark and Johnston 1987:33–34).

In this climate, corporate management throughout the nation sought to boost profits by reducing labor costs through lowering wages and benefits and modifying the conditions of work. In the traditionally unionized heavy industries, management, on the whole was successful at forcing workers to accept disadvantageous contract changes, because a serious decline in the nation's industrial economy gave plausibility to their claims to the need for labor concessions, and reduced the options for workers facing unemployment.

Changes in the proportion of unionized labor in North Dakota generally mirrored those of the nation, rising between 1960 and 1975, only to decline precipitously into the 1980s. In 1975, 19.4 percent of the state's workers were unionized, ranking as the ninth lowest proportion of any state in the country. By 1982, this figure had fallen to 14.2 percent. Despite this steep decrease, North Dakota's ranking in percentage of unionized workers had risen to seventeenth from the bottom (Troy and Sheflin 1985:4–7). This relative boost is apparently due to energy industrial growth and especially the presence of heavily unionized building trades during the construction boom. By the mid-1980s, however, even the energy business was declining again after a decade of explosive growth.

In Mercer County, the gasification plant was the last major construction project of the energy boom, and although Kaiser Engineering built it with union labor, the contract was, by union standards, a poor one. An ironworker at the plant site explained the situation: "The wages are low for a union job. We're getting $2.50 an hour less than for the same work in Minneapolis or Bismarck. . . . They've got the unions over a barrel because there's no work anywhere right now. Just a few years ago, when they built the Coyote plant, they couldn't find enough workers. If the union hadn't signed this contract, it would have been done with nonunion labor."

An increasing proportion of industrial jobs in Mercer County in fact were being done by nonunion labor. All of the older power plants had in-house unions, but the new Antelope Valley Station and adjacent gasification plant were to be operated as nonunion facilities. A similar policy was evident in the coal mines. The older mines all had union representation and collective bargaining. But the new mines owned by Coteau Properties—the Freedom Mine at the gasification site (which in 1984 was the largest producing coal mine in the country) and another one in the next county—were nonunion operations. Coteau was a subsidiary of the North American Coal Mining Company, which also owned the Indian Head Mine at Zap, whose workers were United Mine Workers. In 1974, the Indian Head miners had struck for five and a half months over the issue of letting the UMW automatically into North

American's new mines. The dispute went to federal mediation, and was eventually decided against the union.

As sinking energy prices began to depress the energy sector in the mid-1980s, corporate management took advantage of the opportunity to increase the proportion of nonunion workers still further. Faced with a choice in 1985 of laying off workers in their nonunion Antelope Valley electrical generation plant or in their unionized and older Leland Olds plant, Basin Electric chose to shut down one of the units at Leland Olds. Because this was a mine-mouth plant, shutting down the unit also meant layoffs among the unionized workers in the adjacent Glenharold Mine and its conveyor belt, where the work force was reduced from 165 to 120. The alternative of layoffs at Antelope would have necessitated cuts in the nonunion work force at Coteau's Freedom Mine.

The shortage of industrial work and the declining power of organized labor produced what workers saw as arrogance in the attitude of management. In a speech at a Task Force meeting in 1984, a Great Plains official announced their receiving seven hundred thousand applications for the seven hundred permanent positions at the gasification plant, and boasted that they had been "Santa Claus" to the lucky few who were selected. Commenting later on the presentation, a mine worker complained about the lack of respect in the official's attitude: "They think of themselves as doing a favor to the begging worker on his knees, instead of expecting good work for fair pay. They make money off of the workers, they're not doing them a favor." Another worker remarked on the increasingly condescending attitude of management at the Indian Head Mine: "It's all the *we* attitude: *we* need to do this; *we* need to work together for the good of us all."

The management of labor in Coteau's new nonunion mine reflected a concerted policy to prevent the rise of unionism there. Coteau avoided hiring men who had previously worked in unionized mines (except for those in management positions). Instead, they hired mainly young men fresh off the area's farms and nonunion miners from outside the area. These workers were inexperienced in the local labor union tradition, and in a nonunion facility were isolated from contact with the older generation of local miners who had "fought the good fight" in the 1950s. A worker in a union mine complained: "They simply don't hire union people these days."

Anti-union management at Coteau's Freedom Mine took care to foster positive attitudes towards those aspects of work which differed from mines with union contracts. In their *Employee Work Book*, the operation is characterized not as nonunion, but as "union-free." Similarly, the work agreement is not referred to as a contract, but rather as "guidelines." Higher-paid overtime work, which at the Freedom Mine was mandatory, was renamed "premium time," and was represented as an opportunity to earn more money while also helping out the company during crisis periods. In contrast to the other mines, employee numbers were used, instead of names, to post overtime work assignments, making it more difficult for workers to keep track of whether or not the rotation was fair. Informational pamphlets on pension plans and health plans, which were openly displayed at the other mines, were stored out of sight and were not readily available at the Freedom Mine. A retired railroad employee scoffed: "Oh yeah, they got lots of Freedom over there! When the bosses are due to come inspect the mine, they have to work twelve-hour days to clean up after doing all their regular work."

These management efforts were largely successful, however, and the morale of Freedom miners was quite high. Although the work "guidelines" were unenforceable in the interests of workers and had no provisions for job security, nevertheless the wages and benefits were comparable on the whole to those at unionized mines. As one worker put it, "The mines hate unions, and they'll spend a lot of money to keep them out." Seeing the "harmony of interest" ideal apparently working well for them, Freedom miners felt they had a good deal. They were leary of labor activism because of its potential to upset the harmonious balance they enjoyed. A cautious pliability in dealing with management set them apart from the miners under union contracts, where the conflicting interests of workers and management were openly recognized and negotiated. The Freedom miners saw little need for confrontation, and indeed it seemed there was little need, at least as long as the union contracts in neighboring mines were maintained to set an acceptable standard that Coteau had to match to keep its workers satisfied.

The standard set by union-won contract conditions was eroding, however, as Mercer County's labor unions in the 1980s found themselves fighting losing battles just to keep the status quo. A significant confrontation came in the summer of 1984, when the contract at the Glenharold Mine came up for renegotiation. Basin Electric, which owned the mine, insisted on changes, including the introduction of mandatory overtime, decreases in seniority rights, and a shift from 100 percent medical coverage to 80 percent (workers to pay 20 percent); these were demanded in exchange for a modest salary increase. The union opposed mandatory overtime on the principle that it reduced the number of jobs available to workers. The company found it cheaper to pay a smaller number of workers more for working longer hours than to hire additional men to do the work and pay for their benefits too. Some of the miners were willing to accept these conditions, although there was general agreement that the salary raise was not adequate to cover the medical cuts. The majority opposed the offer, however, especially since it came at a time when large United Mine Workers contracts were coming up for renegotiation in the East and they believed that giving ground here would make it more difficult for other miners to avoid givebacks. So, feeling their backs against the wall, they took a stand and voted to strike.

One hundred and thirty-seven men were out for 133 days, during which time the mine's operations were effectively shut down. The union remained united—there were no strikebreakers and they received support on the picket lines from boilermakers, ironworkers, and members of other construction trades at the gasification site. Workers at the other UMW mine in Zap sent money over to support the striking workers and at least one local bank helped out by deferring their loan and mortgage payments. During this time, contract negotiations remained at an impasse, with neither side willing to concede. The impasse was finally broken when Basin attempted to bring nonunion operators into the mine past picketing workers, who sat down in the road to block their entry. The ensuing confrontation quickly escalated when the local police were reinforced by seventeen state highway patrol car units who began dragging people off the road. Rough treatment of women among the strike supporters touched off an angry melee, in which twenty-seven strike supporters were arrested, nine of them women. Four felony assault charges were filed, and more than twenty misdemeanor charges of blocking a public road. A truckload of National Guardsmen was posted to secure the courthouse during the arraignments that day.

This was the most dramatic labor confrontation in Mercer County since eight years previously, when a similar incident had occurred at the Beulah mine. Friendly businesses closed for the day in sympathy, and public opinion expressed surprise both at the speed with which such large numbers of state police had been called to the scene and with the unexpected aggressiveness of their tactics in support of the strikebreakers. The move paid off for mine management, however. With nonunion workers successfully crossing the picket line, striking workers were forced to accept most of Basin's proposed contract changes for fear of losing their jobs altogether.

Mercer County labor leaders put a bold public face on the strike's outcome. At the meeting to announce the final vote, the president of the striking UMW local claimed, "Now we have a contract we can live with and we can walk with our heads held high because we have beat big business. . . . We would not break. In fact, we got stronger. We stood up to Basin, to the county sheriffs, to the highway patrol, and to Governor Olson. One week ago, Basin lost."

In private, however, local labor leaders saw that the defeat of the Glenharold strikers in 1984 represented a turning point in labor's power here. One of them commented, "With the cuts they took in the strike resolution, it's going to make it damn hard for the other UMW mine [Indian Head] to avoid going backward in their contract that is coming up." The significance of the massive government intervention was not lost on local labor leaders either, especially since they saw President Reagan himself as a chief source of the new anti-labor offensive. "This union-busting trend has been coming down from Washington, ever since the PATCO strike was broken by Reagan," said one leader.

This event fueled the widespread perception in Mercer County of collusion between the industrial corporations, government, and regulatory officials.[4] Some farmers and miners accused the Public Service Commission, for example, of dragging its heels on enforcing environmental regulations, and the Energy Impact Office of operating under a narrow definition of impact that substantially benefitted industries and real estate investors. Questions about the integrity of the Energy Impact Office director, August Keller, were certainly not diminished in 1984, when he left this position of public service to become the Director of Government and Public Affairs for The North American Coal Company, in charge of the mining corporation's public relations and lobbying efforts. Among other assignments, Keller's new job included giving "cheerleading" speeches to North American's mine workers to boost company loyalty. In the same year, a top Public Service Commission official left this post for a job with Burlington Northern, one of the largest coal-owning corporations in the country.

As corporate industrial investment increased in Mercer County, so did the government's efforts to protect this investment. This was apparent not only in the police intervention in breaking the Glenharold strike, but perhaps even more dramatically in the establishment and rapid build-up of National Guard posts in Hazen and Beulah. In November 1976 the Hazen Chamber of Commerce announced the founding of a National Guard unit there, and a prominent businessman became the first enlistee. The following year, Beulah also secured a post and within a year had fifty-one members. For lack of a proper military armory, the Guard was permitted to use the county community center as a base. In 1979, the Beulah Guard received an award as the best in western North Dakota for recruiting and performance. This was no small achievement, as the North Dakota force was ranked first in the nation.

Despite the well-known history of the National Guard as a strike-breaking force, a few miners joined up. At North American's Indian Head Mine in Zap, National Guard members appeared to be unusually willing to ignore the entrenched separation between labor and management. Generally, pro-union miners objected to any promotion of workers into management positions, and this rarely occurred. During the mid-1980s, however, the company introduced a program of choosing certain men to be "temporary supervisors" and sending them out among the other workers, to receive on-the-job management training. Of the four Guardsmen in the Indian Head work force, three were among the six chosen to be temporary supervisors.

The Evolution of Corporate–Community Relations

Mercer County officials had been dealing with industrial corporations (and corporate-like cooperatives) for many years before the energy boom, and had established long-term personal acquaintances with industry representatives who had earned their trust. At first, local people were willing to extend the same kind of trust to the new corporations, but they soon began to realize that these corporations did business differently. As a community official explained: "The County Commissioners didn't have any expertise in dealing with industry. They all had a farm background and were used to very straightforward, open, honest dealings, and they acted that way with industry . . . This is changing now!" Similarly, a labor leader commented on the industries' attitudes toward local people: "They considered the people here just dumb farmers. They thought they could say anything and be believed, have it all their way. It took time for the local people to learn what kind of folks they were dealing with, not to trust them."

Those who closely followed the process came to understand and accept that the fundamental purpose of corporation actions in Mercer County was simply profit, and that their superior financial and political resources enabled them to achieve many of their goals in confrontation with weaker interests. Actually, the energy corporations were not doing anything out of the ordinary for business. Those locals who dealt extensively with them in negotiations over permit conditions and impact mitigation learned to interpret corporate maneuvers according to the legalistic ethic of business rather than the moralistic one of community life. A town official explained: "Our biggest thing is to learn that we're not dealing with your neighbor over the back fence. . . . It's not mean or dirty what they do, it's just business. The guy you are dealing with is doing a job for some board of directors and is out here to get the best deal he can, so if you don't do the same, too bad for you."

Perhaps the most frustrating aspect of dealing with the energy industries for local officials was the lack of personal contact with the corporate representatives and the distance between these agents and those actually making the decisions. A county official complained: "We only saw them when they expected something from the county, like permits, roads. . . . There was no opportunity to get to know them first before they would start asking for things. . . . Over the years what changed was dealing with bigger and bigger outfits. Most of the dealing with the energy people wasn't like dealing with the neighbors. You know, they were from out-of-state. The boss wasn't here. They always had to go ask their bosses about everything, back in Detroit."

Another local man explained the problem: "The way people here deal with corporations is way out of date. Corporations are different these days. They didn't understand that subordinates don't have authority. They would think they had made a deal with the representative here but he had to check it out above him really. . . . Like [the mayor of Beulah]—he'd really prefer to deal with Arthur Seder [the chairman of American Natural Resources] one to one as equals. You know, my town—your company."

Although local officials had to accept the profit rationale behind the industries' actions, the general public continued to judge them according to the moral standards of authentic community members. When the Great Plains Gasification Associates successfully avoided paying most front-end direct financing of impact mitigation, public reaction accused industry of being a "bad neighbor" and an "irresponsible member of the community"—in short, of failing to behave in an ethical manner according to small town civic ideology. At that time an editorial columnist in a local newspaper assessed the local partnership with the energy developers:

> For some time we've questioned its honest intentions and come away believing that industry has a main concern—looking out for number 1. This county has been, to say the least, cooperative with energy development. In fact, we've virtually prostituted ourselves in dealing with industry in many instances. . . . What we have learned thus far in our partnership with energy, is that we had best keep a handle on the situation until our demands are met. Once we give up the lever we have virtually no recourse. When you hear the pleadings made to industry you question whether we haven't been reduced to beggars at the rich man's cuffs. . . . When we have to resort to such action [delaying a permit approval] it proves that our relationship with industry is not the "good neighbor" policy that they are trying to sell the public. . . . Mercer County has acted in good faith. Now it's industry's turn to reciprocate, if they are indeed the good neighbors they claim to want to be. At this point they look like the guy next door who borrows your lawnmower and brings it back broken and out of gas, but with the promise he'll make it right next week.
>
> (*Beulah Beacon* March 10, 1980)

Other residents expressed disillusionment and a sense of betrayal in responding to the newpaper-sponsored opinion survey: "I feel that the Energy Companies in the past made many promises of assistance in housing, schools, hospitals, and numerous other areas of public service, but when it came down to the wire they reneged on their promises because they figured the severance taxes were high enough to handle that. The Energy Companies that ship their end product out of the state should have to pay plenty, because that natural resource is gone forever." "I'm not satisfied with the present conditions, but there is nothing that can be done with yesterday. But hopefully the local powers have learned something from the past. So in future negotiations they will back the energy corporations in the corner and get things our way instead of vice versa, as has happened."

Such disillusion produced a different set of problems for local people. If industry was not a neighbor, then it must be something much more alien and powerful. Not only did the developers have greater resources and the backing of the federal government, but their representatives enjoyed the superior status of well-educated, prosperous, cosmopolitan authority. This made them and their positions more attractive to the urban-oriented business and professional class, and was also effective in intimidating the populist opposition in formal settings such as permit hearings and planning meetings. A town official remarked on the power of this symbolic superiority: "Many people from here don't like to confront the big corporations and push for what they want. It's not that they don't have dreams for how they want things to be, but they give up too easy. They say, 'Well, I don't have much education, how can I talk to those industry guys and tell them what I think they should do?'"

The position of county government, as elected representatives charged with the implementation of industrial development, was fraught with difficulties and contradictions. The consensus of county residents was in favor of some limited development, on condition that the pace of expansion be slow enough to avoid a devastating boom–bust cycle, that local people have preferential status in hirings, and that industry be made to pay the financial costs of its adverse impacts. In addition, agriculturalists were concerned about the enforcement of land reclamation laws, maintenance and dust control on county roads used heavily by industrial traffic, structural damage caused by nearby mine explosions, the effects of strip mining on groundwater supplies, and noxious emissions and toxic pollution produced by the conversion plants. Although they shared these concerns, most county officials felt that these issues were not within their administrative purview. Rather than refuse any new mining permits until a company cleaned up its backlog of unreclaimed mined-out land, for example, county government left enforcement of reclamation law to the Public Service Commission.

The desire of county officials to see the county benefit from a long-term relationship with the industries encouraged them to form close ties with energy interests. This occurred in 1977, for example, when the county agreed to accept a large administrative fee from Basin Electric in return for assistance in financing the purchase of mandatory pollution control equipment. As a nonprofit entity, the county was eligible for short-term tax-exempt low interest loans. The county made the purchase for the companies by issuing revenue bonds, and handled the task of periodic refinancing. The $150,000 administrative fee received from the companies did not, however, go into the county's general administrative fund. Instead, the money went towards the construction costs of a new jail. The jail expansion was itself necessary because of the increased population due to industrial development, so in a sense the county did not receive any net benefits from its role as middleman.

Close ties between industry and the county government were also established for security and law enforcement. The sheriff's office assisted the corporations at times of labor strife, and together with town police forces handled the daily law and order problems associated with the large construction work force. The sheriff himself resigned his post of fifteen years in 1978 to take a job as chief of security at Basin's Antelope Valley Station.

The county and industry also cooperated closely in the planning process. Basin Electric led the way in providing current and forecasted work force numbers and migration patterns for local planners (through the Inter-industry Technical Assistance Team), and in taking responsibility for social impacts not funded by the Energy Impact Office. Basin Electric provided a grant toward the salary of an investigator of child abuse and neglect, and even lobbied in the state legislature for increased social services funding. County officials found it more difficult to win Great Plains' cooperation on social service needs, but appreciated their assistance with work force forecasts.

All but the most adamant opponents of industrial power considered that local government had followed the will of the people to limit industrial growth instead of single-mindedly pursuing the economic benefits of development. A young farmer activist pointed out: "The best thing economically would be to have twelve power plants here—full-scale, no-holds-barred development. But the people didn't want that, so the county tried to let in just enough to keep the economy well enough." Similarly, a Beulah man resolutely opposed to the mayor's politics was nonetheless pleased with the mayor's close relations with industrial officials: "I don't know if it's because he personally likes the industry people as friends, or if he gets things for them because he thinks it is good for the town in the end. He's done a lot of things for them and for the town, like getting money to pay for impact stuff. He's not afraid to ask for things for the town."

On the other hand, to a minority of the local public, any accommodation at all to the energy developers represented a betrayal of local interests. As the County Planning and Zoning Commission approved one permit application after another, an exasperated onlooker exclaimed: "What a bunch of sold-out-to-industry boobies they are!" The opponents of cozy cooperation with developers included some farmers, organized through the Mercer County Landowners Association. They had mounted a vocal block of wholesale opposition to energy development in the early 1970s, and continued to view the developers with profound distrust. This group was quick to point out the unequal nature of the partnership of the energy corporations with the people of the county. In this response to the newspaper's opinion survey, one member vented his frustration:

> I have dust all over my farm some days till it looks like fog from a distance. I can feel it in my eyes. It's unhealthy. "They" will give $100,000 to Cross Ranch [a wilderness park] but won't spray my road nor find me a new well. Both my stock and house wells have almost stopped; I am the closest farmer with a well to Antelope plant. "They" said "they'd" replace any water, but now the word is "Prove it." How can a farmer prove that energy development ran his wells dry except what the workers have said—they opened veins on [the] hillside; I am on [the] hill—and except thru about 50 years experience that those wells have never given any trouble? "They" said it is not substantial evidence. What if I am forced out of livestock?

The expanded class of urban-trained professionals came to play a special role in mediating relations between the corporations and local interest groups. Most professionals were young newcomers to the county, but they soon had several years of residence, home ownership, and churchgoing behind their claims to insider status. This class had taken over key technical posts in the county, providing authoritative information to decision makers on questions of law, public health, social welfare, city planning, and other policy areas. They had more formal education than others in Mercer County, and more analytical views of what was occurring there; they watched local events with interest and, though they remained ambivalent about the benefits of energy development, their work contributed greatly to its smooth progression. By the mid-1980s, this class was clearly an ascendent political force.

The range of relationships established by local groups with the energy industries reflected the complexities and conflicts already present in Mercer County society, arising out of its particular economic history. For its part, capital also selectively sought to establish a variety of relations with local entities, based on a logic of long-run profit maximization. The uneven development generated in part through these uneven relationships was therefore not simply determined by powerful forces emanating from the core of global capitalism and operating through exchange relations, but was also the outcome of the local history of production and its structuring of the usefulness of Mercer County places and people to corporate capital. This local economic history, dialectically related to national capitalist influence, also helped to shape the life experiences, ideologies, and forms of action available to local people in their encounter with developers.

Chapter Eight | The Price of Progress

Industrial growth had been at a peak in Mercer County in the early 1980s, riding the crest of high global energy prices and federal supports. The end of the boom brought a new phase of turbulent restructuring, in which it became clear that progress had brought only a precarious and uneven prosperity contingent on new relations of dependency and debt. By the decade's close the export base of the area had been dramatically changed, from a primarily agricultural economy to one based on the production of energy commodities, with much higher corporate investment and direct state involvement in the local economy. Despite these changes, the basic relation of Mercer County's economy to that of the wider society remained structurally similar—it was still dependent upon outside interests and market forces far beyond the reach of local or democratic control.

In the years beyond the boom, a new order coalesced, in which all of the local towns and interest groups strove to secure a place. Those whom the energy boom had brought into positions of dominance consolidated their position. Others, for whom the experience of uneven development had been more problematic, continued to seek through both confrontation and accommodation a means of survival and a stake in the future.

The Ebb Tide of Industry

At the height of the boom, energy industry growth in Mercer County inspired confidence in its ability to continue providing jobs and income to sustain the burgeoning population. The fortunes of residents and communities were tied to those of the industry, and holding on to their material gains over the boom years depended on its ever-increasing growth in the future. Although the coal industry was notorious for its historical booms and busts, people expected that this more diversified energy commodity base would enjoy more market stability. By 1984, however, as the construction phase was winding down, declining energy prices began to cloud the future of the new plants and mines. Mercer County had been expected to experience a moderate decline at the end of the boom phase as construction workers left and the smaller permanent work forces took their place at the new plants, but the timing of market changes and corporate decisions magnified this downturn into an economic bust. No sooner had the gasification plant opened on July 28, 1984, than a drop in corporate profits threw the newly expanded industries into a period of rapid retrenchment. With profits threatened, capital began pulling out, leaving local residents to face the combined threat of agricultural crisis and industrial decline. As a result, unemployment actually reached higher levels than before the boom: unemployment in the early 1970s had averaged about 5.6 percent, but by 1986 the unemployment rate was 11.2 percent, as compared with a national average of 7.0 percent (*Economic Report of the President* 1988). (For unemployment trends in Mercer County from 1972 to 1986, see Table 4.)

The end of the boom brought hard times for many in Mercer County. Construction workers from outside the area were the first to be laid off. Those who had left their families back home rejoined them, and began their job search anew. Families who had moved to Mercer County with the working father remained there, in many cases, while he sought new employment elsewhere. Temporary workers who had purchased homes could not sell them now, since there was a large surplus on the market and few buyers. A document Basin provided to its employees stated that there were 385 housing units for sale in Mercer County in the summer of 1984, including some two hundred houses and more than one hundred fifty trailers, as well as apartments and townhouses. By 1984, property values were falling on the more expensive homes.[1] One building contractor lamented: "Lots of people are scared to buy right now with rising interest rates. Nobody has enough money now to move up the ladder, not even from a trailer to a home." The opposite trend was more common, with families seeking to sell their homes and move into trailers.

The lack of centralized information about future job possibilities heightened the stress of construction work lay-offs. Workers had to call around for themselves, and use their own judgment about which leads might be worth leaving home to pursue. As one construction worker explained:

Table 4 | Mercer County and North Dakota Unemployment Trends, 1972–1986

Year (annual average)	Mercer County Number Employed	Mercer County Unemployment Rate	North Dakota Unemployment Rate
1972	2,550	6.1	4.9
1973	2,801	5.8	5.1
1974	3,257	4.5	4.6
1975	3,408	5.6	5.2
1976	3,547	5.5	5.1
1977	3,288	5.5	5.5
1978	3,847	3.6	4.3
1979	4,514	4.4	4.0
1980	5,363	5.6	5.0
1981	5,980	6.1	5.0
1982	6,910	4.0	5.9
1983	10,097	3.0	5.6
1984	7,823	7.7	5.1
1985	6,420	9.9	5.9
1986	5,128	11.2	6.3

Source: North Dakota Job Service.

The grapevine is busy all the time, but even with the union it's up to each worker to get himself on local [waiting] benches wherever they want to get work. . . . You have to choose, though, because when you take a job somewhere else they pull your book [remove you from the eligibility list] at your home local. I hear they're going to start hiring out in Idaho soon, but right now I don't want to risk it because I'm number five on the bench here, and we have the house. Out in Idaho and Utah I'm more than 300 on the bench. . . . Even if you get a job you never know how long you will work.

As some laid-off workers and their families moved away, the social services caseload dropped considerably. Even as demand for food stamps dropped, however, cases of child abuse and neglect rose dramatically in the remaining population. Mercer County's child abuse and neglect rate was the highest in the state in 1983, and experts expected it to rise by one-third again in 1984 (*Hazen Star* June 28, 1984). Social workers attributed the elevated rates to the stress endured by those expecting to be laid off, since it did not occur only among those who had already lost their jobs. The number of abuse cases also increased among families supported by insecure service-sector jobs, whose earnings were far below those of construction workers.

There had been persistent rumors since 1983 of the gasification plant's closing because of its unprofitability in the face of falling energy prices. Nervousness over possible lay-offs also ran high among the relatively well-paid "permanent" plant and mine employees. Expecting a long-term stable income, many of these had bought expensive homes, boats, cars, and stereos on credit. No sooner had they established themselves with a comfortable material life than they had to face the psychological stress of living under the threat of losing its financial underpinnings. Those with the highest-level positions had nothing to fear, since their contracts included generous severance clauses, in which the corporation agreed to buy back the house and make a large severance payment should the employee be laid off. A senior official at Tenneco (one of the Great Plains partners) bragged: "A guy could live for two years on what they'd walk away with, so why not? I'd walk away with $100,000 cash in my pocket if my job ended; I really wouldn't mind."

The end of the energy boom came at a time of growing crisis in the agricultural economy, as well. Farmers' production costs had risen throughout the 1970s and 1980s, while farm commodity prices remained stagnant, or even fell, in real terms. With the encouragement of government agencies, land grant universities, and local bankers, many farmers had continued to invest in land and equipment inputs despite high interest rates, in an effort to boost their profitability. But their financial problems were compounded by drought, and after crop prices fell in the early 1980s, a young farmwife despairingly told me: "Farming is a lot more work than compensation. Wheat is three dollars a bushel, but it should be fifteen dollars, for what goes into it. It was three dollars when gasoline costed twenty-five cents a gallon, and it is still only three dollars." Because of the political unpopularity of foreclosures (a moratorium on FHA foreclosures was in effect until 1985), lending institutions instead encouraged a wave of timely sell-offs of land, machinery, and livestock, resulting in further concentration of agricultural capital. The youngest farmers were the hardest hit: Census figures showed a two-thirds drop in the number of operators twenty-five years old and under in Mercer County from 1982 to 1987, and most of these owned none of the land they worked. The numbers of farmers sixty-five years old and over increased by 40 percent over the same period, as youngsters stayed home to work for more established parents delaying their retirement.

Farmers of all ages were in trouble, however, and the fact that operations declined by no more than about 7 percent from 1978 to 1982 can be partly explained by the increase in off-farm employment over the same period from about two-fifths to over one-half of the county's farm operators (U.S. Census of Agriculture 1982), a number which does not include the work of other family members. Most Mercer County farmers had medium-sized family operations, and this class of independent producers was the hardest hit of American farmers in the 1980s (Strange 1988).[2] As in the 1930s, it was no longer enough to work hard and to manage the farm wisely to make a living in agriculture.

Local opinion was nearly unanimous in blaming the farm crisis on structural problems rather than the individual shortcomings of operators. An industry employee who had grown up on a farm explained the situation this way:

> The American farmer can't compete in the world market with our strong dollar, let's face it. We can't sell our stuff. Canada, for example, has a 30 percent advantage on us just on the price of the dollar alone. . . . Our farmers that bought their lands years ago, at a lower dollar figure, they're in business yet, but if you are a young farmer who is just beginning, with the high interest rates, or an older one that was influenced into expanding or buying machinery—this new expensive machinery—there's no way you're going to be in business. And it is inconceivable to me the way that farm machinery has went. Take in 1970, you could have went out and bought the biggest, best combine on the market for $20,000. That same combine today is $120,000. . . . They are geared up for eight-dollar wheat, but it's back down to three now. It is lower than it was in the fifties, the price of wheat. Two and a half to three dollars a bushel. If they could go back with our present inflation—2, 3, 4 percent—our interest rates should be 6 percent. If they could have 6 percent money and $20,000 tractors, sure, they'd be making it!

Some of the survivors, remembering their own sufferings in the 1930s, were sympathetic to the plight of these economic casualties: "It's just pitiful when you pick up the paper and see all the foreclosures of these young farmers. They don't know where to go. Some of them go out West and then there's nothing there so they come back, . . . after they've put in quite a few good years of their life [on the farm] that they're giving up. That's the problem. Where do they go and what do they do?" Not all the local commentary was so sympathetic, however. One Chamber of Commerce member remarked: "The businessmen on Main Street might be more sympathetic to the farmers' crisis if the farmers hadn't been so damn arrogant before. When they were doing well the farmers were so down on others who were less fortunate, it's hard to feel sorry for them now."

Tensions were high in town, with growing animosity between the bankers and the farmers. A local journalist complained that the banks refused to even talk about the farm crisis with reporters and took it personally if the paper printed any remarks about bank practices. Farmers also complained about bankers whom they had known all their lives now refusing to even meet with them. In at least one case, a local bank attempted to distance itself from these lifelong customers by hiring an outside attorney to deal with farm creditors rather than meet with them face-to-face, as in the past.

With indebted farms running at a loss, even the farmers became fully dependent on off-farm income both from coal leases and from service and industrial jobs created by energy development. The case of Ron and Linda was typical of young farmers. In 1985 Ron let his hired man go because he could no longer pay his wages, so he and Linda had to finish harvesting by themselves. He was exhausted, getting up at 5:30 in the morning and working until after 10:00 at night. She worked nights at a club in town—"That's the only way we get groceries"—and helped Ron in the afternoon and on weekends. Despite his vocal opposition to industrial expansion in the county, Ron realized that his wife's job existed only as a result of it. Like most other Mercer County farmers, he had come to view industry—albeit controlled and regulated—as a necessary source of income.

Most of the increase in local service employment had depended on the business of the temporary construction work force. When the job was done, most of these left, but some families stayed on in Mercer County to wait for the next job to appear elsewhere. In the summer of 1984, the ranks of the job seekers were swelled by plant layoffs, the striking Glenharold miners, and farmers looking for extra income. The energy corporations took advantage of high unemployment to move against the mine workers' unions, laying off workers in the older, unionized mines, while expanding their new, nonunion facilities, and demanding concessions in contract negotiations with their remaining union employees. High unemployment also led to friction among job seekers and their resentment against striking miners competing for other work. An underemployed carpenter complained: "They cry murder if someone crosses their picket line to take their work, but they don't give a damn about taking other people's jobs."

These events combined to produce an atmosphere of crisis in the towns. Decreased buying power and the threat of a severe financial crash created nervousness among the county's business people. Every bankruptcy, foreclosure and "timely sell-out" (as near bankrupt liquidations were known) was cause for agitated speculation. Threatened merchants tried to boost sales by offering big discounts; the new furniture warehouse advertised sales at no money down, no interest, and no payment for twelve months. The drop in sales was felt most by owners of those businesses, such as eating and drinking places, hotels, and construction contractors, that had multiplied so rapidly during the construction years. In the town of Hazen, for example, where there had been only two or three liquor licenses before the energy boom, there were eleven in 1984. A bar owner with over twenty years' experience on Main Street commented on the trend: "Business has been very slow since April [1984]. We've got so much competition now, there's a lot more places selling drinks now than used to be. While it was during the boom, the city commission gave out licenses to whoever wanted. They never considered what would happen to all those people when the boom gave out. . . . Some of these guys that came in during the construction and opened up places are complaining now, but not me. I know not to expect any better; that's just how it is in a small town."

The end of the boom brought a wave of business closures in Mercer County, including a tire and an agricultural implements dealership, a home furnishings store, several building contractors, and a number of restaurants. Golden Valley edged back to the brink of extinction when its one remaining store closed in 1984. Many businesses were bought out and reopened as a new wave of late-coming entrepreneurs sought to try their luck.

The appearance of prosperity was everywhere in the boom towns, but the underlying reality was mounting private and public indebtedness. Individuals had made large purchases with the expectation of long-term employment, and the cost of living was steadily rising. In addition to price inflation, people in Mercer County were paying five times as much in property taxes as they had six or seven years before, to pay for the infrastructure required for development.[3] Business owners continued to invest in remodeling and modernizing in an effort to attract trade in the increasingly competitive market.

Available tax revenues were limited, and the required expansion of services had put the county and town governments, as well as the school, police, fire, and water districts, into unprecedented debt.[4] The little town of Zap, for example, had a bonded indebtedness of $77,000 in 1976. By 1984, this had grown to $818,000, at 9 to 11 percent interest. In Hazen, revenues from general property taxes in 1984 were approximately $84,000, while the cost of police salaries alone was over $92,000. School districts suffered from gradual fiscal strangulation, despite the expansion in their tax bases. Enrollments continued to rise, since most of the newcomers were young families with children, but there was a legal limit to the rate at which school district revenues were permitted to grow.

Competition among towns to attract new residents assumed a new urgency, as the need to secure future tax bases to pay for the improvements became acute. A steady trickle of newcomers continued to move into the county, and all the towns vied to become their new home. In hopes of attracting high-paid permanent energy employees who were still commuting from Bismarck, Hazen's business community promoted an image emphasizing their town's supposed cultural advantages, as opposed to what they characterized as the boorish, working class character of Beulah. This strategy met with only middling success since, in the words of one local wit, "They were looking for a champagne set in a beer situation."

Zap, for its part, found it difficult to compete with neighboring Beulah. Not only was Beulah larger and better known, but it also had a full-time planner and the personnel needed to fulfill a long-range plan. Still a solidly working class town, Zap sought to expand low-cost housing, and in 1984 its leaders hoped that the town's newly completed school and gymnasium would help attract new settlers. Lacking the promotional resources of the larger towns, the mayor proposed to compile and distribute a list of available housing to facilitate efforts to stabilize the population at about five hundred. According to him: "There are still a lot of permanent people still in temporary housing and deciding where to settle. That's why now is crucial."

With the construction phase completed, corporate concern over economic impact mitigation quickly evaporated. As the industries lost interest in Mercer County's financial problems, so did the state and federal governments. It became difficult for Mercer County to get funding from the Energy Impact Office to offset the continuing costs of civic expansion. Interest groups in other parts of the state brought pressure to bear in the state legislature to direct monies from the energy taxes elsewhere. In 1984 a bill was introduced to exempt taxes from coal gasification by-products from the gross receipts, thus limiting the revenue sharing funds that Mercer County would receive. Another bill proposed a cap on gross receipts funds to be returned to local entities, for the same purpose. Universities lobbied for Energy Impact Office money to be spent for research on environmental impact mitigation. A Mercer County official explained: "The problem is that now the rest of the state thinks here the streets are paved with gold, that there is no more problem here, even though the financial and other impacts are still severe. They want to redistribute coal severance and conversion taxes over the whole state, instead of funnel them here. [It's not easy to] convince the rest of the state that we're not in the clover yet, even though the boom is past."

This situation provoked a Beulah official to a rare criticism of the state's impact mitigation procedures, in light of the large number of workers commuting from the urban areas in the state capital: "Industry has been very good for the state. They have benefitted tremendously from this gasification project, more so than Beulah probably, through taxation.... We've had to hassle, they haven't, all they've done is to tax, and, you know, reap the benefits. Mandan, Bismarck, the surrounding communities, the larger towns, had the people living there who owned homes, paid taxes, and we had them come through here as construction workers, use our streets and leave, use our facilities and leave."

As grantwriting became less fruitful, civic leaders increasingly fell back on boosterism as the primary vehicle for promoting town development, a trend that might be called "anti-rationalization." In 1984, a meeting was called to revitalize the Beulah Boosters association. One participant commented: "Back to the tried and true, now that the grant money's drying up."

In this atmosphere of economic insecurity, political lines became more starkly drawn. With the future of the energy industries in question, the energy developers' local power seemed, paradoxically, to grow even stronger.[5] The fear of being abandoned by industry made critical views of energy development unpopular among the business elite of the towns. A group of them successfully pressured a local newspaper to fire a writer because of his "anti-industry" stories on continuing environmental and agricultural problems.

A shake-up occurred in the power relations among the Great Plains gasification project partners. Although American Natural Resources was only the second largest partner (holding 25 percent to Tenneco's 30 percent), this Detroit-based subsidiary of Coastal Corporation had been in charge of the gasification project throughout its construction phase. Early in 1985, however, Tenneco flexed its muscles, rearranging the plant management structure and taking a hard-line stance in relations with locals.

Throughout the energy boom the electrical cooperatives and gas pipeline utilities had been the most visible agents of coal conversion development in Mercer County. Tenneco, the fourteenth largest corporation in the world in 1984, had different public relations policies, however. American Natural Resources had worked to maintain friendly relations with local politicians and business leaders, but Tenneco's gloves-off style of dealing with the local people was closer to that of North American Coal. A state senator representing Mercer County complained of the increasingly imperious demands for political support coming from Great Plains, under Tenneco direction, and from Coteau Mining Properties, the North American Coal subsidiary supplying the gasification plant:

Great Plains' lobbying at the last legislative session was really insulting. They never asked for my input, just made demands, told me what they wanted me to vote for. . . . My constituency is not the energy industries, but the communities here. They need Great Plains because they need its taxes to help pay off their debt loads. . . . I told their lobbyists that I would work as hard as I could to see they got taxed at the highest rate possible, and they got mad. Their community relations guy threatened me. He said "We won't forget that, watch out!" They're out to get me in the next election. . . . They're acting stupidly in their public relations lately. They try to rule through fear instead of hope; they use threats like, "Do what we say or we will leave you high and dry." It breaks down the good will.

In the midst of these troubling times, the people of Mercer County had all but lost interest in the formerly engrossing news of technological progress at the gasification plant. When the announcement came on August 2, 1984, of the first commercial delivery of synthetic gas, the culmination of a decade's effort, the news was buried on page seven of the local newspaper.

The end of the industrial boom brought a realization in Mercer County of its new dependence on an uncertain industrial future. Profits were down in all the county's energy industries in 1984; the Montana Dakota Utilities Resources Group (including coal mining, electrical utilities, and gas pipeline companies)[6] reported a drop of over 50 percent in second quarter earnings over the same period the previous year. Strip mining, pipeline, and synfuels project proposals were being discarded throughout the region.[7] The troubled agricultural economy itself was hurting the energy industry; Basin Electric had shut down one of its generating units because of curtailed consumption by their farm customers, and suspended plans to build another one. Although it was still technically a rural electrical cooperative, Basin saw its future with industrial rather than agricultural customers, and now even this new market was threatened.

As the prices of oil and gas fell from 1982 to 1985, so did federal interest in subsidizing synthetic fuel alternatives to imported oil and gas. Since construction of the Great Plains coal gasification plant in Mercer County began in 1981, the spot-market price of natural gas had declined 60 percent by 1985, while that of oil had declined 35 percent. With prices sinking, the Synthetic Fuels Corporation claimed that, despite the state's generous tax benefits, the project was no longer profitable. This conclusion was contested by Congress, but the fact remained that the synthetic gas produced at the Great Plains plant since its opening in July 1984 was priced at over three times the market rate for natural gas. In a statement that seemed like the final irony to farmers who had opposed the project, one plant official was even quoted as regretting the whole operation had ever been started: "We're putting gas into the pipeline every day and, frankly, losing our butts on it. If we had it to do over again, there'd be cows grazing out there" (*Wall Street Journal* May 21, 1985:6). In negotiations with the Synthetic Fuels Corporation, the Department of Energy, and the Federal Financing Bank, Great Plains sought government backing in the form of $720 million in price supports and the deferment of $673 million in payments due on the $1.47 billion federally guaranteed loan.

In spite of the uncertain short-term financial outlook in the mid-1980s, Mercer County residents pinned their hopes firmly on the long-term success of the energy industry. A local mayor expressed this view: "We've always been under the impression that the plant will survive, it will keep going, it will do the job it's meant to do. We're looking forward to the by-product thing that comes with it. . . . It's a slow process. But as the plant gets on line and does its job, other companies will come in and use the by-products that they have, and hopefully will be using them here in the county. And if not, we will live with those interim people that they have got at the Great Plains plant, and in the other plants."

Most people felt that future growth periods lay ahead, within the coming decade, seeing the post-construction phase as merely a breathing space before additional development plans would be realized. A plant worker earnestly explained: "This is going to continue. Someday the prices are going to go back up, or there will be another oil embargo, and then they'll be glad they got this investment here. It may not be profitable right now but they're going to need it in the future. They're not just going to throw it away."

Others expressed optimistic visions of industrial proliferation: "There's five more units planned at AVS, an aluminum plant, there's the Dunn-Nokota coal-to-methanol plant [in neighboring Dunn County]—I hear they already got a fence around the property there." "If it [Great Plains] keeps operating, it's got potential for growth; by-products, complete plastics industries could be generated here. We've got enough thermal hot water in each plant to run six hundred acres of greenhouse." "Someday they'll be sorry they ever burnt a ton of this coal, because they're finding so many other things they can make with it, like nylon. And there are more coal beds, a lot deeper than you can reach by stripping, and someday they might sink a shaft and burn it with a laser beam and extract the gas without even having men underground."

Not everyone was so sanguine, however, about the prospect of a future for Mercer County based on continued industrial growth. As conflicting rumors reached the county about the impending government decision on the Great Plains consortium's request for additional federal subsidies, even industry representatives spoke openly about the potential for an economic collapse. A Basin representative speculated: "If Great Plains shuts its doors, it'll be absolute economic disaster, because the schools are all bonded to the limit to build all the new buildings to house the kids; the county's in debt on roads; the cities were expanded—you got whole subdivisions out there that are on special assessments. If they walk off and abandon all the houses out there, you know, who pays for it?"

Cognizant of the need to further diversify the local economy, a group of young business people formed an association to encourage tourism by promoting the area's historic, scenic, and recreational resources. Although tourism provides mainly low-paying service jobs, which in North Dakota would obviously be seasonal, they considered their promotional campaign to be a way of using existing resources more effectively. Interestingly, their campaign also made extensive use of the energy industry itself as a tourist attraction. All the mines and plants were featured in a flashy pamphlet, in which the corporate public relations messages were taken up and used by locals in their own publicity campaign: "A thriving energy industry and agriculture exist as neighbors in the heart of Mercer County, north and south of Beulah. The energy sites provide tours of the facilities, the most exciting being the Great Plains Coal Gasification Project, the nation's first commercial coal gasification project, known nationwide for its pioneer efforts at energy independence in America" (Highway 200 Association 1985:24).

The gasification consortium took advantage of its advertisement in this pamphlet to justify its bid for further federal assistance, giving assurances of the plant's long-term benefits to the nation:

> The Great Plains plant is intended not only to demonstrate the practicability and feasibility of coal gasification but also to serve as a working laboratory on the prairie . . . a facility where more can be learned about how to best produce a long list of hydrocarbon and other by-products from coal—America's energy treasure chest. The future economic implications of the Great Plains project for America are as open and vast as the North Dakota Prairie[8] on which the project was built.
> (Highway 200 Association 1985:36)

Throughout the spring and early summer of 1985, speculation ran rampant in Mercer County over the government's decision on subsidies to the Great Plains operations. Most people assumed that the funding would indeed be forthcoming, given the heavy investment already committed. The idea that the plant would be idled at this stage seemed ridiculous. As one local put it, "they don't *make* mothballs that big!" Matters came to a head in July 1985, when the Department of Energy rejected the price supports and slashed the budget for backing synthetic fuels projects. The Synthetic Fuels Corporation itself had been abolished and reconstituted as a much smaller program within the Department of Energy. On August 1 of that year, the five gasification partners announced their decision to abandon the coal gasification plant and default on the federally guaranteed loan.

Coming at a time of generalized industrial retrenchment and financial insecurity, this was a devastating blow to Mercer County. Shocked residents held a special church service to pray for the future of the local people. Their economic troubles were just beginning, though, for when the Great Plains consortium lost its bid for federal price supports, the state government reacted by refusing to loan the county additional money from the Coal Impact Trust Fund to cover the continuing costs of expansion, because it was now a poor credit risk. This decision was made in spite of protests that it belied the fund's purpose of helping fiscally threatened communities. Grants from the Energy Impact Office had helped with impact mitigation, but usually in the form of matching funds. The school districts, political subdivisions, and the county itself had relied on loans from the trust fund, and required continued refinancing in order to operate.

When the Great Plains partners abandoned the plant, the unseen role of the federal government in the project suddenly became clearly visible. The Department of Energy took possession, and gained legal title the following spring as the only bidder allowed at the sherrif's sale. Badly shaken Mercer Countians could scarcely believe the news as the vast property was foreclosed and auctioned off on the courthouse steps, the procedure a surreal counterpoint to the comparitively tiny foreclosure auctions of farms, machinery, and small properties that had become so sadly familiar.

The New Order | In the years following the Great Plains Gasification Associates' spectacular default and plant abandonment, a new social, economic, and political order took shape in Mercer County. During the transitional period, instability at Great Plains created three years of uncertainty for all those families, businesses, communities, and local government entities that had come to rely on the income it brought in. During this time, the energy industries as a group consolidated their position of dominance, which only organized labor chose to confront directly. Other miners, agriculturalists, and small town merchants sought to secure their place in the new order through cooperation with the industries. People in Mercer County no longer construed their relations with the corporations along the lines of a boom-time alliance for progress, however, but in more frankly unequal terms of local dependence on impersonal corporate patronage. Despite industry attempts to continue projecting a neighborly image, Main Street leaders felt what little personal recognition and bargaining power they had enjoyed with the industries slipping away. Rather than empowering all local interests, development had in some ways intensified the competitive forces which had historically worked to eliminate the smaller and more vulnerable among the towns, businesses, and farms. The industries represented resources for survival in the form of income and employment, yet these came at the cost of a new dependency and greater assimilation into the urban corporate culture of American mass society.

The default itself in August 1985 left many in Mercer County with a sense of helplessness and despair, a growing realization of their collective dependence on unpredictable forces. And yet the shift to direct government ownership and control of the Great Plains plant was accomplished remarkably smoothly. The local residents' worst fears—that the facility would be shut down altogether—were not realized. Instead, the Department of Energy hired one of the original consortium partners, American Natural Gas, to manage the everyday running of the plant, which continued without interruption. After laying off large numbers of managerial employees, the Department of Energy claimed to actually run the plant at a profit.[9] With the federal government now more directly involved than ever, new funds were authorized for the study of gasification by-products' development and of plans to refurbish the plant to produce jet fuel.

The government had been willing to step in and stabilize what was, after all, a costly investment in national energy independence, but it had no intention of continuing to run the gasification plant as a state enterprise. The Department of Energy began accepting bids from potential purchasers, who hoped to acquire a functioning facility free of its previous debts; by late November 1987, thirteen organizations had submitted official expressions of interest in buying the plant (*Beulah Beacon* November 15, 1987). In an effort to encourage further energy investment in North Dakota, the 1987 state legislature lowered the coal severance tax, a fact which also enhanced the profitability of the Great Plains plant, as well as mining operations.

In August 1988, three years after the default, Basin Electric Power Cooperative was selected to purchase the gasification plant. Basin created a new subsidiary to run the plant, Dakota Gasification Company (DGC), and made special arrangements to insulate themselves from any devastating losses that the risky business might incur. The Department of Energy provided a $75 million trust fund (part of the plant's $150 million reserve fund) and Basin set up a $30 million line of credit to help DGC over any difficulties due to slumping energy prices. As the deal took shape, it was clear that the government had, in effect, used public funds to finance the building of the plant and now was prepared to continue assuming the risk in turning it over to Basin's membership to run for profit. The idea of Basin taking over at Great Plains made sense to Mercer County residents, even if they were nervous at its growing size and managerial remoteness from the membership of the parent cooperative. Although they saw the giant rural electrical cooperative as little different from investor-owned utilities in its behavior, at least it was a familiar company, with a board of directors made up of North Dakotans. Basin's early moves to improve land reclamation and other environmental protection practices and accountability at the Great Plains complex inspired confidence in its stated intention of being a "good neighbor" to the local people.

Basin also set to work immediately to reform the corporate image and what they called the "workplace culture" at Great Plains to suit their rural electrical cooperative style. They hired a local man to head community relations, a former business owner with close ties to Main Street and a seat on the Beulah town council, to project a friendly local face in town. Out at the plant the glossy corporate lobby, world-class in its extravagant business style, was no longer hung with photographs of the innovative plant under construction, but instead with portraits of the cooperative directors and shots of Basin's other power plants. These were placed there because they were more meaningful to the thousands of coop members who visited the plant each year, who could find a familiar face and scene upon the wall. In the educational exhibition rooms of the visitor center, the benches were still tubular in shape to represent gas pipelines, as they had been in the days when pipeline companies owned the plant, but now the pictures on the wall depicted North Dakota pioneer life. One wall was filled by a life-size blowup photograph of a buffalo grazing peacefully on an undisturbed open plain, without a single coal mine or transmission tower in sight.

Among the nearly six thousand visitors at Great Plains annually in the early 1990s were many delegations from nations interested in coal gasification technology. South Africans from the SASOL plant outside Johannesburg, also designed by the Lurgi Company, and the prototype for Great Plains, were frequent guests, and in 1992 the U.S. Agency for International Development sponsored the visit of a thirty-two-member delegation of Eastern European energy specialists from Bulgaria,

Hungary, Poland, and Czechoslovakia seeking ways to use their own low-grade coal. Many other nations also sent agents, including Canada, China, Greece, India, Indonesia, Japan, and Poland. Their gifts were displayed in the visitor center, emphasizing the fact that this remote location had become a busy nexus directly linked to the international business and energy world.

Basin managers were concerned about the disruptive potential of all the changes in fiscal conditions and ownership that workers at the synfuels plant had experienced, which might result in a poorly integrated corporate culture. This, they worried, would make smooth management more difficult and could even hurt plant efficiency, so they conducted research aimed at developing appropriate policy responses. The first phase of their in-house study of corporate culture was complete in 1991. The results were not available to the public, so it is unclear whether conditions in workers' lives outside the plant were considered, but an employee responsible for the study summarized their understanding of what had happened to the workplace culture over the years:

> There have really been three phases. First there was the startup, when everything was new and exciting, and the corporate culture was all about being Number One, being unique, different from any other plant. It was very gung ho. Anything you needed, they'd take the company jet and go and get it.
>
> Then, during the period of uncertainty, from August '85 to August '88, things were very disillusioned and unsettled. Not so much for the fieldworkers (it didn't affect their jobs much) as for those in administration, getting shuffled around, no knowing how long a job would last.
>
> Finally, after Basin came in, they wanted to change the corporate culture to be more in line with them; their way of doing things as an REC [rural electrical cooperative] was different. It was no longer the "Number One" line, but instead a message of being a homegrown co-op, one of a team, made up of like-minded people, with local ties, part of local history, all that. Some people liked the change right away and some have resisted it, wanted to hang on to the excitement of the old way, being Number One and special.
>
> What came out of the encounter was a sort of combination. It's not really like Basin's other plants. For one thing, they are all union, and this one is union-free.

The years from the default to Basin's restabilized management at Great Plains had been a time of uncertainty and economic decline in Mercer County's businesses and public administrative entities. Unemployment in the county rose to a high of 10 percent in March 1988 (when it was 6.4 percent in the state of North Dakota). Many more residents curtailed their spending, not knowing how long their jobs might last, which cut into the income for retail business. What had been a slow increase in business closures since the gasification plant's completion rose dramatically after the Great Plains consortium's default. In just three years, from 1985 to 1988, business and professional listings in the telephone directory declined 28 percent countywide (see Table 5). The uneven distribution of decline reflects the unequal participation of local communities in the energy boom. Declines in individual towns ranged from 23 percent in Beulah, Hazen, and Pick City, those which had the closest ties to corporate management and had grown the most during the boom, to 42 and 56 percent in Golden Valley and Zap, respectively. The same pattern of unequal change appeared in town populations, on which their sustaining tax base depended. Only Beulah, Hazen, and Pick City (the latter with its lakeside vacation homes for the new elite and proximity to the eastward-moving Freedom Mine) experienced net population increases over the decade of the 1980s, while the rest of the towns actually lost population (see Table 6).

Even after the plant's future was secured local businesses on Main Street continued to decline, and, as Table 5 indicates, recovery from the bust period of 1985 to 1988 was unevenly distributed. With the construction crowd gone and mining all but finished in the western part of the county, Beulah and Golden Valley suffered most, but even on the Hazen Main Street empty store fronts continued to appear. Reasons for going out of business varied. In some cases a retiring owner's children refused to continue the business. Other merchants had overextended their investment during the boom and went bankrupt when it ceased.

Table 5 | Mercer County Commercial Telephone Listings, 1985–1991

	1985	1988	1991	Percentage Decline 1985–1988	Percentage Decline 1985–1991
Beulah	211	163	155	23%	26%
Golden Valley	12	7	3	42	75
Hazen	164	127	142	23	13
Pick City	13	10	11	23	15
Stanton	31	21	27	32	13
Zap	16	7	14	56	12
Total	457	335	352	28	23

Source: West River Telephone Directories.

Table 6 | **Mercer County Town Population Changes, 1980–1990**

	1980	1990	Percentage Change
Beulah	2,908	3,363	+16%
Golden Valley	287	239	−17
Hazen	2,365	2,818	+19
Pick City	182	203	+11
Stanton	623	517	−17
Zap	511	287	−44

Source: U.S. Census of Population and Housing, 1980, 1990.

One of these sported a bumper sticker on his car that read, "Lord, let there be another boom in Mercer County and I promise not to piss it all away this time." Still other Main Street merchants fell victim to the trend by which Hazen and Beulah were turning inside out, with more vigorous commercial areas outside of Main Street, closer to the highway and to the new housing additions. These new businesses were mainly owned by newcomers and outside investors, and included fast-food outlets and a large discount store, which competed directly with languishing Main Street, where anchor stores were closing and some of the remaining merchants were already working at second jobs to maintain their income.

Real estate values, which were already lower since the end of the boom, were further depressed by the transition at Great Plains. The Department of Energy had acquired housing property when it took over the plant. It had no interest in such holdings and had quickly sold them off at a loss, further depressing housing prices. The market received another shock when Basin began its tenure at the plant with a wave of layoffs at the management level, newcomers whose expensive new homes hit the market unexpectedly. The middle range of housing values fell when the federal Department of Housing and Urban Development and the Farm Home Insurance Company, which had financed homes at the $50,000 to $60,000 range, began selling them off for as little as $20,000. Homes at all levels of value, from trailers to the large colonials at the Country Club Estates, went back to the towns for taxes, while special assessment payments for services to new housing additions were in arrears in all the towns. By 1991, house values at the upper end of the market had dropped by two-thirds, and those who had bought homes during the boom found themselves trapped, owing more on their homes than their current market value, and considering the option of voluntary foreclosure.

The ripple effect of changes at Great Plains also extended to the finances of Mercer County's towns and schools. The town of Beulah requested $150,000 in assistance from the Energy Impact Office in the fall of 1987, to cover fiscal shortfalls resulting from a 20 percent local tax delinquency rate. The Energy Impact Office objected that this problem was not "energy-related" (*Beulah Beacon* November 25, 1987), although it eventually provided grants to the towns to cover delinquent special assessment payments. The remaining outstanding debt for special assessments was collected from the entire tax base of the communities, including those residents who had nothing to do with the housing developments expansion they now had to pay for. With more and more people moving out, a shrinking number of long-term residents had to shoulder the bloated tax burden.

The school boards in Mercer County were also encountering mounting financial difficulties, and were also placed in the position of begging for assistance in paying for problems that could have been predicted by state authorities. Lowering the state's coal severance tax in 1986 meant less money coming back to the districts here, despite an increase in their share. The Hazen school superintendent went to the state legislature to plead for additional assistance for his beleaguered district. He claimed that students were still crowded into temporary classrooms, and that unless more funds were assigned, class size would soon reach eighty students in the high school and forty to fifty students in the elementary school. The last round of Energy Impact Office grants was made in November 1988, while the area still reeled from the impact of the boom and its aftermath. The system had provided much in the way of infrastructure expansion, but remained only a means of redress for damage done rather than a proactive planning institution offering front-end financing from the industries responsible.

When times were at their worst, a local newspaper columnist captured the prevailing mood of bitterness, anxiety, and awareness of dependency:

> If there is a lesson to be learned from what's happening in Mercer County, it is that being honest and and working hard will not bring success. What your father told you isn't working these days. . . . Coal miners at the Indian Head Mine are on strike, with a big negotiation point being job security. One has to wonder. When farms are going under, both small and large businesses failing, banks closing, and corporations letting senior employees go before retirement, is there any such thing as job security for anyone? . . . Everyone seem dispensable these days and profit pictures dictate what will be done. . . . The process of shaping this county isn't over yet. . . . There is also the light of hope that the resources of the county will

become valuable again and we'll surge back. There hadn't been any "up" in the county for quite a while when the energy industry took off in the mid-seventies. Now we're in a "down" again, but that is still above what it was before it all started. (*Beulah Beacon* December 10, 1987)

Yet in the midst of local economic decline in the late 1980s, the coal business continued to expand. With the help of lowered severance tax rates North American Coal Company (NACCO) made record profits in 1987.[10] purchased from Basin Electric the rights to mine a large tract north of Hazen (a former Consolidation mine site known as North Star), and began leasing land all along the Missouri River in North Dakota in the name of its four subsidiary companies (Coteau, Falkirk, Missouri Valley, and West Plains). Unionized workers at the three older mines in the county (NACCO's Indian Head Mine, Basin's Glenharold Mine, and Knife River's Beulah Mine) saw the writing on the wall. NACCO already had close ties to Basin, selling its coal to use at the Antelope Station and at Great Plains from its nonunion Freedom Mine. With new mines opening to fill the demand for coal, Indian Head and Glenharold could be shut down, wiping out their UMW locals.

Union mine workers' fears were realized in 1987 when NACCO announced its intention to close the Indian Head Mine after seventy years of operation. With contracts up for renegotiation here (and simultaneously at two other UMW strongholds—Pittston Coal in Kentucky and the Dekker Mine in Montana) the stage was set for organized labor's last stand in Mercer County: Indian Head workers looking for some negotiating edge encountered a company that could apparently do without them. NACCO offered no assurance of hiring workers at other operations as they expanded, nor of recognizing their rights to medical benefits. Under their UMW contract, these workers were supposed to receive lifetime medical coverage after twenty years of service to the company. At that rate, all of those working at Indian Head would have been eligible for a health card by 1992, when their average age would be forty-six. North American refused to consider honoring the miners' job transfer rights, in accordance with their unofficial policy of not hiring workers from union operations into nonunion ones. On November 1, 1987, the forty-three Indian Head miners of United Mine Workers local 8880 walked out.

When the strike began, the contract was suspended and workers were angered by the company's move to cut off medical benefits to twenty-one widows and retirees, one remarking "we're just worn out workhorses to them." To demonstrate their determination to stay out "as long as it takes" despite the winter cold, striking miners erected an ice-fishing shack at the mine entrance, complete with an old coal stove.

A skinned fox hung at the gate, with a sign: "scab." Surprisingly, North American found few workers prepared to cross the line, even among nonunion miners laid off at another of their mines nearby. Month after month, the striking miners held their ranks, while North American tried to operate with a skeleton crew of six temporaries and eleven nonunion and supervisory workers from Indian Head. The picket protest was lively. On one occasion thirty were arrested when they managed to block the entrance for three hours. An anonymous supporter disavowed by the union waged a silent campaign of strewing the road entrance with fierce-looking welded "jumping jacks" to puncture the tires of entering vehicles.

With so much at stake, the union continued to support the strike while conducting a series of fruitless talks with North American. As the strike wore on into 1988, the Mercer County Landowners Association and the Dakota Resource Council passed resolutions in support of the strikers, and North American's public relations chief August Keller (whom everyone knew as the former head of the Energy Impact Office) made almost daily television appearances to defend the company's position. In a February rally, miners staged an impressive display of solidarity. Striking miners and their families were joined by members of the asbestos workers, carpenters, plumbers, pipefitters, ironworkers, and electrical workers unions, by some forty striking miners from the Dekker Mine in Sheriden, Wyoming (on strike since October 1987), and Nomonde Ngubo, a United Mine Workers liaison officer with the South African National Union of Mineworkers, of which she was a founding member. Some two hundred marched down Hazen and Beulah's Main Streets and more than three hundred fifty attended a supper and dance following the rally.

This impressive showing was to be the last hurrah of the decade for organized miners in Mercer County. In May 1988 the strikers complied with an order from their national to return to work, where they staged a production slowdown as their final action, still pushing for the job transfer rights that would rescue individual mine workers from unemployment when the mine closed. Shortly thereafter, NACCO imposed a contract that, although it cut medical benefits, did include this important job security clause. As operations wound down at Indian Head over the following years, those who had crossed pickets to work during the strike were hired at newer mines first, and then the union supporters.[11] Organized confrontation had won, for these individuals at least, a stake in the future and a place from which they hoped to rebuild their union in the future.

Basin also announced plans to close the Glenharold Mine by 1994, and since the rural electrical coop would thus be out of the coal mining business, no new labor contract would be considered; their UMW work force thus had no bargaining power and little expectation of being hired by new nonunion facilities. The one remaining organized mine in Mercer County would be Knife River's Beulah Mine, where the UMW had won a close election in 1986. With both Indian Head and Glenharold closed, the United Mine Workers could not hope to hold its narrow margin of support at the Beulah Mine, and might easily be eradicated from the county altogether.[12] In any case, Knife River was losing contracts and laying off workers in 1991, raising for union loyalists the spector that all Mercer County coal operations would be left solely in the hands of NACCO and its subsidiaries.

By 1991 it seemed that organized labor was on the ropes in Mercer County. Their position had been shored up during the construction phase of the energy boom by the support of the other trade unions present then. But now there was simply not enough union labor around for the movement to be self-sustaining. The tradition of Mercer County workers' organizing when they felt aggrieved was far from gone, however, and continued to resurface. Over half of the county government workers voted to affiliate as their own local with the American Federation of State, County, and Municipal Employees (AFSCME), after lengthy and acrimonious contract discussions, followed by unilaterally imposed increases in work hours without extra pay. Pro-union workers were active in the Great Plains synfuels plant, where the first affiliation vote was held in 1992. Employees in the proposed bargaining unit rejected affiliation with the Oil, Chemical, and Atomic Workers International Union in this election, but organizers planned to continue their efforts.

Meanwhile, work conditions in the nonunion mines were acceptable—not up to union standards in the eyes of the diehards, but certainly well above the levels of exploitation that had originally given birth to the local union movement. There was no immediate prospect of organizing successfully there, although union sympathizers there remained vigilant and critical. As one activist acknowledged, "If people are being treated right, there's no need for a union." Another summed up the historical dilemma of dependent workers compelled to bite the hand when it fails to feed them enough: "For all the eternal struggle with the mines to keep them from exploiting people too bad, this place would be a lot worse off without them. They've provided some people with decent paying jobs for a lot of years."

In the new order taking shape in the late 1980s, the energy industries consolidated their position of dominance both within Mercer County and in the state of North Dakota, where Basin, NACCO, and the Lignite Council became the most powerful lobbies in Bismarck.

The strategy of shifting capital investment to new nonunion facilities had strangled the mine workers' labor organizations, and a period of relative calm ensued in which few complaints against the industries were heard. Nonunion workers and the farmers not directly damaged by the mines pursued strategies of cooperation and accommodation with the industries, while those officials running local affairs took on the task of sustaining the development they had once sought to rein in.

There were several reasons for lowered levels of opposition to the energy industry among farmers. Many of them were near retirement age and willing to accept compensation and move to town. Others had come to depend on extra income from the industrial economy. One farmer explained their quiescence in 1991: "People have adjusted to the energy industry. It's become familiar. No one is struggling with it any more. Farmers are just trying to survive; they're more worried about *that*. Besides, a lot of them work at the mines and plants at the same time. That's what lets them keep on farming." Even the Landowners Association adopted a more cooperative stance, emphasizing its role as a mediator in farmer–industry disputes. Such disputes remained alive, particularly in the neighborhood north of Hazen affected by the activities of NACCO's subsidiary, Coteau. Despite legal assistance from the Dakota Resource Council, farmers there continued to be stymied in efforts to prove company culpability for wells gone dry and damage to buildings they claimed resulted from nearby blasting. They also protested the closing of farm-to-market roads due to mine activities.

With the older generation of farmers retiring and farms continuing to fail at the rate of one-thousand a year in the state, the pre-boom style of farming was no longer so prevalent. Experts predicted another major "housecleaning" of family farmers in western North Dakota in the next generation, with only the large, complex operations of mixed grain and livestock likely to survive. Successfully running such enterprises takes well-developed financial and business management skills similar to those of an industrial agribusiness concern. An example of one of these operations is Martin's, who has a cow/calf and wheat-growing enterprise on six thousand acres. He no longer does the hands-on field work himself, but hires two farmhands to, as he puts it, "drive tractors around," while he manages the business—tracking markets, planning strategies, researching programs, and doing paperwork. Martin also occasionally helps his father out with paperwork and planning at his nearby farm, since the older man's fifth-grade education is insufficient to manage them successfully.

There were also few complaints at the new union-free mines and plants, aside from some ex-union men still smarting from the strike.

Management took pains to promote a harmonious climate, emphasizing company spirit and encouraging workers to think of themselves as white collar professionals rather than laboring proletarians. Promoting a corporate culture of teamwork and cooperation among the growing industrial work force, the energy industries successfully defused the immediate potential for new labor mobilization. In this sense the remaining mine workers appeared, like the large farmers, to be assimilating to the business culture of big capital.

Work productivity was so high at Coteau's Freedom mine that by September 1991, with the removal of the mine's seventy-fifth million ton of coal, this became the largest mine in North Dakota history, and the tenth largest in the nation. The 226 employees had achieved this landmark in only eight years of operation, one and a half years ahead of the originally projected date. Company officials predicted the facility would be handling approximately 15.5 million tons of coal annually by the mid-1990s.

The new class of more highly trained and better-paid professionals and managers were not complaining in 1991. This group had always been most at home with the rational, technocratic culture of development, planning, and urbanization. One unusually disgruntled supervisory-level plant worker described his colleagues' attitudes this way: "Everybody around here has completely bought into the whole development thing. . . . Nobody is complaining because they've bought into it and also because at this point, they've got no choice. Lots of people bought expensive homes at top dollar, and now they're stuck with it. They took on a lot of debt, and now the real estate prices are down and they can't move out."

The demeanor of the town and county workers performing the everyday technical, managerial, and office functions changed dramatically as the new order became routine. When these urban trained technocrats were new to their position of running things in the county, they had been a beleaguered crew, daily assaulted by the conflicting demands of developers and local residents, striving to ride the tiger of the energy boom while mitigating its environmental and economic damage. In 1991, by contrast, they worked calmly in their newly modernized and computerized offices, pursuing on their own initiative the tasks that had been forced so unpleasantly on them before. Development, it appeared, was no longer something that was happening to them, but rather something that they were engaged in doing for themselves. When I marveled at the change, one administrator musingly agreed, and said: "I guess, after a while, it becomes us."

For those in positions of public responsibility this period represented a new phase in the sequence of problems they had faced over the course of energy development. First had been environmental concerns, then problems associated with the construction boom. That was followed by the period when the continued existence of the gasification plant itself was in question. Now, the principal concern for the county and its towns was the sustainability of economic growth, and how to hold on to the improvements they had made.

The towns had achieved their goal of modernizing their infrastructural facilities during the boom, but the merchants of Main Street had been hard hit by the economic bust following the Great Plains plant's abandonment, and were still working hard to recover in the early 1990s. Where once boom growth had been handed to them on a silver platter, chambers of commerce and town governments now had to struggle to keep the gains of the last decade and to pursue community economic development on their own. They remained committed to their historic vision of future progress based on the expansion of local business, but faced a daunting task. Towns had received large amounts of property back in tax default, and found few buyers—even for commercial plots priced at just one dollar. They continued plans to develop local tourism, especially at the lake and in Beulah and Zap, where closed-down mines might be refurbished as industrial museums, but the latter were risky and time-comsuming ventures to launch.

The most promising developments were those taking place at the gasification and electric plant site, where a fish farm using heated water from the generators began production in 1992 and a series of by-products projects and contracts were being developed. The Dakota Gasification Company planned to begin selling krypton and xenon to Union Carbide in the early 1990s, and hoped to start selling phenol, argon, naphtha, methanol, and diesel fuel over the next few years. Although high transportation costs to markets made some of these ventures unlikely, the company pursued financing grants from the federal Department of Energy's Clean Coal Technology Fund. The best of the energy industry spin-offs, in terms of a more integrated local development strategy, was a proposed ethanol plant that would be a producer-owned cooperative using locally grown grain and waste heat from Great Plains. People in Mercer County were quick to see the advantages of this plan, and positive local attitudes towards cooperatives—as opposed to outsider-owned corporations—contributed to universal support for this project.

Old rivalries among the towns persisted, and each worked on its own plans to attract more residents and businesses. Competitive pressures among them were as fierce as ever, and they had not benefitted equally from energy development. The larger towns of Hazen and Beulah had secured the greatest share of vital resources for future survival in the form of expanded tax base and commercial activity, while Golden Valley, Zap, Stanton, and Pick City found themselves ill-equipped for the challenge. Over the course of the boom, however, all had acquired greater expertise and information about how to pursue and manage development, and they shared an understanding that economic security lay in broadening the economic base to include more than just dependence on agriculture, retail trade, and the energy industries. Together with towns in neighboring Oliver County, Mercer County municipalities commissioned a costly professional study of what sorts of light industry would be best suited to the area with the intention of courting likely targets, and they even formed a combined organization, the Mercer Oliver Economic Development group. The need to pool financial resources motivated this rare cooperative measure among neighboring towns, but did not dispel the underlying competitive ethos of business. The persistence of competitive thinking was best expressed by a town official in Beulah: "Our ultimate goal is future growth, from new light industry. It's not going to come from energy industry. And it won't come without a struggle, because every town in the U.S. is competing for businesses."

Even at the level of a single town, commercial groups found the coordinated planning of active community development difficult. Consensus was elusive, and the project of aggressively seeking out companies and convincing them to relocate in Mercer County was beyond the experience of local boosters. A community development leader in Hazen explained, "It's hard to overcome the psychological barrier. We've relied on the things we knew worked: agriculture, mining coal. It's hard to go over the threshold to being entrepreneurial."

Conclusion

Economic restructuring is a continual and ongoing feature of capitalism, one in which there are always conflicting interests and processes at work. I have argued that this is a fundamental dynamic of social change not only in the Third World, where economic development is most often studied by anthropologists, but also in places like Mercer County. The conflicts and changes explored in this account do not end with the establishment of what I have characterized as a new order, but their future course will be contingent on the possibilities it presents.

Questions about the sustainability of the local economy remained at the time of my last visit late in the summer of 1991, just as they had been a concern since the settlers first arrived. Indeed, in many ways, life appeared to go on much as it had before the energy boom: the August heat, the heavy grain trucks crawling townward with the harvest, the heady scent carried on the evening breeze from mile after mile of open grassland; the weather-beaten faces of shy farmers in their greasy caps and long hair, resting in a cafe after delivering a load of hard-gotten grain, looking so different from their sleek, underexercised, and self-assured "neighbors" of the town. Some of the basic attitudes and problems among the lifelong locals had not changed dramatically, despite the shifting field of resources and powers. Farming here had always been a hard living, with high attrition, and after the boom it was still that way. Miners had always sought protection from perceived abuse by organizing, while management sought to depoliticize them, and this tension continued among the workers, ready to erupt in the future. The merchants of Main Street had always wanted growth, and this was still their goal. The county's economy had always been dependent on outside interests, and this was as true as ever. Most of the wealth produced from its natural resources and the hard work of its people had always been drained away to enrich others, and this was still the case. And most of the young people finishing high school had always left for greater job opportunities elsewhere and, after a brief lull in the early 1980s when the new permanent work force was being hired, the youth drain continued. In the older neighborhoods and smaller towns, it seemed that the community life of the preboom days had somehow survived. Neighbors still visited and looked after the elderly, gangs of children still roamed freely on their bikes, and wedding dances still brought networks of relations and friends together.

And yet the pattern of social and political relationships among those in Mercer County had been rearranged, not only in terms of the relative positions of farmers, miners, and merchants, but also in the prevailing patterns of community sociability. In the larger towns especially, large numbers of newcomers had never really mixed with the general population. The raw ugliness of the new neighborhoods was softened by maturing grass, trees, and flowerbeds but the lives of residents there remained molded by the suburban stamp rather than that of the small town. An older native of the county described what he saw as the unneighborly behavior of these transplanted urbanites:

> All these new people don't mix with the old. They get a house and just stay there with their wife and children and don't even mix with the folks downtown. They've just got a different way. I know of a for-instance: A family moved in next door to this fellow, with a moving truck. He came

over to help them out and they acted real strange, didn't want him there, interfering, didn't want to know him. Now around here, you go over to your neighbor, you visit, if you've got some vegetables or something you bring that over. But not these people. They just go to work, go home to their family, and don't want to know about anybody else.

The newcomers had mixed mainly with members of the upper ranks in local society, and especially with those leaders most involved in promoting continued modernization. Those newcomers who had chosen to join the community in this way found in church and school activities the avenue for involvement in local affairs. Assuming positions of responsibility had brought some into the circle of elite leadership, with whom they shared an urban-oriented lifestyle and values. The other previous residents were still there, but increasingly on the margins of civic life. The generation that had founded the towns was becoming an all-but-invisible and voiceless class of anachronistic old-timers, distinguished not simply by age but by their uncertain place in the new order.

The ultimate consequences of progress in economic and environmental terms were still far from clear, however. The fiscal health of families, towns, school districts, and the rest of the constituent elements of the county depended entirely on sustaining the growth and diversification of commerce and industry in competition with the rest of rural America, a project subject to forces beyond the control of anyone in Mercer County. The long-term environmental impact of the energy industry activities also remained difficult to predict. In 1991 the first of the land tracts reclaimed from strip mining was going back into production. So far, only hay was planted on it, and the Public Service Commission would not even allow its use as cattle pasture. Doubt remained whether it would ever be approved for crops.[13]

Meanwhile, the backlog of unreclaimed land at Indian Head and Glenharold was rapidly being reduced, with the impending shutdown of these facilities. According to the responsible county official, the quality of reclamation had improved markedly, particularly at Coteau's Freedom Mine, where two native North Dakotans had been hired to supervise environmental protection and restoration. He also approved of Basin's environmental practices at the gasification plant, citing their use of biocides in the cooling tanks, and claimed the operation was easier to work with than before: "Their environmental people are becoming local. They're not as flashy, but they're doing better work."

For many reasons, the energy boom had clearly not become the unmitigated social, economic, and environmental disaster that it might have been. The legacy of local history—the conflicts, goals, values, and life experiences of Mercer County's people had shaped their response to energy development and enabled them to achieve, despite the institutional limits to their power, a livable compromise. The active part taken by local residents in contending with the forces of big capital had helped them get out of the development opportunity much of what they wanted, without losing their potential for wariness and organized opposition should the need arise.

Bitterness and conflict remained, however. The goals and interests of some had been met, while others, who never found the idea of modernization appealing, felt their values and needs had been pushed aside and submerged. Despite the ascendency of urban culture, something of the historical diversity of the ideological currents there survives. For Mercer County people, the goal of economic growth remains in dynamic tension with other values, and the resulting conflicts will continue to be an engine of change as they seek to make their future.

Notes

Chapter One

1. Among these are Albrecht et al. 1988; Apgar and Brown 1988; Beaulieu 1988; Borich et al. 1985; Breimyer 1990; Deavers et al. 1986; Dillman and Hobbs 1982; Fitchen 1987, 1991; Hefferman and Hefferman 1986; O'Hare 1988; and Porter 1989.
2. It is important to remember, however, that by the time of the energy boom the area that includes Mercer County was already "developed," in the sense of being fully integrated into an advanced capitalist society, so the internal periphery concept is less useful for understanding the recent processes at work there.
3. The most famous of these is Robert and Helen Lynd's classic, *Middletown*, which appeared in 1928 and was followed in 1937 by a sequel documenting changes brought on by the Great Depression. Rapid urbanization in the 1920s and 1930s inspired the Chicago school of urban ethnography, under the leadership of Robert Park (Park 1915; Park and Burgess 1925; Warner et al. 1941–1949; Wirth 1925; Whyte 1955, 1961; Zorbaugh 1929), while rural community studies were infused with a critical enthusiasm for documenting ethnographically the consequences of the Great Depression in the countryside (e.g., Bell 1942). This tradition has continued in both urban and rural community studies, generating a broad and varied literature on the relationship between industrial growth and decline and social changes in affected communities (e.g., Cassity 1989; Caudill 1962; Hareven and Langenbach 1978; Hatch 1979; Nash 1989; Sanders and Lewis 1976; Vidich and Bensman 1968; and Young and Newton 1980).
4. Walker has pointed out the futility of traditional regional and community development strategies such as creating multipliers, generating linkages, and preventing economic leakage in the face of spatial differentiation and capital mobility (1990:33).
5. The limitations of cities' attempts to attract major new industry have been studied by Alan Pred, who points out the difficulty of preventing the expected benefits in terms of income, profits, and linkages from going instead to middle class suburbs, other cities' financial districts, or to suppliers in other regions (Pred 1977), while a strategy relying on smaller

entrepreneurs is weak because they have little control over growth. The Gunns (1991) and others recommend instead community efforts to use local capital (from savings, pensions, grant money, etc.) to make local investments, and for workers to buy out control over closing factories.

6. The phrase "common sense" is used here, in Antonio Gramsci's sense, to refer to the inventory of traditional ideas that constitute what is assumed to be true in practical knowledge (1971:326).

7. Stuart Hall has explained how linguistic or semiological analysis combines with the more historical Gramscian approach to ideology to demonstrate that the logic of particular discourses in the West depends on their reference to such "preconstructed" elements of hegemonic bourgeois "common sense." This helps create a version of reality recognizable to the audience, so that the message is taken for simple fact—a phenomenon known as the "reality effect." In Hall's words, "Statements about economic relations thus lost their conditional and premised character, and appeared simply to arise from 'how things are.' . . . But this 'reality-effect' arose precisely from the circularity, the presuppositionless character, the self-generating nature, of the process of representation itself" (1982:76).

8. See, for example, June Nash's study of Bolivian tin miners (1979), Aihwa Ong's on Malaysian factory women (1987), and Michael Taussig's work on Colombian plantation workers (1980).

9. Other studies of the dynamic interplay between the structuring forces of industrial growth and local culture include David Thelen's *Paths of Resistance* (1986) and Daniel Walkowitz's *Worker City, Company Town* (1978).

10. Marxist economists Harry Magdoff and Paul Sweezy describe the corporate/government relation as "symbiotic" (1981:81).

11. Wilson, a General Motors chief executive and an Eisenhower administration Secretary of Defense, made this statement in an address to the Senate Armed Forces Committee in 1952 (Andrews 1989:32).

12. The similarity of this trend to that occurring in the oil-exporting agricultural nations of the Middle East is striking. See Antoun and Harik 1972; Katouzian 1978; and Owen 1981.

13. The lake is named for the famous Shoshone woman, captive in a Hidatsa (Gros Ventre) town in what is today Mercer County, whom Lewis and Clark hired as a guide in their exploratory trek west into Montana. Sakakawea became known to the rest of the country as "Sakajawea."

14. Although gender is not an explicitly developed analytical dimension in this account, its implicit significance is very great. In focusing on formal arenas of economic activity and public life where male actors are at center stage, this work inevitably contains a bias towards presenting masculine perspectives and activities as normative. This is not so much a result of sexism on my part—indeed I have tried to offset this bias where possible—but because male hegemony pervaded the subject of my study. Male dominance was a property of the system of relations that came into play in the energy boom, although it was rarely expressed as overt gender discrimination. The historic leadership of men (and suppression of women) in these formal economic and political institutions has produced a situation in which it is mainly their concerns and experiences that are articulated in ideological formulations, and their interactional styles that set the norms operating in formal organizations and civic life.

Chapter Two

1. Others included the Assiniboin, Chippewa, Cree, and Teton and Yanktonai Dakotas.
2. See Hibbard (1939) for a history of federal land policies, and Davies (1958) on the role of real estate in U.S. economic growth.
3. These laws were widely abused by speculators, and did not prevent concentrated land ownership in much of the West (Gates 1945), but they worked more or less as intended in Mercer County.
4. Laura Ingalls Wilder gives a richly detailed account of pioneer life in such dwellings in her autobiographical novels, *On the Banks of Plum Creek* and *Little House on the Prairie* (1953a, 1953b).
5. The majority of homesteaders were German-Russians, but they spoke at least four different German dialects. There were also some Scandinavians and native-born Americans, especially near the Missouri River, a small settlement of Irish near Hazen, and a few families from other European nations. In 1890, North Dakota had the highest percentage of foreign born residents of all the Plains states, at 45 percent (U.S. Census 1893).
6. In 1885 the land that is today Oliver County was separated from Mercer by legislative act. In 1889 the county auditor succeeded in securing an additional 24 townships, of present-day Dunn County, but these were lost in 1898 through the negligence of county officials, who had never bothered to assess property or collect taxes there (*The Common* August 10, 1972).
7. See Hudson (1985, chs. 5, 6) for a detailed account of railway track, town, and elevator location strategies in North Dakota.
8. Don Harrison Doyle (1978) describes the importance of boosterism in providing the energetic and unified effort needed to successfully launch the Illinois frontier town he studied.
9. The Brazilians were presumably ethnic Germans from Russia from the South American contingent, who then later joined relatives or friends in Mercer County.
10. For extensive accounts of pricing abuses, see Morlan (1955) and Nelson (1964).
11. For an account of the national scope of this movement, see Lawrence Goodwyn's *The Populist Moment* (1978) and Seymour Martin Lipset's *Agrarian Socialism* (1950).
12. The Independent Party had accepted the Populist platform and ran successfully against the Republicans in 1893, winning every state office except secretary of state. But the legislative assembly remained under the control of a Republican majority and the reform efforts promoted by the Populist program were stymied by the delaying tactics of the railroad and milling interests in the state legislature (Robinson 1966:223–224). By 1895 they had all but defeated Populism in North Dakota.
13. See Burdick (1944) for a historical account of political action by North Dakota farmers.
14. This is A. V. Chayanov's (1966) term for the use of unpaid family labor in family-owned or -operated farms (peasant or capitalistic).
15. In one large mine, wages stayed at 30 cents an hour from 1932 to 1943, and rose to only 65 cents an hour in 1946.
16. As of 1991, community economic planners in Zap, some of them retired

miners, hoped to excavate and restore at least part of this abandoned coal camp to serve as a historical tourist attraction.
17. This has been a recurring tactic in labor struggles in the United States and elsewhere.
18. See Allen (1966, ch. 4) for more on the history of coal mining in the American West.
19. A German term used in Mercer County as elsewhere for the informal yet stable groups of women who gather to drink coffee and gossip, either on a rotating basis in each other's homes, or in a cafe. It is gender-specific, and implicitly devalues the significance of women's communication.

Chapter Three

1. Here, I follow Eric Wolf, who suggests the explanation of coexisting alternative cultural forms by reference to the political and economic forces at work in specific social-historical contexts (1982:387).
2. This low level of collective identity and class consciousness characterizes service workers nationwide (Mills 1951) and may be explained in terms of their dispersal among many different employers and the high level of differentiation within the class, which includes white collar professionals as well as field hands, food service workers, and mechanics.
3. This shift was documented by rural sociologists of the time, in works such as those by Bell 1934; Gillette 1940; Holmes 1932:73–75; Landis 1940:385; Smith 1940; Taylor 1942; and Wheeler 1949.
4. Their conception of the family as a nuclear one, in which primary kin ties gradually weaken as offspring reach social maturity and found new families of their own, is consistent with the primary-kin familism that Heller and Quesada found throughout the western United States (1977).
5. See Taylor 1933 for a summary of these studies. These traits resemble those reported to be characteristic of peasant personality (cf. Blum and Blum 1965; Foster 1967; F. Friedmann 1967), and may be explained by the difficulty of survival under economically marginal conditions with limited land resources.
6. See Jefferson's *Notes on the State of Virginia* (1787). One of the clearest expressions of this agrarian moral ideology can be found in Bruce Anderson's *The Farmer Seeks Jeffersonian Democracy* (1943).
7. As Marx pointed out in *The Eighteenth Brumaire of Louis Bonaparte* (1852), this is a basic difficulty of political organizing among small-farming peasants as well.
8. Forty-five percent of the nonmining wage workers earned all their income from wage work, and another 15 percent worked to supplement farm income (U.S. Census 1970).
9. During the union drives of the 1930s in Appalachia, the Progressive Mine Workers, then a small union headquartered in Illinois, was invited into the mines by coal companies as a competing union in an effort to prevent the stronger United Mine Workers from gaining complete control (Caudill 1962:202).
10. In this they resemble the coal miners of Yorkshire, England, as described by Norman Dennis et al. (1956:33), and of Harlan County, Kentucky, described by Shaunna Scott (1988). Mann (1973) also explores the problem of consciousness among Western miners.

11. Lazonick (1980) dates the historical origin of this ideological formulation of the harmony of interests between labor and capital to the period following the fall of the Chartist pan-labor movement in England in 1842. Arguing that the will of labor must be consistent with the goals of capital for the productive system to function, he describes the various means by which this will was changed, such as through education, undermining the family as a production unit, and the application of patriarchal organization to the factory. By the mid-nineteenth century, Lazonick says that organized labor was co-opted by economic prizes, gave up its claims to political power, and adopted bourgeois values of working within the system. It was after the failure of the Chartist movement that organized labor formed a series of separate, industry-specific unions and it has, at least in the advanced capitalist societies, focused its efforts on narrow economic goals ever since.
12. Such ambivalence pervades both American society and its media treatment of labor unions. For an analysis of the origins of the negative image of labor unions in the United States, see Mills' *The New Men of Power* (1948).
13. Such arguments blaming the labor force for the decisions made by corporate managers are widespread and time-honored in the U.S. (see Mills 1948), and obscure the real causes of economic insecurity in a system where capital always seeks the highest possible profits (O'Connor 1979:x).
14. At the time of this research the town of Stanton was seeking to establish a comparable street fair, "Knife River Days," organized around the theme of the encounter between Lewis and Clark and the nearby Native Americans. Their visits are re-enacted in a pageant featuring actors from the Three Affiliated Tribes, designed to emphasize the area's culturally plural heritage and promote Anglo-Native cooperation and mutual respect.
15. See Sinclair Lewis's *Babbitt* (1922) for an outstanding novelistic portrayal of the booster ethos in the Midwestern United States.
16. When I remarked to a minister at a rural church upon the silent discipline and the general lack of interaction among Mercer County churchgoers packed together in the pews, he laughed and explained, "Of course you don't want to talk to other people in the church. The guy sitting next to you might be trying to steal your farm!"
17. This is the sense in which Ferdinand Toennies (1963) used the term "Gemeinschaft" in his work *Community and Society*, and characterizes the societies that Henry Maine saw as based on "status" rather than "contract" (Maine 1871, 1905). It also is related to what Max Weber (1964) identified as "communal" rather than "associative" behavior.

Chapter Four

1. C. Wright Mills' classic, *The Power Elite* (1956), sparked a generation of research into the question of consolidated power in the highest ranks of American political, economic, and military institutions, including E. Digby Baltzell's *The Protestant Establishment* (1964), William Domhoff's *Who Rules America?* (1967) and *The Power Elite and the State* (1990), Mintz and Cohen's *America Inc.* (1971), Thoman Dye's *Who's Running America?* series (1976–1990), Creel Froman's *The Two American Political Systems* (1984), and many more. For a critical summary, see Kerbo and Fave 1979.
2. The "ruling class" thesis, of course, is not required to explain the

246 | Notes to Chapter Four

hegemonic influence of this dominant class alliance through historical cultural leadership.

3. In this empirically oriented analysis, I follow Theda Skocpol in viewing states not as "mere analytic aspects of abstractly conceived modes of production, or even political aspects of concrete class relations and struggles" (1979:31), but rather as real organizations that extract resources from territories and people, and seek to control them.

4. The technology for gasifying coal, using oxygen and steam, was invented in Nazi Germany in the 1930s, where its development enjoyed state support as a part of the war preparation effort. See Rasch (1984) for more on the early development of the gasification process. The German engineering firm which developed the process, Lurgi, split into East and West German corporations after the war. The East German firm went on to design coal gasification plants in Yugoslavia, while the West German Lurgi (a subsidiary of the giant Metall Gesellschaft of Frankfurt) designed the SASOL plant in South Africa and then the Great Plains plant in Mercer County. For a summary description of the technological process of converting solid fuel to combustible gas see Wionczek et al. 1982:35.

5. This Garrison Diversion Project was a plan inspired by the Pick-Sloan Missouri Basin Program, authorized by the Flood Control Act of 1944. Little has been done to realize its grandiose proposals, but the Diversion Project remains a powerful political symbol of the great potential for future economic development in North Dakota.

6. These included the federal Department of Interior (13 percent), the Bureau of Indian Affairs (7 percent), the State of North Dakota (6 percent), the Federal Land Bank (3 percent), the Bank of North Dakota (3 percent), and the Burlington Northern Railway (8 percent).

7. According to Tanzer (1974) this crisis was not caused by actual shortages in world energy supplies, but rather by the manipulation of supply by monopolies and by changes in international political relations.

8. The Carter administration promoted a crash program for synthetic fuels development from oil shale, tar sands, coal, and residual crude oil, aiming to replace two million barrels of imported oil a day by 1992.

9. Since the Synthetic Fuels Corporation was originally a creature of the Democratic Party, the latter continued to support the idea of federally subsidized synfuels development during the Reagan presidency. Prominent western Democrats, such as House Minority Leader Jim Wright of Texas and Pete Domenici of New Mexico, argued for it while in the Republican administration the Office of Management and Budget Director David Stockman and Interior Secretary James Watt opposed it on conservative ideological grounds. They argued against providing price supports and loan guarantees to projects such as the Mercer County coal gasification plant, calling this "corporate welfare," and proposed that market price should decide whether synfuels was an idea whose time had come.

10. Michigan-Wisconsin was later renamed American Natural Gas, and is a subsidiary of American Natural Resources, acquired by the Coastal Corporation in 1985.

11. The rural electrical cooperatives operating throughout the Great Plains are run by the federal Rural Electrification Administration, the result of a New Deal program to bring affordable electricity to all the scattered farms and ranches of the nation. The electrification program began in the 1930s,

under Democratic Party leadership, although much of the project in North Dakota was not completed until the 1950s. See Doyle and Reinemer 1979 for a complete account.
12. John Richards and Larry Pratt (1979) offer an excellent account of similar energy development on the Canadian Plains, focusing on the entrepreneurial role of provincial government.
13. The coal conversion privilege tax bill levied a tax of 2.5 percent on the earnings of conversion plants other than electrical generation stations (such as charcoal briquetting). Power plants were to be taxed at the rate of 25 hundredths of a mill for each kilowatt hour of electricity produced for sale (a mill is one-tenth of a cent). Gasification plants were to pay 2.5 percent of gross receipts or 10 cents per thousand cubic feet of synthetic gas produced for sale, whichever was greater.
14. The first $100,000 paid by each plant goes to the county in which it is located; the second $100,000 is split evenly by the county and the state's general fund; of the next $300,000, 25 percent goes to the county and 75 percent to the state; the next $500,000 is divided into 15 percent for the county and 85 percent for the state; all the money over $1 million is divided, 10 percent for the county and 90 percent for the state's general fund. Such tax money coming into the county was to be divided so that 15 percent went to the cities according to their population, 40 percent went to the county's general fund, and 45 percent went to its school districts according to average daily attendance.
15. The North Dakota Research Foundation, the North Dakota Economic Development Commission, and the Business and Industrial Development Department.
16. Native Americans on the Fort Berthold reservation north of Mercer County were the most affected by the creation of the Lake Sakakawea reservoir. The Mandan, Hidatsa, and more recently the Arikara had been agricultural peoples, but the inundation claimed most of their farmland, forced the relocation of established communities, and dramatically raised unemployment and economic dependence on government entitlements.

Chapter Five

1. This optimism might have been dampened by more knowledge of the long-term experiences of other boomtowns. Earlier American impact studies had pointed out the pattern of initial high hopes giving way to disappointment and disillusion over the course of project development (Breese et al. 1968; Chapin et al. 1954.). The significance of timing was also pointed out by John Gilmore (1976) in his study of energy boom communities in the American West. Short-term studies of public attitudes made in the early stages of project implementation reflect the hopeful anticipation of desirable effects while minimizing the likelihood of undesireable ones (Little 1978:71; Sundstrom et al. 1977). Such optimism is less evident in post-construction studies of energy boomtowns (Garrison 1970; Gold 1974b:138–141; Pardy et al. 1977; Wadsworth and Conrad 1966).
2. The same methodology is followed even in more independent impact studies (as in Leistritz and Hertsgaard 1980; Luken 1974).
3. According to a 1974 report by the Environmental Policy Center in Washington, D.C., extensive reserves of deep low-sulphur coal (1 percent

or less sulphur content) in Appalachia has four times the energy-producing potential of strippable lignite in the West. Citing a study by Michael Rieber of the University of Illinois Center for Advanced Computation, the report claims that estimates of western coal are normally based on tons rather than heating value. And yet the lignite of Mercer County has such a high water content that 35 percent of its weight is water. If measured on a BTU sulphur-adjusted scale, the amount of low-sulphur coal reserves is reduced by 85 percent. The federal sulphur dioxide emission standards limit the amount released per million BTU of heat. Having a lower heating value per pound, western coal, despite its low 0.7 percent sulphur content, actually has the effect of high-sulphur coal when burned (Environmental Policy Center 1974).
4. The Coyote plant has the last old-fashioned cyclone boiler system built in the United States. The boiler temperature is not hot enough to reduce emissions to very elemental particles, and its smokestack releases a bright yellow-brown stream of nitric oxide gases, discoloring the skyline for miles around.
5. The Mitre study is entitled *Health and Environmental Impacts of Coal Technologies: Background Information on Processes and Pollutants*.
6. In his work *Legitimation Crisis* (1975), Jürgen Habermas developed this argument, linking ideology and discourse to the hegemonic dominance of established power structures.
7. See Goodman (1971) and Plotkin (1987) for a full critique of the classist uses of zoning regulation.
8. See Plesuk (1981) and West (1977) for examples of citizen-involvement programs.

Chapter Six

1. An additional 263 construction workers were local residents.
2. Social segregation of mobile home residents was common in western energy boomtowns. According to Massey and Lewis's study most mobile home dwellers' friendships remained among themselves, and they had relatively fewer voluntary association memberships in town (1979:86).
3. This behavior is consistent with the attitudes described by Herbert Appelbaum in his ethnography of construction workers; according to his analysis, workers behave in a positive manner on what they consider to be "good jobs," but a "bad project promotes all the negative behavior that goes with construction mistakes, losses, and a bad reputation for the contractor, the men and the supervision" (1981:47).
4. This income disparity heightened the ambivalence people in Mercer County felt towards the intruders. An interesting comparison can be made with the case of European "guestworkers" who migrate from countries with high unemployment, such as Spain, Portugal, Italy, Turkey, and the Balkan Republics, to work at low-paying manual labor in more prosperous countries such as Switzerland and Germany. They are regarded by their hosts as an inferior race and as bearers of all manner of social ills. Mexican migrant workers in the U.S. Southwest experience similar social discrimination and stigma. In Mercer County, local residents also despised the visiting workers, but in this case the outsiders held the most desirable jobs.

5. The editor of the *Hazen Star* who conducted the survey in the Fall of 1981 made the complete survey responses available to me. Local weekly newspapers published only a brief summary of the results. All references to a newspaper survey in this and later chapters are based on this unpublished source.
6. Karl Marx's main complaint about capitalism was its alienation of intrinsically human attributes. He wrote in *Economic and Philosophical Manuscripts* (1844) that not only were industrial workers deprived of the meaningful expression of their humanity through labor as creative activity and through control over their labor power and the products they create, but also that competition and exploitation make all people in the system become estranged from one another.
7. In his work *The Division of Labor in Society* (1893), Émile Durkheim sets out a model of complex society as held together by the functional interdependence of its parts. When people and institutions become highly specialized, like functionally specialized organs in a body, survival depends on maintaining the stability and cooperation of the whole. For him, this "organic" solidarity, in which all are fully integrated into the social whole, depends in part on the coercive power of social norms and accepted cultural (especially religious) values and practices.
8. In his famous study, *Suicide* (1897), Durkheim found that suicide rates were highest where social integration was lowest—under conditions of social disorganization, where there was a loss of norms, or anomie. Translated to the level of individuals, this analysis would indicate that those at greatest risk for taking their lives are those suffering from anomic life situations, such as having lost loved ones, a familiar home, supportive community, or a long-held job.
9. Subsequent American community studies, of which there are a large number, more or less confirm the general pattern noted in these classics. A notable exception is Thomas Bender's *Community and Social Change in America* (1978), in which (although it is not a community study) he argues that "community" is not lost with urbanization, but merely replaced by different forms of small group involvement—in churches, ethnic associations, and so on.

Chapter Seven

1. Business categories with more modest growth than the "boom" types included: auto and mechanical services; food and drink retailers; health care; law and finance; recreation; transportation; and general retail and services.
2. A similar occurrence of older merchants selling out to younger entrepreneurs has been reported in Langdon, North Dakota, the site of ABM missile testing and installation 1970–1974 (Luken 1974:9)
3. Local pundits uncharitably remarked that "industry couldn't elect a mayor, so they bought one ready-made."
4. The extent of such connections is explored in Mintz and Cohen 1971, ch. 7. Nader and Serber (1976) discuss the informal power mechanisms through which regulatory agencies are captured by the industries they seek to regulate.

250 | Notes to Chapter Eight

Chapter Eight

1. According to the county tax assessor, the prices of houses in the $30,000–50,000 range retained their value, but those in the $50,000–65,000 range dropped 5 to 7 percent in that year, while those in the $65,000–90,000 range fell about 10 percent. Above that range, it was a buyer's market, with prices negotiable.
2. Both Barlett (1987) and MacLennan and Walker (1980) predict the eventual extinction of medium-sized family farms in the U.S. as the rural class structure becomes increasingly polarized between large mixed and small highly specialized operations.
3. Before the energy boom, property assessments had been kept well below fair market value to reduce tax burdens. Residents also claim that rates were unevenly distributed; as one put it, "How much tax you paid depended on who you were friends with."
4. This is a predictable symptom of boom growth, described by Harry Caudill in the Kentucky coal boomtowns of the late 1910s (Caudill 1962:97–98) and by numerous accounts of Western energy boomtowns of the 1970s.
5. This apparently paradoxical situation is actually common, and has a system-maintaining effect.
6. Specifically, Montana-Dakota Utilities Resources Group consists of Montana-Dakota Utilities Co., Knife River Coal Mining Co., Williston Basin Interstate Pipeline Co., and Fidelity Gas Co.
7. Energy development projects abandoned in 1984–1985 in this area included an extension of the Colstrip Mine in eastern Montana, a proposed Exxon carbon dioxide pipeline, and Tenneco's proposed gasification plant in nearby Golden Valley County, North Dakota.
8. Industry-produced materials often referred to the local landscape inaccurately as "prairie," apparently because the word evokes more romantic associations than "plains," the more correct geographic term.
9. This fact seemed to confirm rumors that the Great Plains consortium had indeed maintained a top-heavy managerial staff, at least in part to enhance the unprofitability of the operation to support their claim for federal assistance.
10. Around this time NACCO was expelled from Ohio, the corporation's home state, for alleged price fixing. Its headquarters were moved to Dallas, Texas, but its subsidiary Powhatan's mines continued to operate in the East. The Mercer County union miners' nemesis, Bob Murray, left NACCO in the scandal to run Powhatan Mines.
11. Indian Head mine workers were hired at two NACCO subsidiaries: Coteau Properties' Freedom Mine north of Beulah and the Falkirk Mine in the next county to the east.
12. Losing a UMW vote at the Beulah Mine would have repercussions at Knife River's two other mines in Montana, where elections had also been won by narrow margins, since the company had won a ruling that all their mines should have common elections and representation.
13. The semi-arid climate contributed to the marginality of Mercer County agricultural land, and large tracts of nonmined land were being put to fallow in the early 1990s under the federal grasslands recovery program.

Bibliography

Albrecht, Don E., Steve H. Murdock, Kathy Schiflett, Rita R. Hamm, F. Larry Leistritz, and Brenda Eckstrom. 1988. "The Consequences of the Farm Crisis for Rural Communities." *Journal of the Community Development Society* 19(2):119–135.
Albrecht, S. L. 1978. "Socio-Cultural Factors and Energy Resource Development in the West." *Journal of Environmental Management* 7:73–90.
Allen, James B. 1966. *The Company Town in the American West*. Norman: University of Oklahoma Press.
American Ethnologist. 1978. Special issue on political economy 5(3).
Amin, Samir. 1976. *Unequal Development: An Essay on the Social Formations of Peripheral Capitalism*. New York: Monthly Review Press.
Anderson, Bruce. 1943. *The Farmer Seeks Jeffersonian Democracy*. Baltimore: King Brothers.
Andrews, Robert. 1989. *The Concise Columbia Dictionary of Quotations*. New York: Columbia University Press.
Antoun, Richard, and Iliya Harik, eds. 1972. *Rural Politics and Social Change in the Middle East*. Bloomington: Indiana University Press.
Apgar, William C. Jr., and H. James Brown. 1988. *The State of the Nation's Housing, 1988*. Cambridge, Mass.: Harvard University Joint Center for Housing Studies.
Appadurai, Arjun. 1990. "Disjuncture and Difference in the Global Cultural Economy." *Public Culture* 2(2):1–24.
Appelbaum, Herbert A. 1981. *Royal Blue: The Culture of Construction Workers*. Case Studies in Cultural Anthropology. New York: Holt, Rinehart and Winston.
Atherton, Lewis. 1966 (orig. 1954). *Main Street on the Middle Border*. Bloomington: Indiana University Press.
Baltzell, E. Digby. 1964. *The Protestant Establishment: Aristocracy and Caste in America*. New York: Random House.
Barlett, Peggy. 1987. "The Crisis in Family Farming: Who Will Survive?" in Michael Chibnik, ed., *Farm Work and Fieldwork: American Agriculture in Anthropological Perspective*, pp. 29–57. Ithaca: Cornell Univeristy Press.
Beaulieu, Lionel J., ed. 1988. *The Rural South in Crisis: Challenges for the Future*. Boulder, Colo.: Westview Press.

Bell, Earl H. 1934. "Social Stratification in a Small Community." *Scientific Monthly* February:157–164.
———. 1942. *Culture of a Contemporary Rural Community: Sublette, Kansas*. Rural Life Studies no. 2. Washington, D.C.: U.S. Department of Agriculture Bureau of Agricultural Economics.
Bender, Thomas. 1978. *Community and Social Change in America*. Baltimore: Johns Hopkins University Press.
Bennett, John W. 1969. *Northern Plainsmen: Adaptive Strategy and Agrarian Life*. Chicago: Aldine.
Berg, Francie. 1977. *North Dakota: Land of Changing Seasons*. Hettinger, N.D.: Flying Diamond Books.
Bergland, Bob. 1988. "Rural Mental Health: Report of the National Action Commission on the Mental Health of Rural Americans." *Journal of Rural Community Psychology* 9(2):29–39.
Berry, Susan. n.d. "Planning Social Change: Anthropologists and the Social Impact Assessment Process." N.p.: photocopy.
Beulah, North Dakota: Golden Anniversary 1914–1964. N.p.: Jubilee Book Committee.
Beulah Beacon. 1977, 1978, 1979, 1980, 1982, 1987. Garrison, N.D.: BHG.
Bismarck Tribune. 1974, 1975. Bismarck, North Dakota.
Blood, Robert O., and Robert L. Hamblin. 1958. "Effects of Wives' Employment on Family Power Structure." *Social Forces* 36(4):347–352.
Bluestone, Barry, and Bennett Harrison. 1982. *The Deindustrialization of America: Plant Closings, Community Abandonment, and the Dismantling of Basic Industry*. New York: Basic Books.
Blum, Richard, and Eva Blum. 1965. *Health and Healing in Rural Greece*. Stanford: Stanford University Press.
Borich, Timothy O., James R. Steward, and Harlowe Hatle. 1985. "The Impact of a Regional Mall on Rural Main Street." *Rural Sociology* 5(1):6–9.
Breese, Gerald, Russell J. Klingenmeier, Jr., Harold P. Cahill, Jr., James E. Whelan, Archer E. Church, Jr., and Dorothy E. Whiteman. 1968. *The Impact of Large Installations on Nearby Areas: Accelerated Urban Growth*. Beverly Hills: Sage Publications.
Breimyer, Harold F. 1990. "Prospects for Rural America as the Nation Matures: An Agricultural Economist's Prognosis." *Rural Sociologist* 10(3):3–9.
Brenneise, Nathan, ed., 1979. *Hardships, Blessings, Opportunities: A History of the Brenneise Family*. N.p.
Brunner, Edmund de S., Gwendolyn Hughes, and Marjorie Patten. 1927. *American Agricultural Villages*. New York: Doran.
Burdge, Rabel J., and Sue Johnson. 1977. "Sociocultural Aspects of the Effects of Resource Development," in James McEvoy III and Thomas Dietz, eds. *Handbook for Environmental Planning*, pp. 241–278. New York: Wiley.
Burdick, Usher. 1944. *History of the Farmers' Political Action in North Dakota*. Baltimore: Wirth Brothers.
Burg, N. C. 1978. *Economic Development in Non-Metropolitan Areas: Special Socio-Economic Problems of Rapid-Growth Communities: A Selected Bibliography*. Exchange Bibliography no. 1497. Monticello, Ill.: Council of Planning Libraries.
Cardoso, Fernando Enrique. 1972. "Dependency and Development in Latin America." *New Left Review* 74:83–95.

Carnes, Sam, and Paul Friesma. 1973. *Urbanization and the Northern Great Plains*. Denver: Northern Great Plains Resources Program.

Cassity, Michael. 1989. *Defending a Way of Life: An American Community in the Nineteeth Century*. Albany: State University of New York Press.

Caudill, Harry M. 1962. *Night Comes to the Cumberlands*. Boston: Little, Brown.

Chapin, F. Stuart, Jr., Theodore W. Wirths, Alfred M. Danton Jr., and John C. Gould. 1954. *In the Shadow of a Defense Plant: A Study of Urbanization in Rural South Carolina*. A Final Report of the Savannah River Urbanization Study. Chapel Hill: University of North Carolina Institute for Research in Social Science.

Chayanov, A. V. 1986 (orig. 1966). *The Theory of Peasant Economy*. Daniel Thorner, Basile Kerblay, and R. E. F. Smith, eds. Madison: University of Wisconsin Press.

Christiansen, Bill, and Theodore H. Clack, Jr. 1976. "A Western Perspective on Energy: A Plea for Rational Energy Planning." *Science* 194:578–584.

Clark, G. L., and K. Johnston, 1987. "The Geography of U.S. Union Elections 1: The Crisis of the U.S. Unions and a Critical Review of the Literature." *Environment and Planning A*. 19(1):33–57.

Clemente, Frank. 1975. *What Industry Really Means to a Small Town*. University Park: Pennsylvania State University and the U.S. Department of Agriculture.

Clemente, Frank, and G. F. Summers. 1973. "Industrial Development and the Elderly: A Longitudinal Analysis." *Journal of Gerontology* 28:479–483.

Common, The. 1972, 1978, 1979. Supplement to the *Beulah Beacon* and *Hazen Star*. Garrison, N.D.: BHG.

Community Service Program. 1975. *A Study of Impact of Coal Development in the Deiber-Birney-Ashland Area*. Missoula: University of Montana Press.

Cortese, Charles F., and Jane Archer Cortese. 1978. *The Social Effects of Energy Boomtowns in the West: A Partially Annotated Bibliography*. Exchange Bibliography no. 1557. Monticello, Ill.: Council of Planning Libraries.

Cortese, Charles F., and Bernie Jones. 1976. *Boom Towns: A Social Impact Model with Propositions and Bibliography*. Washington, D.C.: National Research Council Committee on Nuclear and Alternative Energy Systems.

———. 1977. "The Sociological Analysis of Boomtowns." *Western Sociological Review*. 8(1):76–90.

Council on Environmental Quality. 1979. *Tenth Annual Report of the Council on Environmental Quality*. Washington, D.C.: U.S. Government Printing Office.

Dakota Counsel. 1982. Dickinson, N.D.: Dakota Resource Council.

Dalstead, Norman, F. Larry Leistritz, Thor A. Hertsgaard, Ronald Frasse, and Richard Anderson. 1974. *Economic Impact of Alternative Energy Development Patterns in North Dakota*. Denver: Northern Great Plains Resources Program.

Davenport, Joseph III, and Judith A. Davenport, eds. 1980. *The Boom Town: Problems and Promises in the Energy Vortex*. Wyoming Human Services Project. Laramie: University of Wyoming Department of Social Work.

Davenport, Judith A., and Joseph Davenport III, eds. 1979. *Boom Towns and Human Services*. University of Wyoming Publication number 43. Laramie: University of Wyoming Department of Social Work.

Davies, Pearl J. 1958. *Real Estate in American History.* Washington, D.C.: Public Affairs Press.

Deavers, Kenneth L., Robert A. Hoppe, and Peggy J. Ross. 1986. "Public Policy and Rural Poverty: A View from the 1980s." *Policy Studies Journal* 15(2):291–309.

Dennis, Norman, Fernando Enriques, and Clifford Slaughter. 1956. *Coal Is Our Life: An Analysis of a Yorkshire Mining Community.* London: Eyre and Spottiswoode.

Denver Research Institute and Resource Planning Associates. 1979. *Socioeconomic Impacts of Western Energy Resource Development.* Denver: University of Denver Press.

Dick, Everett. 1954 (orig. 1937). *The Sod-House Frontier, 1854–1890: A Social History of the Northern Great Plains from the Creation of Kansas and Nebraska to the Admission of the Dakotas.* Lincoln, Neb.: Johnson.

Digger, The. 1981. N.p: Knife River Coal Mining Company (in-house newsletter).

Dillman, Don A., and Daryl J. Hobbs, eds. 1982. *Rural Society in the United States: Issues for the 1980s.* Boulder, Colo.: Westview Press.

Dixon, Mim 1978. *What Happened to Fairbanks? The Effects of the Trans-Alaska Oil Pipeline on the Community of Fairbanks, Alaska.* Boulder, Colo.: Westview Press.

Domhoff, William. 1967. *Who Rules America?* Englewood Cliffs, N.J.: Prentice-Hall.

———. 1990. *The Power Elite and the State: How Policy Is Made in America.* New York: A. de Gruyter.

Dorst, John D. 1989. *The Written Suburb: An American Site, An Ethnographic Dilemma.* Philadelphia: University of Pennsylvania Press.

Douglass, Harlan Paul. 1919. *The Little Town, Especially in Its Rural Relationships.* New York: Macmillan.

Doyle, Don Harrison. 1978. *The Social Order of a Frontier Community: Jacksonville, Illinois, 1825–1870.* Urbana: University of Illinois Press.

Doyle, Jack, and Vic Reinemer, eds. 1979. *Lines Across the Land.* Washington, D.C.: Environmental Policy Center.

Dumont, Louis. 1986. *Essays on Individualism: Modern Ideology in Anthropological Perspective.* Chicago: University of Chicago Press.

Durkheim, Émile. 1933 (orig. 1893). *The Division of Labor in Society*, trans. George Simpson. New York: Macmillan.

———. 1963 (orig. 1897). *Suicide: A Study in Sociology*, trans. John Spaulding and George Simpson. London: Routledge and Kegan Paul.

Dye, Thomas R. 1976, 1979, 1983, 1986, 1990. *Who's Running America?* Englewood Cliffs, N.J.: Prentice-Hall.

Economic Report of the President. 1988. Washington, D.C.: U.S. Government Printing Office.

Environmental Policy Center. 1974. *Facts on Coal in the United States.* Washington, D.C.: EPC.

Family Violence Specialist: A Funding Proposal. 1981. Stanton, N.D.: Mercer County Social Services.

Federal Writers Project of the Works Progress Administration for the State of North Dakota. 1938. *North Dakota: A Guide to the Northern Prairie State.* Fargo, N.D.: Knight.

Fernández-Kelly, M. Patricia, and Anna Garcia. 1985. "The Making of an

Underground Economy: Hispanic Women, Home Work, and the Advanced Capitalist State." *Urban Anthropology* 14(1–3):59–90.
Ferrell, Mary Zey, O. C. Ferrell, and Quentin Jenkins. 1973. "Social Power in a Rural Community." *Growth and Change* 4(2):3–6.
Fink, Deborah. 1987. "Farming in Open Country, Iowa: Women and the Changing Farm Economy," in Michael Chibnik, ed. *Farm Work and Fieldwork: American Agriculture in Anthropological Perspective*, pp. 121–144. Ithaca: Cornell University Press.
Finsterbusch, Kurt, and Charles P. Wolf, eds. 1977. *Methodology of Social Impact Assessment*. Stroudsburg, Pa.: Dowden, Hutchinson, and Ross.
Fitchen, Janet M. 1987. *Poverty in Rural America: A Case Study*. Boulder, Colo.: Westview Press.
———. 1991. *Endangered Spaces, Enduring Places: Change, Identity, and Survival in Rural America*. Boulder, Colo.: Westview Press.
Foster, George M. 1967. "Introduction: Peasant Character and Personality," and "Peasant Society and the Image of Limited Good," in Jack Potter, May Diaz, and George Foster, eds. *Peasant Society: A Reader*, pp. 300–323. Boston: Little, Brown.
Foucault, Michel. 1980. *Power/Knowledge: Selected Interviews and Other Writings, 1972–1977*, ed. Colin Gordon. New York: Pantheon.
Frank, André Gunder. 1975. *On Capitalist Underdevelopment*. New York: Oxford University Press.
Freudenberg, William R. 1979. *Humans in the Impact Zone: A Report on the Social Consequences of Energy Boomtown Growth*. New Haven, Conn.: Yale University Department of Sociology.
Friedman, Elizabeth. 1978. *Crest Street: A Family/Community Impact Statement*. Durham, N.C.: Duke University Institute of Policy and Public Affairs.
Friedmann, F. G. 1967. "The World of 'La Miseria'," in Jack Potter, May Diaz, and George Foster, eds. *Peasant Society: A Reader*, pp. 324–335. Boston: Little, Brown.
Friedmann, Harriet. 1978. "Simple Commodity Production and Wage Labor in the American Plains." *Journal of Peasant Studies* 6(1):71–100.
———. 1980. "Household Production and National Economy: Concepts for the Analysis of Agrarian Formations." *Journal of Peasant Studies* 7(2):158–184.
Friesma, H. Paul, and Paul J. Culhane. 1976. "Social Impacts, Politics, and the Environmental Impact Statement Process." *Natural Resources Journal* 16(2):339–356.
Frisch, Michael H. 1972. *Town into City: Springfield, Massachusetts, and the Meaning of Community, 1840–1880*. Cambridge: Harvard University Press.
Froman, Creel. 1984. *The Two American Political Systems: Society, Economics, and Politics*. Englewood Cliffs, N.J.: Prentice-Hall.
Galpin, Charles J. 1915. *The Social Anatomy of an Agricultural Community*. Research Bulletin no. 34. Madison, Wisc.: University of Wisconsin Agricultural Experiment Station.
Gans, Herbert. 1967. *The Levittowners: Ways of Life and Politics in a New Suburban Community*. New York: Random House Vintage.
Garrison, C. R. 1970. *The Impact of New Industry on Local Government Finances in Five Small Towns in Kentucky*. Agricultural Economic Report

no. 191, Washington, D.C.: U.S. Department of Agriculture Economic Research Service.
Gates, Paul. 1945. *Frontier Landlords and Pioneer Tenants.* Ithaca, N.Y.: Cornell University Press.
Giddens, Anthony. 1979. *Central Problems in Social Theory: Action, Structure, and Contradiction in Social Analysis.* Berkeley and Los Angeles: University of California Press.
Gillette, J. M. 1940. "Socio-Economic Submergence in a Plains State." *Rural Sociology* 5:57–68.
Gilmore, John S. 1976. "Boom Towns May Hinder Energy Resource Development: Isolated Communities Cannot Handle Sudden Industrialization and Growth Without Help." *Science* 191:536.
Gilmore, John S., and Mary K. Duff. 1974. *The Sweetwater County Boom: A Challenge to Growth Management.* Denver: University of Denver Research Institute.
———. 1975. *Boomtown Growth Management: A Case Study of Green River—Rock Springs, Wyoming.* Boulder, Colo.: Westview Press.
Gold, Raymond L. 1974a. *A Comparative Case Study of the Impact of Coal Development on the Way of Life of People in the Coal Areas of Eastern Montana and Northeastern Wyoming.* Missoula: University of Montana Institute for Social Science Research.
———. 1974b. "Social Impacts of Strip Mining and Other Industrializations of Coal Resources," in Charles Wolf, ed., pp. 123–146. *Social Impact Assessment.* Stroudsburg, Pa.: Environmental Design Research Association.
Goodman, Robert. 1971. "The Scientific Method: Salvation from Politics," in Robert Goodman, ed. *After the Planners*, pp. 143–170. New York: Simon and Schuster.
Goodwyn, Lawrence. 1978. *The Populist Moment: A Short History of the Agrarian Revolt in America.* New York: Oxford University Press.
Graber, E. E. 1974. "Newcomers and Oldtimers: Growth and Change in a Mountain Town." *Rural Sociology* 39:504–513.
Gramsci, Antonio. 1971. *Selections from the Prison Notebooks of Antonio Gramsci*, ed. and trans. Quintin Hoare and Geoffrey Nowell Smith. New York: International Publishers.
Gray, Irwin. 1969. "Employment Effect of a New Industry in a Rural Area." *Monthly Labor Review* 92:26–30.
Greenstein, Michael. 1978. *Effects of Rapid Social Change in Western Energy Boomtowns.* Boulder: University of Colorado Institute of Behavioral Science.
Gunn, Christopher, and Hazel Gunn. 1991. *Reclaiming Capital: Democratic Initiatives and Community Development.* Ithaca, N.Y.: Cornell University Press.
Habermas, Jürgen. 1975. *Legitimation Crisis.* Boston: Beacon.
Haights, Eric, James Mak, and Gary Walton. 1975. *Western River Transportation: The Era of Early Internal Development, 1810–1860.* Baltimore: Johns Hopkins University Press.
Hall, Stuart. 1982. "The Rediscovery of 'Ideology': Return of the Repressed in Media Studies," in Michael Gurevitch, Tony Bennett, James Curran, and Janet Woollacott, eds. *Culture, Society, and the Media*, pp. 56–90. London: Methuen.

Hannerz, Ulf. 1987. "The World in Creolization" *Africa* 57(4):546–559.
Hareven, Tamara, and Randolph Langenbach. 1978. *Amoskeag: Life and Work in an American Factory City.* New York: Pantheon.
Hart, Henry C. 1957. *The Dark Missouri.* Madison: University of Wisconsin Press.
Hart, Keith. 1982. *The Development of Commercial Agriculture in West Africa.* Cambridge: Cambridge University Press.
Harvey, David. 1985. *The Urbanization of Capital.* Baltimore: Johns Hopkins University Press.
Hatch, Elvin. 1979. *Biography of a Small Town.* New York: Columbia University Press.
Hazen Star. 1976, 1977, 1978, 1979, 1984. Garrison, N.D.: BHG.
Hefferman, William D., and Judith B. Hefferman. 1986. "Impact of the Farm Crisis on Rural Families and Communities." *Rural Sociologist* 6(3):160–170.
Heilbroner, Robert. 1985. *The Nature and Logic of Capitalism.* New York: Norton.
Heiman, Michael. 1988. *The Quiet Revolution.* Albany: State University of New York Press.
Heller, Peter L., and Gustavo M. Quesada. 1977. "Rural Familism: An Interregional Analysis." *Rural Sociology* 42(2):220–240.
Henry, Jules. 1963. *Culture Against Man.* New York: Random House.
Hibbard, Benjamin H. 1939. *A History of Public Land Policies.* New York: P. Smith.
Highway 200 Association. 1985. The Sakakawea Trail: Travelers' Guide to *Highway 200.* Garrison, N.D.: *Beulah Beacon/Hazen Star.*
Hobsbawm, Eric J. 1977. "Ideology and Social Change in Colombia," in June Nash, Juan Corradi, and Hobart Spaulding, eds. *Ideology and Social Change in Latin America,* pp. 185–199. New York: Gordan Breach.
Hofstadter, Richard. 1955. *The Age of Reform: From Bryan to F.D.R.* New York: Random House Vintage.
Holmes, Roy H. 1932. *Rural Sociology.* New York: McGraw-Hill.
Hopper, Kim, Ezra Susser, and Sarah Conover. 1985. "Economics of Makeshift: Deindustrialization and Homelessness in New York City." *Urban Anthropology* 14(1–3):183–236.
Hudson, John C. 1982. "Towns of the Western Railroads." *Great Plains Quarterly* 2(1):41–54.
———. 1985. *Plains Country Towns.* Minneapolis: University of Minnesota Press.
Hunter, Louis. 1969. *Steamboats on the Western Rivers.* Cambridge, Mass.: Harvard University Press.
Inter-industry Technical Assistance Team. 1984. *Mercer County Socioeconomic Impact Mitigation Assessment: Final Report.* (photocopy)
Jacobs, Mike. 1975. *One-Time Harvest: Reflections on Coal and Our Future.* Jamestown: North Dakota Farmers Union.
Jefferson, Thomas. 1964 (orig. 1787). *Notes on the State of Virginia.* New York: Harper and Row.
Jirovec, Ronald. 1979. "Preparing a Boom Town for the Impact of Rapid Growth," in Judith A. Davenport and Joseph Davenport III, eds. *Boom Towns and Human Services,* pp. 79–90. Laramie: University of Wyoming Department of Social Work.

Katouzian, M.A.H. 1978. "Oil Versus Agriculture: A Case Study of Dual Resource Depletion in Iran." *Journal of Peasant Studies* 5(3):347–369.

Kerbo, Harold, and L. Richard Fave. 1979. "The Empirical Side of the Power Elite Debate: An Assessment and Critique of Recent Research." *The Sociological Quarterly* 20(1):5–22.

Kolb, John H. 1959. *Emerging Rural Communities.* Madison: University of Wisconsin Press.

Krawetz, N. M. 1981. *Overseas Energy Projects and Huntly.* Monitoring Social and Economic Impact, Huntly Case Study Final Report Series. Hamilton, New Zealand: University of Waikato.

Landis, Paul. 1940. *Rural Life in Process.* New York: McGraw-Hill.

Lazonick, William. 1980. "The Subjection of Labor to Capital: The Rise of the Capitalist System." *Review of Radical Political Economics* 10(1):1–31.

League of Women Voters. 1978. *The Impacts of Western Coal Development.* Washington, D.C.: League of Women Voters Educational Fund.

Leistritz, F. Larry, and T. A. Hertsgaard. 1980. *Environmental, Economic, and Social Impacts of a Coal Gasification Plant in Western North Dakota.* Bulletin no. 509. North Dakota Agricultural Experiment Station. Fargo: North Dakota State University Press.

Leistritz, F. Larry, Steve H. Murdock, and Arlen G. Leholm. 1982. "Local Economic Changes Associated with Rapid Growth," in Bruce A. Weber and Robert E. Howell, eds. *Coping with Rapid Growth in Rural Communities,* pp. 25–61. Boulder, Colo.: Westview Press.

Lewis, Sinclair. 1961 (orig. 1922). *Babbitt.* New York: Harcourt, Brace, Jovanovich.

Liebow, Elliott. 1967. *Tally's Corner: A Study of Negro Streetcorner Men.* Boston: Little, Brown.

Lipset, Seymour M. 1950. *Agrarian Socialism.* New York: Doubleday.

Little, Ronald L. 1975. "Rural Industrialization: The Four Corners Region," in Lewis Carter and Louis Gray, eds. *Social Implications of Energy Scarcity: Social and Technological Priorities in Steady-State and Constricting Systems.* Pullman: Washington State University Department of Sociology and Social Research.

———. 1977. "Some Social Consequences of Boom Towns." *North Dakota Law Review* 53(3):401–425.

———. 1978. "Energy Boom Towns: Views from Within," in S. Davis and R. Matthews, eds. *Native Americans and Energy Development.* Cambridge Mass.: Anthropology Resource Center.

Logan, J. R., and Harvey L. Molotch. 1988. *Urban Fortunes: The Political Economy of Place.* Berkeley and Los Angeles: University of California Press.

Luken, Ralph A. 1974. *Economic and Social Impacts of Coal Development in the 1970s for Mercer County, North Dakota.* Prepared for the Old West Regional Commission. Washington, D.C.: Thomas E. Carroll Associates.

Lynd, Robert, and Helen Lynd. 1928. *Middletown: A Study in Modern American Culture.* New York: Harcourt, Brace.

———. 1937. *Middletown in Transition: A Study in Cultural Conflicts.* New York: Harcourt, Brace.

McKeown, R. L. and A. Lantz. n.d. *Rapid Growth and Impact on Quality of Life in Rural Communities: A Case Study.* Denver: Denver Research Institute.

McLean County Independent. 1973. Washburn, North Dakota.

MacLennan, Carol. 1985. "Political Response to Economic Loss: The Automotive Crisis of 1979–1982." *Urban Anthropology* 14(1–3):21–57.

MacLennan, Carol, and Richard Walker. 1980. "Crisis and Change in United States Agriculture: An Overview," in Roger Burbach and Patricia Flynn, eds. *Agribusiness in the Americas*, pp. 21–40. New York: Monthly Review Press.

Magdoff, Harry, and Paul Sweezy. 1981 (orig. 1977). *The Deepening Crisis of U.S. Capitalism*. New York: Monthly Review Press.

Maine, Henry. 1871. *Village Communities in the East and West*. New York: Holt.

———. 1905. *Ancient Law*, 10th ed. London: Murray.

Mann, Michael. 1973. *Consciousness and Action Among the Western Working Class*. London: Macmillan.

Marcus, George. 1986. "Contemporary Problems of Ethnography in the Modern World System," in James Clifford, and George Marcus, eds. *Writing Culture: The Politics and Poetics of Ethnography*, pp. 163–193. Berkeley and Los Angeles: University of California Press.

Marcus, George, and Michael Fischer. 1986. *Anthropology as Cultural Critique*. Chicago: University of Chicago Press.

Markusen, Ann. 1978. "Socioeconomic Impact Models for Boomtown Planning and Policy Evaluation." Paper presented at the Western Regional Science Association Meetings, 1978.

———. 1980a "The Political-Economy of Rural Development: The Case of Western U.S. Boomtowns," in Frederick Buttel and Howard Newby, eds. *The Rural Sociology of Advanced Societies: Critical Perspectives*, pp. 405–430. Montclair, N.J.: Allenheld, Osmun.

———. 1980b. "Class, Rent, and Sectoral Conflict: Uneven Development in Western U.S. Boomtowns." *The Review of Radical Political Economics* 10(3):117–129.

Markusen, Ann, and Amy Glasmeier. n.d. "The Case Against Energy Impact Aid." N.p: photocopy.

Marx, Karl. 1961 (orig. 1844). "Alienated Labor," in *Economic and Philosophical Manuscripts*, trans. T. B. Bottomore, in Erich Fromm, ed. *Marx's Concept of Man*. New York: Frederick Ungar.

———. 1977 (orig. 1852). *The Eighteenth Brumaire of Louis Bonaparte*, trans. second edition (Hamburg 1869). New York: International Publishers.

Massey, Doreen. 1988. *Global Restructuring, Local Responses*. Wallace W. Atwood Lecture Series no. 4, Clark University Graduate School of Geography. Worcester, Mass: Clark University Press.

Massey, Garth. 1978. *Building a Power Plant: Newcomers and Social Impact*. Laramie: University of Wyoming Center for Urban and Regional Analysis.

Mercer County Atlas. 1918. N.p.: Ogle and Company.

Miller, E. Willard, and Ruby Miller. 1980. *The American Coal Industry and Economic, Political, and Environmental Aspects*. Public Administration Series Bibliography no. P-572. Monticello, Ill.: Vance Bibliographies.

Miller, Elva E. 1928. *Town and Country*. Durham: University of North Carolina Press.

Mills, C. Wright. 1971. *The New Men of Power: America's Labor Leaders*. New York: Augustus M. Kelly.

———. 1951. *White Collar: The American Middle Classes*. New York: Oxford University Press.

———. 1956. *The Power Elite*. New York: Oxford University Press.

———. 1959. *The Sociological Imagination*. New York: Grove Press.

Minot Daily News. 1987. Minot, North Dakota.

Mintz, Morton, and Jerry S. Cohen. 1971. *America, Inc.: Who Owns and Operates the United States*. New York: Dell.

Morlan, Robert L. 1955. *Political Prairie Fire*. Minneapolis: University of Minnesota Press.

Murdock, Steve H., and F. Larry Leistritz. 1979. *Energy Development in the Western United States*. New York: Praeger.

Murdock, Steve H., F. Larry Leistritz, and Eldon Schreiner. 1982. "Local Demographic Changes Associated with Rapid Growth," in Bruce A. Weber and Robert E. Howell, eds. *Coping with Rapid Growth in Rural Communities*, pp. 63–69. Boulder, Colo.: Westview Press.

Nace, Theodore C. 1978. "State Politics and the Northern Plains Coal Boom, 1971–1975: Montana, Wyoming, and North Dakota." N.p.: photocopy.

———. 1979. "An Analysis of the Agricultural, Environmental, and Ratepayer Impacts of Rural Electric Generation and Transmission Policy in North Dakota," in Jack Doyle and Vic Reinemer, eds., *Lines Across the Land*, pp. 550–577. Washington, D.C.: Environmental Policy Center.

Nader, Laura. 1974. "Up the Anthropologist—Perspectives Gained from Studying up," in Dell Hymes, ed. *Reinventing Anthropology*, pp. 284–311. New York: Random House.

———. 1980. "The Veritical Slice: Hierarchies and Children," in Gerald M. Britan and Ronald Cohen, eds. *Hierarchy and Society*. Berkeley, Calif.: Ishi Press.

Nader, Laura, and David Serber. 1976. "Law and the Distribution of Power," in Lewis Coser and Otto Larsen, eds. *The Uses of Controversy in Sociology*, pp. 273–291. New York: Free Press.

Nash, June. 1979. *We Eat the Mines and the Mines Eat Us*. New York: Columbia University Press.

———. 1981. "Ethnographic Aspects of the World Capitalist System." *Annual Review of Anthropology* 10:393–423.

———. 1985. "Deindustrialization and the Impact on Labor Control Systems." *Urban Anthropology* 14(1–3):151–182.

———. 1989. *From Tank Town to High Tech: The Clash of Community and Industrial Cycles*. Albany: State University of New York Press.

Nellis, L. 1974. "What Does Energy Development Mean for Wyoming?" *Human Organization* 33:229–238.

Nelson, Bruce. 1964. *Land of the Dakotahs*. Lincoln: University of Nebraska Press.

Newman, Katherine. 1985. "Urban Anthropology and the Deindustrialization Paradigm" and "Turning Your Back on Tradition: Symbolic Analysis and Moral Critique in a Plant Shutdown." *Urban Anthropology* 14(1–3):5–19 and 109–150.

———. 1989. *Falling from Grace: The Experience of Downward Mobility in the American Middle Class*. New York: Random House Vintage.

Nonpartisan Leader, The. 1916. Bismarck: North Dakota Nonpartisan Political League Party.

North Dakota Magazine. 1906. Bismarck: North Dakota Chamber of Commerce.

Northwest Orient Passages. 1982. N.p.: Northwest Orient Airlines (March).
O'Connor, James. 1973. *The Fiscal Crisis of the State.* New York: St. Martin's Press.
———. 1979. "Foreword," in John Young and Jan Newton. *Capitalism and Human Obsolescence: Corporate Control Versus Individual Survival in Rural America,* pp. ix–xiv. Montclair, N.J.: Allenheld, Osmun; New York: Universe.
O'Hare, William P. 1988. *The Rise of Poverty in Rural America.* Washington, D.C.: Population Reference Bureau.
Olson, Philip. 1964. "Rural American Community Studies: The Survival of Public Ideology." *Human Organization* 24(4):342–350.
Ong, Aihwa. 1987. *Spirits of Resistance and Capitalist Discipline: Factory Women in Malaysia.* Albany: State University of New York Press.
Ortner, Sherry. 1984. "Theory in Anthropology Since the Sixties." *Comparative Studies in Society and History* 26(1):126–166.
Owen, Roger. 1981. "The Arab Economies in the 1970s." *MERIP Reports,* October–December 1981, pp. 3–13.
Pardy, B. J., Elizabeth Peele, B. H. Bronfman, and D. J. Bjornstadd. 1977. *A Post-Licensing Study of Community Effects at Two Operating Nuclear Power Plants.* Final Report. Oak Ridge, Tenn: Oak Ridge National Laboratory.
Park, Robert. 1915. "The City: Suggestions for the Investigation of Human Behavior in the City Environment." *American Journal of Sociology* 20(5):577–612.
Park, Robert, and E. W. Burgess. 1925. *The City.* Chicago: University of Chicago Press.
Peele, Elizabeth. 1974. "Social Effects of Nuclear Power Plants," in Charles P. Wolf, ed., *Social Impact Assessment,* pp. 113–120. Stroudsburg, Pa.: Environmental Design Research Center.
Peterson, George L., and Robert S. Gemmell. 1977. "Social Impact Assessment: Comments on the State of the Art," in Kurt Finsterbusch and Charles P. Wolf, eds. *Methodology of Social Impact Assessment,* pp. 374–387. Stroudsburg, Pa.: Dowden, Hutchinson, and Ross.
Piven, Frances Fox, and Richard A. Cloward. 1979. *Poor People's Movements: Why They Succeed; How They Fail.* New York: Random House Vintage.
Plesuk, Brian, ed. 1981. *The Only Game in Town: Public Involvement in Cold Lake.* Edmonton, Alberta: Department of the Environment.
Plotkin, Sidney. 1987. *Keep Out: The Struggle for Land Use Control.* Berkeley and Los Angeles: University of California Press.
———. 1990. "Enclave Consciousness and Neighborhood Activism," in Joseph Kling and Prudence Posner, eds. *Dilemmas of Activism: Class, Community, and the Politics of Local Mobilization,* pp. 218–239. Philadelphia: Temple University Press.
Porter, Kathryn H. 1989. *Poverty in Rural America: A National Overview.* Washington, D.C.: Center on Budget and Policy Priorities.
Pred, Alan. 1977. *City-Systems in Advanced Economies.* London: Hutchinson.
———. 1984. "Place as Historically Contingent Process: Structuration and Time-Geography of Becoming Places." *Annals of the Association of American Geographers.* 74(2):279–297.
Rasch, Manfred. 1984. "On the Prehistory of the Liquefaction of Coal up to

1945," in *Energy and History*. Proceedings of the Eleventh Symposium of the International Cooperation in History of Technology Committee. Duesseldorf: ICHTC.

Redfield, Robert. 1941. *The Folk Culture of Yucatan*. Chicago: University of Chicago Press.

Richards, John, and Larry Pratt. 1979. *Prairie Capitalism: Power and Influence in the New West*. Toronto: McClelland and Stewart.

Ridgeway, James. 1973. *The Last Play: The Struggle to Monopolize the World's Energy Resources*. New York: Dutton.

Robinson, Elwyn. 1966. *History of North Dakota*. Lincoln: University of Nebraska Press.

Rodgers, Joseph Jr. 1976. *Environmental Impact Assessment, Growth Management, and the Comprehensive Plan*. Cambridge, Mass.: Ballinger.

Rose, Dan. 1989. *Patterns of American Culture: Ethnography and Estrangement*. Philadelphia: University of Pennsylvania Press.

Roseberry, William. 1989. *Anthropology and Histories: Essays in Culture, History, and Political Economy*. New Brunswick, N.J.: Rutgers University Press.

Rostow, Walter W. 1960. *The Stages of Economic Growth: A Non-Communist Manifesto*. Cambridge: Cambridge University Press.

Sahlins, Marshall. 1976. *Culture and Practical Reason*. Chicago: University of Chicago Press.

Saloutos, Theodore. 1946. "The Rise of the Nonpartisan League in North Dakota, 1915–1917." *Agricultural History* 20:43–61.

Sanders, Irwin T., and Gordon F. Lewis. 1976. "Rural Community Studies in the United States: A Decade in Review." *Annual Review of Sociology* 2:35–53.

Sanderson, Ezra Dwight. 1932. *The Rural Community: The Natural History of a Sociological Group*. Boston: Ginn.

Santos, T. dos. 1973. "The Crisis of Development and the Problem of Dependency in Latin America," excerpted in in H. Bernstein, ed. *Underdevelopment and Development*, pp. 76–77. Harmondsworth: Penguin.

Schneider, H. K. 1975. "Economic Development and Anthropology." *Annual Reviews in Anthropology* 3:271–292.

Schneider, Jane and Peter Schneider. 1975. *Culture and Political Economy in Western Sicily*. New York: Academic Press.

Schriner, Eldon C., Faye Keogh, and Tom Gallagher. 1976. *The Social Impacts Associated with an Electrical Generating Plant Located in Mercer County, North Dakota*. Fargo: North Dakota State University Department of Sociology.

Scott, Shaunna. 1988. *Where There Is No Middle Ground: Community and Class Consciousness in Harlan County, Kentucky*. Ph.D dissertation, Department of Anthropology, University of California, Berkeley.

Shapiro, Isaac. 1989. *Laboring for Less: Working but Poor in Rural America*. Washington, D.C.: Center on Budget and Policy Priorities.

Shaw, R. Paul. 1979. "A Note on Shifts in Parity, Poverty, and Sources of Farm Family Income in North America." *Economic Development and Social Change* 27(4):645–652.

Sherrill, Robert. 1972. "Energy Crisis: The Industry's Fright Campaign." *The Nation* June 26, 1972:816–820.

Skinner, G. William. 1964. "Marketing and Social Structure in Rural China, Part I." *Journal of Asian Studies* 24(1):3–44.

Skocpol, Theda. 1979. *States and Social Revolutions.* New York: Cambridge University Press.

Smith, C. L., T. C. Hogg, and M. J. Reagan. 1976. "Economic Development: Panacea or Perplexity for Rural Areas?" *Rural Sociology* 36:173–186.

Smith, C. T. 1980. "Community Wealth Concentration: Comparisons in General Evolution and Development." *Economic Development and Social Change* 28:801–817.

Smith, Henry Nash. 1950. *Virgin Land: The American West as Symbol and Myth.* New York: Random House Vintage.

Smith, T. Lynn. 1940. "Trends in Community Organization and Life." *American Sociological Review* 1:325–344.

———. 1947 (orig. 1940). *The Sociology of Rural Life.* New York: Harper.

Spradley, James. 1970. *You Owe Yourself a Drunk: An Ethnography of Urban Nomads.* Boston: Little, Brown.

Strange, Marty. 1988. *Family Farming: A New Economic Vision.* Lincoln: University of Nebraska Press; San Francisco: Institute for Development Policy.

Summers, G. F. and Frank Clemente. 1976. "Industrial Development, Income Distribution, and Public Policy." *Rural Sociology* 41:248–268.

Sundstrom, Eric, John Lounsberry, C. Richard Schuller, James Fowler, and Thomas Mattingly, Jr. 1977. "Community Attitudes Toward a Proposed Nuclear Power Generating Facility as a Function of Expected Outcomes." *Journal of Community Psychology* 5(3):199–208.

Sunkel, Osvaldo 1972. "Big Business and 'dependencia.'" *Foreign Affairs* 50:517-531.

Tanzer, Michael. 1974. *The Energy Crisis: World Struggle for Power and Wealth.* New York: Monthly Review Press.

Taussig, Michael. 1980. *The Devil and Commodity Fetishism in South America.* Chapel Hill: University of North Carolina Press.

Taylor, Carl C. 1933. *Rural Sociology: Its Economic, Historical, and Psychological Aspects*, rev. ed., New York: Harper.

———. 1942. "Rural Life." *American Journal of Sociology* 42:841–853.

Thelen, David P. 1986. *Paths of Resistance: Tradition and Dignity in Industrializing Missouri.* Oxford: Oxford Univiversity Press.

Toennies, Ferdinand. 1963. *Community and Society*, trans. Charles P. Loomis. New York: Harper.

Tocqueville, Alexis de. 1945 (orig. 1835). *Democracy in America*, ed. Phillips Bradley, trans. Henry Reeve. New York: Random House.

Tremblay, Kenneth R., Jr., Charles L. Schwarz, and Don Dillman. 1981. "Understanding the Boom Town Problem: Value Conflict Between Oldtimers and Newcomers," in Judith A. Davenport and Joseph Davenport III, eds. *Proceedings of the First International Symposium on the Human Side of Energy.* Laramie: University of Wyoming Department of Social Work.

Troy, Leo, and Neil Sheflin. 1985. *Union Sourcebook: Membership, Structure, Finance Directory.* West Orange, N.J.: Industrial Relations Data and Information Services.

Tucker, William P. 1947. "Populism Up-to-Date: The Story of the Farmers' Union." *Agricultural History* 21:198–208.

Uhlman, Julie M. 1978. *Providing Human Services in Energy-Impacted Communities*. Laramie: University of Wyoming Press.

United States Bureau of the Census. 1893. *Report on Population of the United States at the 11th Census*. Washington, D.C.: U.S. Government Printing Office.

———. 1969, 1974, 1982, 1987. *U.S. Census of Agriculture*, 1, part 34. Washington, D.C.: U.S. Government Printing Office.

———. 1960, 1970, 1980. *General Social and Economic Characteristics: North Dakota*. Washington, D.C.: U.S. Government Printing Office.

———. 1960, 1970, 1980, 1990. *U.S. Census of Population and Housing*. Washington, D.C.: U.S. Government Printing Office.

Useem, John, Pierre Tangent, and Ruth Useem. 1942. "Stratification in a Prairie Town." *American Sociological Review* 7:331–342.

Vidich, Arthur, and Joseph Bensman. 1968. *Small Town in Mass Society*. Princeton, N.J.: Princeton University Press.

Voeller, Joseph B. 1940. *The Origin of the German-Russian People and Their Role in North Dakota*. M.A. thesis, University of North Dakota, Grand Forks.

Wadsworth, H. A., and J. M. Conrad. 1966. *Impact of New Industry on a Rural Community*. Indiana Agricultural Experiment Station Research Bulletin No. 811. W. Lafayette, Ind.: Purdue University.

Walker, Richard A. 1980. "Two Sources of Uneven Development Under Advanced Capitalism: Spatial Differentiation and Capital Mobility." *Review of Radical Political Economics* 10(3):28–38.

Walker, Richard, Michael Storper, and Ellen Gersh. 1978. "The Limits of Environmental Controls: The Saga of Dow in the Delta." Berkeley: University of California, Department of Geography.

Walkowitz, Daniel J. 1978. *Worker City, Company Town: Iron and Cotton Worker Protest in Troy and Cohoes, New York, 1855–1884*. Urbana: University of Illinois Press.

Wall Street Journal. 1985. New York: Dow, Jones and Company.

Wallerstein, Immanuel. 1976. *The Modern World-System*. New York: Academic Press.

Warf, Barney. 1988. "Regional Transformation, Everyday Life, and Pacific Northwest Lumber Production." *Annals of the Association of American Geographers* 78(2):326–346.

Warner, W. Lloyd, J. O. Low, Paul S. Lunt, and Leo Srole. 1941–1949. *Yankee City* Series. Chicago: University of Chicago Press.

Webb, Walter Prescott. 1931. *The Great Plains*. New York: Grosset and Dunlap.

Weber, Bruce A., and Robert E. Howell, eds. 1982. *Coping with Rapid Growth in Rural Communities*. Boulder, Colo.: Westview Press.

Weber, Max. 1946. *From Max Weber: Essays in Sociology*, trans. and ed. by Hans H. Gerth and C. Wright Mills. New York: Oxford University Press.

———. 1964. *The Theory of Social and Economic Organization*, trans. Talcott Parsons. New York: Free Press.

West, James. 1945. *Plainville, U.S.A.* New York: Columbia University Press.

West, S. A. 1977. *Opportunities for Company-Community Co-operation in Mitigating Energy Facility Impacts*. Cambridge, Mass.: Massachusetts Institute of Technology Energy Impact Project.

Wheeler, Wayne. 1949. *Social Stratification in a Plains Community*. Minneapolis, Minn.: Privately published.

White, William T. 1977. "Yaquina Bay: A Case Study in Social Impact Assessment," in Kurt Finsterbusch and Charles P. Wolf, eds. *Methodology for Social Impact Assessment.* pp. 155–159. Stroudsburg, Pa: Dowden, Hutchinson, and Ross.
Whyte, William Foote. 1955. *Street Corner Society: The Social Structure of an Italian Slum*, 2nd ed. Chicago: University of Chicago Press.
———. 1961. *Men at Work.* Homewood. Ill.: Dorsey.
Wilder, Laura Ingalls. 1953a. *On the Banks of Plum Creek.* New York: Harper.
———. 1953b. *Little House on the Prairie.* New York: Harper.
Wionczek, Miguel S.; Gerald Foley; and Ariane Van Buren. 1982. *Energy in the Transition From Rural Subsistence.* Boulder, Colo.: Westview.
Wirth, Lewis. 1956 (orig. 1925). *The Ghetto.* Chicago: University of Chicago Press.
Wolf, Charles P. 1974. "American Anthropologists and American Society," in Dell Hymes, ed. *Reinventing Anthropology*, pp. 251–263. New York: Random House.
———. 1975. "Social Impact Assessment." *Environment and Behavior* 7:259-404.
Wolf, Eric. 1982. *Europe and the People Without History.* Berkeley and Los Angeles: University of California Press.
Yamaguchi, S., and I. Kuczek. 1984. "The Social and Economic Impacts of Large-Scale Energy Projects on the Local Community." *International Labor Review* 23(2):149–165.
Young, John A., and Jan M. Newton. 1980. *Capitalism and Human Obsolescence: Corporate Control Versus Individual Survival in Rural America.* New York: Universe Books; Montclair, N.J.: Allenheld, Osmun.
Zorbaugh, Harvey. 1929. *The Gold Coast and the Slum.* Chicago: University of Chicago Press.

Index

Acid rain, 126
Advertising, 18, 48, 111–112, 222
Agency. *See* Social action
Agrarian populism. *See* Populism
Agriculture: and climate, 20, 43, 70; economic decline of, 12, 42–45, 48, 192, 214–215, 233; economics of farm operation, 65, 67–68, 215, 233; and energy development, 113, 114, 116, 124–125, 220; history of, 2, 27–28, 30, 31, 36; market, 39, 43–44, 47, 70, 187–188, 214; policy, 18, 187. *See also* Farm crisis; Farmers; Farming; Grain market; Great Depression
Aiken, Sen. Conrad, 97
Air quality, 100, 117; impact of development on, 124, 126–127, 184, 207; nitric oxide pollution, 248 n.4; regulations, 19, 139, 191; and sulphur in coal, 247–248 n.3. *See also* Pollution
Alcohol drinking, 69–70, 172; alcoholism, 128, 158; bars, 54, 76, 156–157; function of, 70, 92; as recreation, 54, 87, 91, 152, 157
Alienation, 85, 166–168, 171; theory on, 164–165
American Natural Gas Corporation (ANG). *See* American Natural Resources Corporation
American Natural Resources Corporation (ANR), 104, 206, 219; American Natural Gas (subsidiary), 118, 189; corporate organization of, 246 n.10; Michigan-Wisconsin Pipe Line Company, 103, 104, 111, 112, 114
Antelope Valley Station, 111, 186, 208; construction of, 155; environmental impact of, 127, 209; naming of, 117; nonunion policy of, 200, 201
Anthropology, 3–4, 7–9, 61, 89, 94
Anticorporation Farming Law, 44–45, 47
Anti-unionism, 51, 78, 82, 199–204, 245 nn. 12, 13
Arikara. *See* Three Affiliated Tribes
Assimilation. *See* Insiders versus outsiders; Newcomers; Permanent employees
Atherton, Lewis, 35

Bank of North Dakota, 41, 45, 47, 102, 246 n.6
Banking, 84, 88, 172, 193, 203; and development, 105, 196; and farming, 37, 42, 45, 47, 54, 216
Basin Electric Power Cooperative, 107, 179, 196, 220; employee relations, 152, 201, 202, 203, 226; facilities of, 110, 111, 186, 208, 224–225; impact of, 108–109, 152, 189, 208, 212; organizational structure of, 76, 109; public relations, 114, 117, 134, 195, 225. *See also* Rural electrical cooperatives
Bender, Thomas, 249 n.9
Bennett, John, 65
Beulah, 21, 79, 83–84; boom growth of, 56, 152, 168, 178, 179, 184, 192, 195–199, 204; civic and political life of, 34, 51, 57,

Beulah (*cont.*)
  87, 88, 159, 178, 194, 208–209; history of, 33, 55, 56, 57; rivalry with Hazen, 57, 91, 117, 218
Beulah Mine, 38, 76–77, 78, 117
Bluestone, Barry, 12, 159
Boomtowns, 119, 149; planning, 121, 128, 129; studies of, 12, 123, 129, 159, 247n.1
Boosterism: activities, 87, 197; function of, 35–36, 86, 143, 219, 243n.8; ideology and values of, 57, 60, 88, 130, 133, 135, 145, 168, 180, 197, 245n.15
Bureau of Land Management, 122, 131
Bureaucracy, 142, 147, 166; corporate, 18, 76, 94, 206; government, 9, 22, 136; power, 9, 18, 94
Bureaucratization, 141, 169, 171; of public life, 149, 172; theory on, 166
Burlington Northern Railway, 101, 204, 246n.6
Business people: customer and employee relations of, 86, 170–171, 172–173; family and ownership, 84, 85, 193, 194; history and careers of, 36, 83–84, 85–86; ideology and values of, 48, 51, 52, 82, 87–88, 133, 180, 183, 205, 215; industry relations of, 123, 196–197, 224; role of, in community and development, 82–83, 87, 164, 195, 197
Businesses (small): change with boom, 115, 149, 176, 192–194; closures of, 217, 227–228; employee relations in, 84, 85, 86, 172–173, 180; history of, 32–33, 35, 55, 83–85; national franchises, 56, 172, 193. *See also* Competition; Real estate
Bust, 218, 223, 228, 229, 235; business impact of, 216–217, 226–227, 228; and Great Plains crisis, 212, 220–223; and local government finances, 217, 218–219, 223, 227, 229. *See also* Debt; Farm crisis; Unemployment
Butz, Earl, 187

Capital accumulation, 12, 17, 96, 111, 120
Capitalism, 8, 10, 16, 43, 165; and monopoly, 60, 80, 166; and world-system, 4, 6, 7, 8, 210
Carter, Jimmy, 103, 136
Chambers of Commerce, 57, 74, 87, 112, 170, 178, 204; function of, 79, 86, 87, 93, 172; history of, 35, 36; relations with developers, 195, 196, 197
Children, 30, 55, 63, 172, 174, 177; abuse and neglect of, 174, 208, 213; in business families, 84, 85–86, 180; in construction work families, 150, 151, 154, 155, 163; in farm families, 65, 66; upbringing of, 28, 44, 46
Churches, 32, 37, 58, 91, 177, 198. *See also* Religion
Class: change with development, 166, 167, 176, 178–179, 182, 183, 199; class system, Mercer County, 37, 38, 57, 90; conflict, 76, 79–81, 82, 111, 118, 161, 191; consciousness, 65, 75, 76, 79, 80, 88; prejudice, 90, 158, 160; symbols of, 58, 90, 161, 179, 207; theory and study of, 4, 8, 15, 62, 81, 95; working class, 49, 51, 74, 81. *See also* Elites; Social inequality
Coal (lignite), 2, 28, 100, 101, 139
Coal companies. *See* Mining companies
Coal conversion, 2, 19, 100, 105, 126. *See also* Coal gasification; Electricity generation
Coal Conversion Counties (CCC), 135
Coal gasification, 2, 94, 96, 104, 220; byproducts, 113, 221, 224, 235; history of, 246n.4
Coal Impact Office. *See* Energy Impact Office
Coal leasing, 118, 169, 189, 216; farmers' attitudes toward, 108, 133, 135, 186–187, 188, 192; federal role in, 102, 122
Coal miners. *See* Miners
Coal mining. *See* Mining
Colonialism, 4, 5, 7, 26, 41
Community, local control of, 1, 59, 94–95, 96; decline in, 13, 123, 162, 166, 167
Community development, 2, 12, 25, 116, 143, 233, 235; entrepreneur's role in, 35, 83, 143, 235–236; financing of, 13, 35, 84, 128, 132, 134, 138, 143, 197, 219, 223; planning, 130, 144, 146, 241nn.2, 4
Community economy, 1, 120, 160, 168, 191, 229
Community ideology, 62, 81, 86, 90, 92–93, 113–114; and corporations, 113, 168–169, 205, 206–207

Community studies, 10, 14, 166, 193, 241n.3
Competition, 51, 60, 91, 165, 166; inter-business, 171, 193, 194; inter-farm, 31, 45, 69, 73; inter-town, 35, 36, 57, 86, 133, 135, 179, 197, 218, 235–236
Conflict, 2, 59, 61, 73, 119, 120, 191; change with boom, 140, 142, 171; with energy industries, 105, 115; management of, 89, 91, 144, 169. *See also* Class; Insiders versus outsiders; Town–country relations
Consolidation Coal Corporation, 76, 98, 113
Construction, 114, 129, 138; boom, 2, 155, 192, 200
Construction workers, 46, 150–151, 208, 248 nn.1–4; attitudes toward, 129, 156, 157–158, 163, 164, 170, 176; family life of, 21, 151, 152–153, 154–155, 173, 212, 213; housing, 151–152, 153–154, 164, 198; impact of, 128, 149–150, 159, 160, 168, 172, 216; work and leisure, 155–157, 159, 194, 212–213. *See also* Insiders versus outsiders; Labor unions, in construction trades; Migration, of construction workers; Mobile home parks
Conversion. *See* Coal conversion
Cooperation, 60, 93, 96, 191; in business, 35, 86; among farmers, 45, 72, 73, 190; in industry, 115, 116, 136, 194, 206, 209; inter-town, 179, 236; among miners, 48, 77, 81
Cooperatives. *See* Farmers Union Cooperative; Rural electrical cooperatives
Corporate–community relations, 10, 95, 140, 168–170, 205–210. *See also* Public relations
Coteau Properties, 139–140, 189, 200, 201, 202, 219
County Commission, 23, 162, 197; administration of, 71, 134–135, 185; and industries, 136, 139, 140, 185, 205; public participation of, 71, 136
Coyote Station, 110–111, 116, 117, 127, 152, 200
Crime, 59, 128, 129, 157, 158, 171
Culture, 7–8; corporate, 226, 233–234. *See also* Political culture; Urban culture

Dakota Gasification Company (DGC), 224
Dakota Resource Council, 135, 138, 185, 186, 189, 231
Debt: farm, 68, 188; private, 217, 234; public, 217, 222, 223, 234
Deindustrialization, 12, 13
Democratic Party, 105, 106, 110, 247n.11; and energy industry, 103, 107, 109, 133; history of, 47, 48
Department of Energy (federal), 103, 134, 221, 223, 224
Department of Interior (federal), 105; secretaries of, 102, 246n.6
Dependency, 52, 182, 220, 224, 229, 239; theory, 5, 6
Depersonalization. *See* Alienation; Rationalization
Dog Town, 37, 164
Domination. *See* Power
Dorgan, Byron, 106
Dorst, John, 176
Drugs, 56, 91, 129, 159, 158
Dumont, Louis, 61
Durkheim, Émile, 164–165, 249nn.7, 8
Dust Bowl. *See* Great Depression

Economic democracy, 14–15, 19, 94–95, 147, 211
Economic development, 2–3, 4, 7, 11, 31, 95, 102, 106–107, 182
Economic morality. *See* Community ideology; Morality; Values
Economic restructuring, 1, 10–14, 150, 211
Education, 30, 74, 85, 90, 207, 209; administration and financing of, 71, 172, 217, 229; changes with boom, 128, 143, 176, 198
Electricity generation, 19, 21, 126, 200; boomtime expansion of, 2, 109, 175; history of, 55, 57, 107, 108, 192; technical process of, 75, 113. *See also* Antelope Valley Station; Coyote Station; Garrison Hydroelectric Dam
Electricity transmission lines. *See* Transmission lines
Elites, 83, 90, 92, 160, 161, 166, 176; and development, 6, 146–147, 178–180, 196, 199, 238. *See also* Power elite

270 | Index

Employment. *See* Jobs
Energy boom, 6, 21, 25, 56, 119, 121, 200, 212; changes brought by, 167, 180–181, 192, 198; government role in, 17, 94, 95, 133–134; regional, 2, 104–105. *See also* Boomtowns; Economic development
Energy boomtowns. *See* Boomtowns
Energy corporations, 98–100, 187, 188, 207; government relations, 11, 102, 185, 204, 205; and local elites, 105, 146, 194, 197; oil companies, 52, 97; power of, 17–18, 105, 193, 232; public relations, 115–116, 169–170, 195, 206. *See also* Corporate–community relations
Energy development, financing of, 102, 106, 118, 137; government role in, 103–104, 111, 138, 208, 221, 222–223, 225
Energy Development Board (EDB), 134, 136, 141
Energy development impact. *See* Impact
Energy Impact Office (EIO), 132, 136, 137, 138, 143, 184, 197, 204, 218, 223, 229
Energy policy, 2, 17, 18, 94, 96, 103, 246nn. 8, 9, 11; alternative energy, 19, 220; and corporate relations, 11, 95, 103; at state level, 105, 109; strategic concerns of, 19, 94, 95, 97, 102. *See also* Synthetic Fuels Corporation
Energy prices, 97, 100, 103, 201, 212, 220; oil crisis highs, 2, 11, 96, 211. *See also* Oil crisis
Energy Research and Development Administration (ERDA), 134
Entertainment. *See* Recreation
Environmental degradation, 118, 124–125, 126; mining-related, 5, 48, 57, 124, 133, 139, 188
Environmental impact statements, 110, 121–123, 126–127, 128
Environmental legislation, 19, 52, 75, 102, 110, 122, 130, 133, 191
Environmental protection, 101, 103, 108–109, 120, 189, 204, 225, 238; whistleblowing, 14. *See also* Air quality; Environmental impact statements; Land reclamation; Regulation of energy development
Environmental Protection Agency (EPA), 131
Environmentalists, 103–105, 127, 132, 133, 135, 185, 189, 190. *See also* Dakota Resource Council
Ethnic groups, 26, 73, 90, 176–177; among settlers, 26, 37, 39, 243nn. 5, 9. *See also* Germans from Russia; Native Americans
Ethnography, 3, 4, 6–7, 10, 15, 61, 94

Family, 30, 115; business, 84, 85–86, 193, 196; change of, with development, 123, 166, 168, 171, 172, 173–174, 194; of construction workers, 150, 151, 152–155, 156, 160, 212; of farmers, 45, 65–66; of miners, 73, 74–75; stress, 128, 153, 174, 213–214; values and symbolism, 93, 112, 118, 169, 197. *See also* Farming, family
Family farmers. *See* Farming, family
Farm crisis, 11, 31, 34, 42, 44–45, 233; of 1980s, 1, 19, 68, 188, 192, 212, 214–216
Farm economy. *See* Agriculture
Farmers, 65–66, 141, 162; and economics, 64, 67–71, 89, 159–160, 187–188, 214–215; and industry, 107, 108, 120, 125–126, 133, 138–140, 145, 147, 189–190, 209; and politics, 18, 39, 71–73, 88, 135–136, 185, 191–192; social position of, 34, 53, 63–64, 84–85, 90, 167, 180, 182–185; and strip mining, 124, 125, 186–187, 188, 207. *See also* Farming, family; Mercer County Landowners Association
Farmers Alliance, 39
Farmers Union Cooperative, 36, 43, 57, 72, 73, 107, 109, 133; history of, 40, 43, 47
Farming: corporate, 1, 45; family, 1, 42, 45, 63–73, 190, 191, 233, 250n.2. *See also* Agriculture
Farmland. *See* Land
Federal Power Commission, 103
Fieldwork (anthropological), 2, 3, 21–22, 23–24
Financing. *See* Community development, financing of; Energy development, financing of
Ford, Gerald, 102
Foreclosures: farms, 44–45, 47, 188, 214, 215; Great Plains, 223; homes, 228
Fort Berthold Indian Reservation, 26, 33, 102, 247n.16
Fort Union coal formation, 20

Foucault, Michel, 62
Frank, André Gunder, 4
Freedom Mine, 139, 155, 234; labor management, 200, 201–202
Frisch, Michael, 166
Future, 115, 116, 117, 133, 221

Galpin, Charles, 85
Garrison Hydroelectric Dam, 20, 33, 55, 56, 101, 107, 110, 199
Gasification. *See* Coal gasification; Great Plains coal gasification plant
Gender roles, 7, 50, 84, 91, 175, 177, 242n.14; in family, 66, 75, 153, 175; in work, 38, 65, 160
Germans from Russia, 20, 40, 41, 47, 49, 55, 56; history of, 28–29; as settlers, 29–30, 36, 37
Glenharold Mine, 77, 201, 202–203, 216
Global warming, 126
Golden Valley, 55, 140, 198, 217; history of, 33, 55, 192
Golf clubs, 90, 177, 179–180
Gossip, 57–58, 69, 76, 80, 89, 91
Government, federal, 11, 42, 204; role in development, 17, 94, 207, 223, 224
Government, Mercer County, 23, 32, 33, 88, 185; role in development, 120, 138, 205–208. *See also* County Commission
Government, State of North Dakota, 41, 208, 218
Government, town, 23, 54, 84, 178, 195; role in development, 129, 134, 138, 195, 198
Government assistance. *See* Social services
Grain market, 11, 31, 39, 41, 43
Gramsci, Antonio, 15, 242nn.6, 7
Great Depression, 11, 25, 43–46, 49, 64, 102, 107, 241n.3
Great Plains coal gasification plant, 2, 155, 195, 222, 226; employment at, 154, 159, 160, 175, 200, 201, 203; financing of, 103, 104, 137, 194, 214, 220, 221, 222, 223, 224; impacts of, 126, 127, 128, 238; organizational structure of, 111, 224, 225; permits for, 109, 138, 140; public relations, 113, 116, 117, 225
Great Plains Gasification Associates (GPGA), 127, 152, 208; financing of, 104, 222, 223; organizational structure of, 109, 117, 219; public relations, 113, 118, 195; role in local society, 179, 206, 222
Great Plains region, 20, 190; energy boom in, 121, 123, 129, 195
Greater North Dakota Association, 47

Hall, Stuart, 242n.7
Harmony of interest. *See* Cooperation
Harrison, Bennett, 12, 159
Hazen, 21; boom growth of, 56, 57, 178, 179, 184, 192, 197–198, 199, 204; civic life in, 57, 87, 88, 194, 196; history of, 33, 48, 55, 107, 192; rivalry with Beulah, 57, 91, 117, 195, 218
Health, 30, 164, 176, 209; hospital, 128–129, 198; union benefits, 78, 202, 230
Hegemony, 72, 119, 120, 144–148, 182, 210; theory on, 14–18, 96, 242n.7, 248n.6
Hidatsa. *See* Three Affiliated Tribes
Homestead Act, 27
Hospitals. *See* Health
Housing, 86, 170, 179, 188, 218; boom expansion of, 124, 128, 146, 192, 195, 196; frontier, 27–28, 30; of work force, 150, 151–155, 161, 162, 163, 164, 195, 212. *See also* Mobile home parks; Real estate

Ideology, 46, 60, 61, 62, 74, 80, 115, 210; agrarian, 42, 133; business, 87, 88, 168; hegemonic, 15, 16, 18, 120, 144, 145; study of, 13, 61, 242n.7. *See also* Boosterism; Community ideology; Labor unionism
Immigration. *See* Migration
Impact: anticipation of, 121–130; assessment of, 121, 122–123; definition of, 132, 137; environmental, 122, 124–127, 136, 209, 233, 238; social and economic, 122–123, 128–130, 137, 172. *See also* Environmental impact statements
Impact mitigation, 116, 130, 132, 137, 145, 207; conflict over, 184–185, 198; financing of, 130, 132, 138, 139, 218–219, 223, 229; negotiating, 138, 140, 205–206
Indian Head mine, 38, 52, 76, 131, 204; unions at, 77, 200, 201, 204, 230–231
Individualism, 16, 60, 88, 186; of farmers, 46, 65, 67, 70, 72, 73, 141, 142, 190

Industrial location decisions. *See* Location decisions
Industrialization, 5, 31, 190; attitude toward, 85, 107, 109–110, 135, 149, 187, 221; promotion of, 47, 52, 106–107; and secondary development, 106, 107; and social change, 23, 93, 164–166, 175, 182–183, 193
Inequality. *See* Social inequality
Inflation, 132, 149, 162, 170–171, 188, 198
Insiders versus outsiders, 157, 161, 195; and assimilation, 22, 160, 176–178, 209; attitude toward outsiders, 134, 157–158, 170, 171; conflict, 119, 129, 141, 159, 161, 164; outsider experience, 154, 162–163
Inter-industry Technical Assistance Team (ITAT), 134, 136, 194, 208
Internal periphery, 5, 241n.2

Jacobs, Mike, 43
Jaycees, 87, 88, 177, 178
Jobs, 1, 17, 116, 149, 159, 165, 194; and economic development, 14, 116, 120, 122, 146; for locals, 113, 114, 115, 116, 129, 147, 159–160, 163, 173–175, 207; off-farm, 54, 65, 108, 160, 174, 186, 188, 215, 216; permanent, 160, 175; and unions, 49–50, 74, 201, 202. *See also* Unemployment

Kaiser Engineering Corporation, 155, 200
Kapas, Ted, 134
Keller, August, 204, 231
Kinship, 22, 54, 70, 74, 89, 90, 183
Knife River, 27, 55
Knife River Coal Mining Company, 76, 98, 116, 186–187, 232; history of, 38, 78

Labor history, 7, 13, 39–40, 204; mining, 36, 48–52, 78, 201, 244n.9. *See also* Labor unions, among mine workers; Mining, history of
Labor unionism, 16, 39, 60, 61, 146, 232; among mine workers, 73–75, 77–79, 80–82, 201
Labor unions, 7, 11, 12, 199–205
—in construction trades, 120, 156, 200, 203, 231, 232
—among mine workers, 76, 77; decline of, 133, 199–205, 216, 230–233; organizing, 39, 49, 50–52, 78, 81, 232; relations with business, 36, 51, 79; social position of, 51, 73, 82, 199. *See also* Labor history; Labor unionism; United Mine Workers
Land, 21, 34, 161, 162, 190, 195; farmland, 19, 27, 28, 30, 45, 64, 65, 68–70, 187, 191, 192; mined, 57, 74, 188, 189. *See also* Real estate
Land reclamation, 108–109, 113, 116, 124, 133, 187, 238; conflict over, 136, 169, 190; enforcement of, 19, 110, 120, 131, 188, 189, 191, 207–208; regulations, 75, 95, 102
Land speculation. *See* Real estate
Land use, 19, 132, 141, 143, 162, 196; conflict over, 19, 161, 185, 191; local control of, 96, 120, 139, 185
Landowners association. *See* Mercer County Landowners Association
Langer, William, 47
Law. *See* Legislation
Law enforcement. *See* Police
Legislation, 27, 81, 146; energy, 105–106, 110, 112, 132, 137, 218; environmental, 19, 52, 75, 102, 110, 122, 130, 133, 191; populist, 40–41, 45
Legitimacy, 17, 136, 190; and development, 111, 122, 142, 145; of state, 16, 96, 120
Leland Olds power station, 55, 107, 201
Lignite. *See* Coal
Lignite Council, 112, 232
Link, Gov. Arthur, 104, 105, 109, 124, 132
Little Moscow, 49
Lobbying, 135, 136, 208; pro-development, 102, 111–112, 204, 220, 232
Local control. *See* Community, local control of
Location decisions, 8–9, 12
Lurgi Company, 225, 246n.4
Lynd, Helen, 166
Lynd, Robert, 166

McKenzie, Alexander, 40
Mandan. *See* Three Affiliated Tribes
Marx, Karl, 164–165, 166, 244n.7, 249n.6
Mass media, 22, 113, 120, 121
Mass society, 22, 175, 180, 224
Men, 23, 57, 159, 178, 242n.14; construction workers, 150–153, 156, 157, 173; and employment, 65, 74, 75, 84; in farm

families, 65–66. *See also* Construction workers; Miners
Mercer County Government. *See* Government, Mercer County
Mercer County Impact Alleviation Task Force. *See* Task Force
Mercer County Landowners Association (MCLA), 135–136, 137, 138, 186, 191–192, 231, 233
Merchants. *See* Business people
Methodology, 3, 4, 7, 9, 23–24, 26; of environmental impact studies, 121, 122
Michigan-Wisconsin Pipe Line Company. *See* American Natural Resources Corporation
Micro–macro linkages, 3, 6, 9, 13, 15
Middletown, 166, 241n.2
Midwestern Miners, 77
Migration, 7, 12, 26, 48, 72, 208; of construction workers, 21, 149, 150–151, 152–153, 154, 155, 160, 162–163; of farmers, 42, 44, 48; of settlers, 26–30, 32, 36; of youth, 84, 115, 116, 129, 174, 237
Mills, C. Wright, 86, 95, 165, 166, 245n.12
Mine worker unions. *See* Labor unions, among mine workers
Mineral leasing. *See* Coal leasing
Mineral rights, 52, 101, 102, 107, 110, 187, 191
Miners, 38, 49, 73–82, 173, 202, 216; and development opposition, 120, 133, 191; social status of, 37–38, 73, 90, 164. *See also* Labor unions, among mine workers
Mining, 2, 37, 88, 97, 221; boom growth of, 104, 111, 117, 135; history of, 20, 36, 38, 48–52, 77–79; process, 75–76. *See also* Strip mining
Mining companies, 76, 230, 231–232; community relations, 82, 147, 188–189, 192
Minnkota Power Cooperative, 108
Missouri River, 20, 21, 26, 55, 101, 107
Mobile home parks, 21, 146, 164, 198; of construction work families, 150, 152, 153–154, 163
Modernization, 4, 119–120, 130, 145, 166, 197
Monopoly capitalism. *See* Capitalism
Montana-Dakota Utilities (MDU), 76, 110, 220, 250n.6
Morality, 157, 170–171, 172; agricultural, 126, 133, 190, 191; communitarian, 92–93, 169, 206; legalistic, 169, 170, 205; religious, 115, 158, 177. *See also* Community ideology; Values
Municipal services. *See* Public services

Nace, Theodore, 109
Nader, Laura, 9, 94
Nash, June, 6, 12, 13, 81, 242n.8
National Guard, 56, 203, 204
National Labor Relations Board, 199
Native Americans, 21, 26, 145, 187. *See also* Three Affiliated Tribes
Natural resources, 4, 5, 9, 27, 101, 146; agricultural, 20, 68; fossil fuels, 20, 33, 52, 97, 100, 104, 105
Neighboring, 74, 92, 154; change with the boom, 141, 158, 167–168, 171, 237–238; rural, 31, 34, 45, 65, 174; used in public relations, 117, 118, 168–169, 198; values, 30, 86, 89, 92, 161, 206
Newcomers, 142, 160, 162, 173; assimilation of, 160, 161, 175, 176–181; difference from local norms, 160, 161, 162, 174, 237–238; influence of, 143, 146, 167, 178–180, 193–194, 209; towns' efforts to attract, 168, 197–198
Nonpartisan Political League (NPL), 40–41, 47, 71
Nonunion mines and plants, 100, 133, 199–202, 232–234
North American Coal Corporation (NACCO), 38, 76, 169; allegations against, 131, 250n.10; labor relations, 200, 230–232; public relations, 189, 204
North Central Power Study, 104
North Dakota Lignite Council. *See* Lignite Council
North Dakota State Bank. *See* Bank of North Dakota
Northern Pacific Railway Corporation, 39, 101, 105; role in settlement, 27, 30, 33

O'Connor, James, 96
Oil crisis, 2, 94, 96, 103, 113
Olson, Allan, 135, 203
Olson, Philip, 93
Opposition, 4, 18, 120, 208–209, 219; containment of, 96, 118, 120, 130, 136, 142, 146; farmers', 105, 133, 135, 209, 220, 233; in formal arenas, 109, 138, 140,

Opposition (cont.)
147, 207; theory about, 7, 17. See also Social action
Outsiders. See Insiders versus outsiders

PATCO, 199, 204
Permanent employees, 150, 160–162; assimilation of, 163, 175–178; towns' efforts to attract, 196, 197–198, 218. See also Newcomers
Permits, 18, 130, 132, 142, 144; and corporate–community relations, 138, 205–206; local control over, 96, 114–115, 134, 138, 147, 207, 208; at state level, 105, 109, 110
Pick City, 55, 56, 110, 199
Pipelines, 101, 124, 125, 128, 135
Planning, 106, 121; at county level, 123–148, 164, 168, 208; public participation in, 121, 122, 123–124, 133–138, 144–145, 147–148; structure of, 18–19, 52, 95, 120; theory about, 5–6, 14, 119–120
Planning and zoning: county, 23, 134, 139–140, 142, 174, 178, 209; town, 23, 135, 140, 146, 163–164, 195, 196. See also Zoning
Plant closings, 1, 11
Police: boom expansion of, 128, 129, 208; labor confrontation with, 129, 203, 208; rationalization of law enforcement, 128, 129, 208
Political culture, 16, 42, 60–62, 182; of farmers, 36–40, 42–43, 71–73; of merchants, 87–89; of miners, 79–82, 202; of service workers, 244n.2
Pollution, 126–127, 191, 207. See also Air quality; Environmental degradation; Solid waste; Toxic waste; Water
Populism: ideology of, 16, 60, 71, 115, 118, 141, 146; legacy of, 47, 71–72, 117, 190, 207
Populist movement, 39–42, 47, 243n.11
Power: of business elite, 83, 88–89, 166; corporate, 14, 18, 166, 169, 189, 205; of farmers 63, 107, 124, 136, 183, 185; hegemonic, 15, 144–145, 182; local, 18, 19, 96, 102, 120, 136, 138, 139, 206–207; of organized labor, 12, 14, 51, 73, 81, 199–201, 204; theory about, 4, 6, 9, 19, 61–62, 94, 210

Power elite, 95, 245n.1, 245–246n.2
Power plant. See Electricity generation
Pred, Allan, 241n.5
Professionals, 142, 176, 180, 192, 207, 209, 234
Progress: ideology of, 16, 18, 87, 115, 120, 145, 168; and modernization, 14, 87, 117, 149
Progressive Mine Workers (PMW), 50, 77, 244n.9
Prostitution, 156, 157
Public participation. See Planning, public participation in
Public relations, 18, 147, 204, 225; community relations, 134, 169, 219–220; landowner relations, 147, 185–191; merchants, 173; selling development, 111–118
Public Service Commission (PSC), 110, 135, 139, 185, 188, 204; enforcement by, 125, 131, 208
Public services, 53, 71, 149; and boom expansion, 122, 128, 129, 143, 149; financing of, 128, 132, 198, 207

Quality of life, 1, 47, 59, 114, 137, 167, 168; coverage in environmental impact statements, 120, 122, 123

Railways, 47, 101–102, 105, 128; role in settlement, 11, 26–27, 31, 33
Ranchers. See Farmers
Rationalization, 166; in community life, 170, 171–173; in planning, 120, 134, 140–142, 146, 147. See also Bureaucratization
Reagan, Ronald, 103, 199, 204
Real estate, 35; and boom growth, 192, 194–196; housing values, 228, 250n.1; interest in energy development, 105, 146, 182, 192, 194, 196–197, 204; land speculation, 22, 27, 32
Recreation, 21, 23, 199; athletics, 91, 143; bars and clubs, 54, 76, 156, 159, 177, 179; before the boom, 34–35, 54, 58, 87; boom time changes in, 143, 147, 167, 180, 184
Redfield, Robert, 198
Regulation of energy development, 95, 102, 105, 118, 130

Religion, 30, 32, 37, 58, 91, 174, 177; and morality, 16, 115. *See also* Churches
Republican Party: business links with, 71, 88; versus populism, 40–41, 47–48, 71; and state legislature, 109
Residential class segregation: during boom, 146, 152, 160, 164, 166; of miners, 37, 49, 78
Resistance. *See* Opposition
Right-to-work laws, 81, 100, 156
Roads, 73, 146, 149, 180; and farmers' equity concerns, 162, 184–185; industry impact on, 128, 132, 139, 184, 207
Rose, Dan, 10
Rostow, W. W., 4
Rural decline, 1, 88, 149, 166, 183
Rural electrical cooperatives, 47; Democratic Party links with, 107, 108, 133, 246–247n.11; as energy developers, 55, 76, 105, 108, 111, 117, 225

Sahlins, Marshall, 61
Sakakawea, Lake, 21, 56, 101, 179, 185, 247n.16
SASOL, 225, 246n.4
Schools. *See* Education
Seder, Arthur, 104, 118, 206
Segregation. *See* Residential class segregation
Services. *See* Education; Police; Public services; Social services; Water
Social action, 19, 25, 61, 190, 239; hegemonic influence on, 102, 210; ideology, relation to, 62, 145; theory about, 7, 8, 62. *See also* Labor unions, among mine workers; Opposition; Planning, public participation in
Social change, 22, 114–115; in community life, 150, 164–181, 238; expectations about, 123, 145, 149; study of, 2, 4, 6–8, 10–11, 13, 17, 241n.3
Social inequality, 62; increase with development, 6, 166, 175, 176; social mobility, 63, 73–81; status ranking, 57, 63, 73, 89–90. *See also* Class; Community ideology
Social mobility. *See* Social inequality
Social services, 46, 71; energy development–related, 137, 139, 171, 173–174, 213; funding of, 208

Solid waste, 111, 126, 127, 129
South Russia, 28–29, 30, 77, 83
Stanton: energy boom influence on, 192, 196, 198; history of, 32, 33, 55, 57; industrial character of, 79, 82, 108
State, the, 14, 17, 95–96, 111, 132; definition of, 95, 246n.3. *See also* Legitimacy
Status. *See* Social inequality
Strikes. *See* Labor unions, among mine workers
Strip mining: and boom expansion, 2, 100, 109, 111, 113, 116; and farming, 19, 113, 116, 119, 124, 133, 186–187, 207–208; history of, 48, 51, 78; procedure, 20, 75. *See also* Environmental degradation; Land reclamation
Surface mining. *See* Strip mining
Synthetic Fuels Corporation (SFC), 2, 17, 103, 220, 221, 246n.9

T-towns, 33
Task Force, 134, 135, 136, 137, 201
Taxes, 160, 184, 218–219; on coal industries, 95–96, 105–106, 132, 207, 220, 224–225, 247nn.13, 14; local, 122, 144, 198, 217; municipal tax base, 129, 162, 168, 197, 229; tax gap, 128, 138; tax incentives, 12, 100, 111
Temporary work force. *See* Construction workers
Tenneco, 219–220
Three Affiliated Tribes, 26, 102, 245n.14, 247n.16
Tourism, 21, 56, 199, 235; industrial, 222, 235, 243–244n.16
Town–country relations: ascendency of towns, 167, 183–185, 189; pre-boom interdependence, 34–35, 53–54; status differences, 63, 85, 90
Townley, Arthur C., 41
Toxic waste, 111, 126, 127, 207
Trailer parks. *See* Mobile home parks
Transmission lines, 19, 101, 124, 125, 132, 135, 186, 188

Unemployment, 10, 11, 74, 106, 124; in construction work families, 153, 154, 155, 160, 212–213; during bust, 212, 216, 226; managerial lay-offs, 214, 228; and union power, 81, 200, 216

Uneven development: in Mercer County, 2, 10, 18, 198–199, 210, 224, 227, 235–236; and planning, 120, 123, 147; theory about, 5–6, 7–8, 12
Unions. *See* Labor unions
United Mine Workers (UMW): decline of, 200, 203–204, 230–232, 250n.12; organizing in Mercer County, 49–51, 77, 79
United Power Association (UPA), 108, 110
Urban culture, 54; and local elites, 162, 207; and newcomers, 84, 146, 176, 179–180, 234, 237–238
Urbanization, 175, 192, 241n.3; and alienation of farmers, 85, 167, 184, 190; promoted by business class, 133, 180, 183

Values, 16, 30, 46, 58, 80, 122; community, 89, 92–93, 115, 170, 172; farm, 54, 191; use of, by corporations, 113, 117
Vertical slice, 9–10, 94, 95
Voluntary associations, 23, 54, 58, 72, 87, 90, 166, 177–178, 179

Walker, Richard, 8–9, 13
Wallerstein, Emmanuel, 4
Warner, Lloyd, 166
Water: groundwater supply, 124, 139, 170, 188, 209; industrial use of, 21, 100, 101, 109, 110; quality, 117; services, 128, 129
Weber, Max, 164, 165–166, 245n.17
Wedding dances, 54, 168
Welfare. *See* Social services
Wolf, Eric, 6, 9, 244n.1
Women, 23, 34–35, 57, 156, 159, 174, 177–178; in construction families, 151, 153, 154; employment of, 175; in farm families, 65–66; labor struggle participation of, 50, 75, 203; as settlers, 28, 29, 30, 31
Work: construction, 155–156; farming, 66–71; at Great Plains, 226; mining, 75–79, 201–202; small business, 84, 85–87
Workers. *See* Construction workers; Miners; Permanent employees
World-systems, 4–7, 9

Yankee City, 166

Zap: businesses in, 85; community development in, 198, 218; history of, 33, 55, 56; miners in, 51, 82; mines nearby, 38, 48, 49, 78; recreation in, 156
Zap-In, 56, 86, 156
Zoning: and class segregation, 164, 248n.7; conflict over, 161; industrial, 115, 138, 139–140; public participation in, 147; regulations, 140, 141, 142, 146